The Coburg Conspiracy

The Coburg Conspiracy

VICTORIA AND ALBERT –
ROYAL PLOTS AND MANOEUVRES

Richard Sotnick

To Alan

Warm wishes,

Richard Sotnick.

08 - 05 - 13

Ephesus Publishing

First published in Great Britain in 2008 by Ephesus Publishing
This edition published in 2010

10 9 8 7 6 5 4 3 2 1

A CIP catalogue record for this book is available from the British Library

Printed and bound in Great Britain by LPPS Ltd

ISBN: 0-9557125-1-3
ISBN: 978-0-9557125-1-7

**Visit *The Coburg Conspiracy* website at
www.thecoburgconspiracy.co.uk**

It is the first law of history that it shall not dare to state anything that is false, and consequently that it shall not shrink from stating anything that is true.

Cicero, *De Oratore*, Book 2, 15

This book is dedicated to my wife Ruth, who encouraged me to learn German late in life in order to pursue my investigation into the history of the Saxe-Coburg-Gotha family; my three daughters, Juliet, Lisa and Karen, who have acted as proof readers and critical advisers; and especially to my young grandsons, Harry and Sam, representatives of the next generation, in the hope that their knowledge of history may help them more easily to understand the mistakes of their predecessors.

Richard Sotnick, London

Contents

List of illustrations

Acknowledgements

I owe much gratitude to the many who encouraged and actively helped me. To my school friend Dr John Sweetman, himself a historian; Dr Robert Bases and Ann Burger, both of New York; Dr Nöth, Director of Landesarchiv Coburg, and his very helpful staff; and the staff at the Archives at Gotha. Dr Josef Dreesen in Holsthum, Eifel, Germany, made time in his busy life to give me his opinion on letters and documents, and shared historic observations on the period; Roland Geiger, whom I was fortunate to meet on my visits to St Wendel, introduced me to Luise's life there; Gabriella Weil patiently taught me German and translated original documents and letters with enthusiasm. Thanks too to Michael Hunter, the curator at Osborne House, Isle of Wight, and his staff; the German Institute, London; the Goethe-Institut, London; Schloss Ehrenburg Coburg; Schloss Friedenstein Gotha; the Rosenau near Coburg; the British Library, where I spent three years of study; the Royal Historical Manuscripts Commission; Susanne McDadd for her encouragement, suggestions for the primal text, and professionalism; Cathy Douglas for her continued advice and assistance during the many drafts of the manuscript; Rabbi Reuven Livingstone; Joe Little (*Majesty Magazine*); Rusty Sotnick; Lynne Goldwyn; Simon Shulman for his image scanning and map design; Lawrence Bloom; and a host of friends too numerous to mention for their support and advice. Most particularly I owe much to my wife Ruth, who insisted I devote a major part of my recent life to this work, and has read, re-read, made suggestions and calmed me during frequent computer crises.

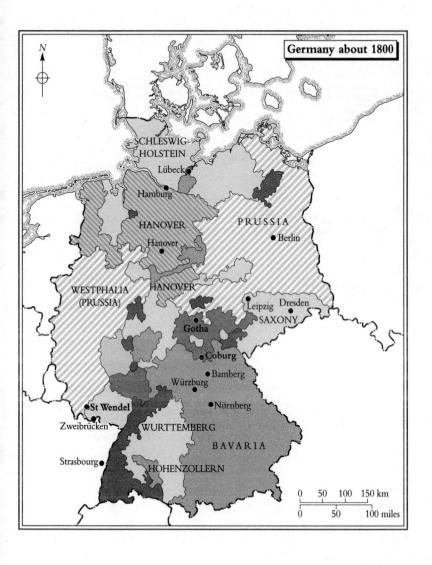

Germany about 1800

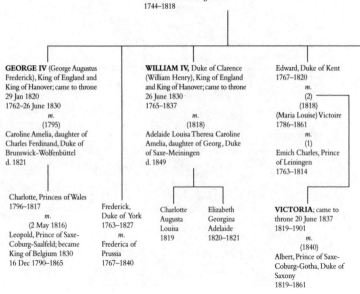

The descendants of George III

GEORGE III (George William Frederick), King of England and King of Hanover; came to throne 25 Oct 1760
1738–1820

m.
(8 Sept 1761)
(Sophia) Charlotte, daughter of Charles Ludwig Frederick, Duke of Mecklenburg-Strelitz
1744–1818

GEORGE IV (George Augustus Frederick), King of England and King of Hanover; came to throne 29 Jan 1820
1762–26 June 1830
m.
(1795)
Caroline Amelia, daughter of Charles Ferdinand, Duke of Brunswick-Wolfenbüttel
d. 1821

Charlotte, Princess of Wales
1796–1817
m.
(2 May 1816)
Leopold, Prince of Saxe-Coburg-Saalfeld; became King of Belgium 1830
16 Dec 1790–1865

WILLIAM IV, Duke of Clarence (William Henry), King of England and King of Hanover; came to throne 26 June 1830
1765–1837
m.
(1818)
Adelaide Louisa Theresa Caroline Amelia, daughter of Georg, Duke of Saxe-Meiningen
d. 1849

Frederick, Duke of York
1763–1827
m.
Frederica of Prussia
1767–1840

Charlotte Augusta Louisa
1819

Elizabeth Georgina Adelaide
1820–1821

Edward, Duke of Kent
1767–1820
m.
(2)
(1818)
(Maria Louise) Victoire
1786–1861
m.
(1)
Emich Charles, Prince of Leiningen
1763–1814

VICTORIA; came to throne 20 June 1837
1819–1901
m.
(1840)
Albert, Prince of Saxe-Coburg-Gotha, Duke of Saxony
1819–1861

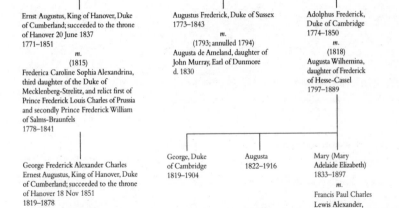

Ernst Augustus, King of Hanover, Duke of Cumberland; succeeded to the throne of Hanover 20 June 1837
1771–1851

m.
(1815)
Frederica Caroline Sophia Alexandrina, third daughter of the Duke of Mecklenberg-Strelitz, and relict first of Prince Frederick Louis Charles of Prussia and secondly Prince Frederick William of Salms-Braunfels
1778–1841

George Frederick Alexander Charles Ernest Augustus, King of Hanover, Duke of Cumberland; succeeded to the throne of Hanover 18 Nov 1851
1819–1878

m.
(1843)
Mary, daughter of Joseph, Duke of Saxe-Altenburg
d. 1907

Augustus Frederick, Duke of Sussex
1773–1843

m.
(1793; annulled 1794)
Augusta de Ameland, daughter of John Murray, Earl of Dunmore
d. 1830

George, Duke of Cambridge
1819–1904

Augusta
1822–1916

Adolphus Frederick, Duke of Cambridge
1774–1850

m.
(1818)
Augusta Wilhemina, daughter of Frederick of Hesse-Cassel
1797–1889

Mary (Mary Adelaide Elizabeth)
1833–1897

m.
Francis Paul Charles Lewis Alexander, Prince and Duke of Teck
1837–1900

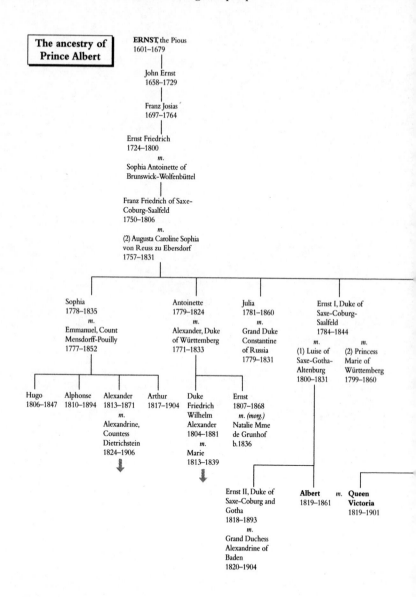

The ancestry of Prince Albert

ERNST, the Pious
1601–1679

John Ernst
1658–1729

Franz Josias
1697–1764

Ernst Friedrich
1724–1800
m.
Sophia Antoinette of
Brunswick-Wolfenbüttel

Franz Friedrich of Saxe-
Coburg-Saalfeld
1750–1806
m.
(2) Augusta Caroline Sophia
von Reuss zu Ebersdorf
1757–1831

Sophia
1778–1835
m.
Emmanuel, Count
Mensdorff-Pouilly
1777–1852

Antoinette
1779–1824
m.
Alexander, Duke
of Württemberg
1771–1833

Julia
1781–1860
m.
Grand Duke
Constantine
of Russia
1779–1831

Ernst I, Duke of
Saxe-Coburg-
Saalfeld
1784–1844
m.   *m.*
(1) Luise of   (2) Princess
Saxe-Gotha-   Marie of
Altenburg   Württemberg
1800–1831   1799–1860

Hugo
1806–1847

Alphonse
1810–1894

Alexander
1813–1871
m.
Alexandrine,
Countess
Dietrichstein
1824–1906

Arthur
1817–1904

Duke
Friedrich
Wilhelm
Alexander
1804–1881
m.
Marie
1813–1839

Ernst
1807–1868
m. (morg.)
Natalie Mme
de Grunhof
b.1836

Ernst II, Duke of
Saxe-Coburg and
Gotha
1818–1893
m.
Grand Duchess
Alexandrine of
Baden
1820–1904

Albert
1819–1861

m.   **Queen
Victoria**
1819–1901

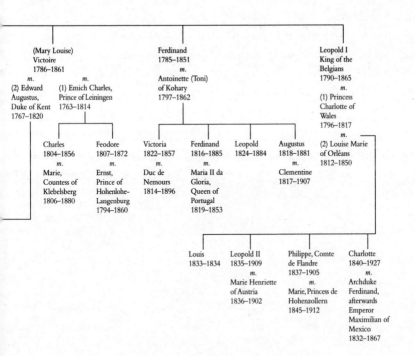

(Mary Louise)
Victoire
1786–1861
m.
(2) Edward
Augustus,
Duke of Kent
1767–1820

m.
(1) Emich Charles,
Prince of Leiningen
1763–1814

Ferdinand
1785–1851
m.
Antoinette (Toni)
of Kohary
1797–1862

Leopold I
King of the
Belgians
1790–1865
m.
(1) Princess
Charlotte of
Wales
1796–1817
m.
(2) Louise Marie
of Orléans
1812–1850

Charles
1804–1856
m.
Marie,
Countess of
Klebelsberg
1806–1880

Feodore
1807–1872
m.
Ernst,
Prince of
Hohenlohe-
Langenburg
1794–1860

Victoria
1822–1857
m.
Duc de
Nemours
1814–1896

Ferdinand
1816–1885
m.
Maria II da
Gloria,
Queen of
Portugal
1819–1853

Leopold
1824–1884

Augustus
1818–1881
m.
Clementine
1817–1907

Louis
1833–1834

Leopold II
1835–1909
m.
Marie Henriette
of Austria
1836–1902

Philippe, Comte
de Flandre
1837–1905
m.
Marie, Princesse de
Hohenzollern
1845–1912

Charlotte
1840–1927
m.
Archduke
Ferdinand,
afterwards
Emperor
Maximilian of
Mexico
1832–1867

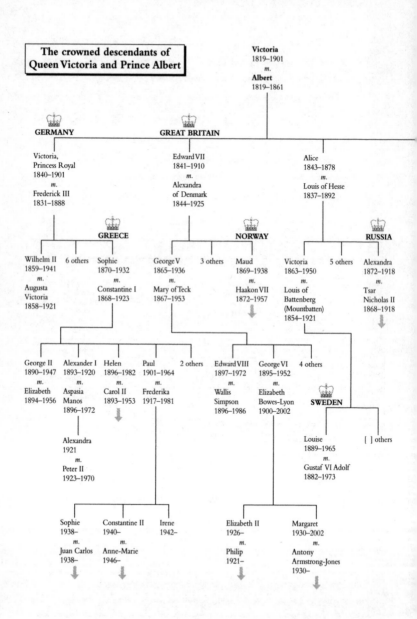

The crowned descendants of Queen Victoria and Prince Albert

Victoria
1819–1901
m.
Albert
1819–1861

GERMANY

GREAT BRITAIN

Victoria,
Princess Royal
1840–1901
m.
Frederick III
1831–1888

Edward VII
1841–1910
m.
Alexandra
of Denmark
1844–1925

Alice
1843–1878
m.
Louis of Hesse
1837–1892

GREECE

NORWAY

RUSSIA

Wilhelm II
1859–1941
m.
Augusta
Victoria
1858–1921

6 others

Sophie
1870–1932
m.
Constantine I
1868–1923

George V
1865–1936
m.
Mary of Teck
1867–1953

3 others

Maud
1869–1938
m.
Haakon VII
1872–1957

Victoria
1863–1950
m.
Louis of
Battenberg
(Mountbatten)
1854–1921

5 others

Alexandra
1872–1918
m.
Tsar
Nicholas II
1868–1918

George II
1890–1947
m.
Elizabeth
1894–1956

Alexander I
1893–1920
m.
Aspasia
Manos
1896–1972

Helen
1896–1982
m.
Carol II
1893–1953

Paul
1901–1964
m.
Frederika
1917–1981

2 others

Edward VIII
1897–1972
m.
Wallis
Simpson
1896–1986

George VI
1895–1952
m.
Elizabeth
Bowes-Lyon
1900–2002

4 others

SWEDEN

Alexandra
1921
m.
Peter II
1923–1970

Louise
1889–1965
m.
Gustaf VI Adolf
1882–1973

[ ] others

Sophie
1938–
m.
Juan Carlos
1938–

Constantine II
1940–
m.
Anne-Marie
1946–

Irene
1942–

Elizabeth II
1926–
m.
Philip
1921–

Margaret
1930–2002
m.
Antony
Armstrong-Jones
1930–

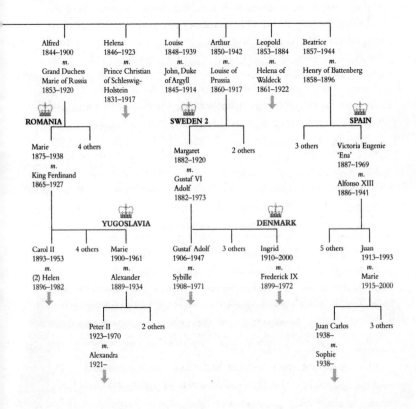

Alfred
1844–1900
m.
Grand Duchess
Marie of Russia
1853–1920

ROMANIA

Helena
1846–1923
m.
Prince Christian
of Schleswig-
Holstein
1831–1917

Louise
1848–1939
m.
John, Duke
of Argyll
1845–1914

Arthur
1850–1942
m.
Louise of
Prussia
1860–1917

SWEDEN 2

Leopold
1853–1884
m.
Helena of
Waldeck
1861–1922

Beatrice
1857–1944
m.
Henry of Battenberg
1858–1896

SPAIN

Marie
1875–1938
m.
King Ferdinand
1865–1927

4 others

Margaret
1882–1920
m.
Gustaf VI
Adolf
1882–1973

2 others

3 others

Victoria Eugenie
'Ena'
1887–1969
m.
Alfonso XIII
1886–1941

YUGOSLAVIA

DENMARK

Carol II
1893–1953
m.
(2) Helen
1896–1982

4 others

Marie
1900–1961
m.
Alexander
1889–1934

Gustaf Adolf
1906–1947
m.
Sybille
1908–1971

3 others

Ingrid
1910–2000
m.
Frederick IX
1899–1972

5 others

Juan
1913–1993
m.
Marie
1915–2000

Peter II
1923–1970
m.
Alexandra
1921–

2 others

Juan Carlos
1938–
m.
Sophie
1938–

3 others

Preface

Had I not been destined to enter a family law practice, I'd have liked to study history. The stories of personalities, with all their strengths and weaknesses – some with true vision, some with great powers of oratory, all fending off rivals and, quietly or otherwise, manoeuvring themselves into influential positions – have long had me under their spell. So after a career in law, local politics and the fascinating world of international string quartet competitions and music education, I reclaimed my life as an historian manqué.

Following a meeting with Lord Louis Mountbatten in October 1975, I had nursed a desire to investigate the Coburg family. I was able to start in September 2000. After three years of research, which took me to New York, Coburg, Gotha and St Wendel, I carefully considered the structure of this book. It was not easy, since there are two distinct areas of interest.

The first – explaining the family background and dealing substantially with Leopold, the founder of the international Coburg dynasty – is primarily set in England. The second concentrates on the German courts at Coburg, Gotha and St Wendel, with particular reference to the lifestyles of Albert's parents, Ernst I and Duchess Luise. It also addresses the question of Albert's legitimacy, which involves several candidates for paternity and includes two formal courts of enquiry into Luise's putative adultery.

These parts interlock, and each deserves close examination. By arranging them as I have, and with the help of the genealogical trees, I hope I have made the complexities of the Coburg family easier for the reader to follow.

The title was conceived as a challenge to the orthodox histories. I contend that there are two discrete yet related Coburg conspiracies. First, Leopold's opportunistic ambition – combined with sheer luck – developed into a deliberate strategy to acquire hegemony among the European royal houses, as shown by the correspondence between the leading members of the family and their advisers. Then there is the conspiracy of silence surrounding Albert's paternity, which is referred to in von Zach's obituary of Luise.

Nothing is black and white – most things are drawn in subtle shades of grey – but I believe I have produced enough evidence here to present a tenable theory.

Richard Sotnick
London, October 2007

Chronology

THE COBURGS IN ENGLAND

29 March 1815	Arrival of Stockmar in England
2 May 1816	Leopold's marriage to Charlotte
29 March 1817	Death of Charlotte and child
29 May 1818	Marriage of Duke of Kent to Victoire
24 May 1819	Birth of Victoria
26 August 1819	Birth of Albert
21 May 1830	Leopold declines Greek crown
14 July 1831	Leopold accepts Belgian crown
18 May 1837	Accession of Victoria to throne
10 February 1840	Marriage of Victoria to Albert
14 December 1861	Death of Albert

GERMAN COBURGS

21 December 1800	Birth of Luise
20 December 1816	Engagement of Luise to Ernst 1, Duke of Coburg
31 July 1817	Marriage of Luise to Ernst 1
29–30 August 1824	Riots in Coburg
2 September 1824	Legal separation of Luise and Ernst
27 March 1826	Divorce of Luise and Ernst
18 October 1826	Marriage of Luise to Maximilian von Hanstein
30 August 1831	Death of Luise

CHAPTER I

Royal Marines Officers' Mess, Eastney, Portsmouth

Among the twenty-eight officers of the Royal Marines in full mess uniform, resplendent with shining brass buttons, gold braid and medals, I was the only person wearing black tie – and so was a curiosity to many of the guests.

It was the evening of 31 October 1975, and the occasion was the inaugural dinner of the 1664 Club. The Royal Marines were leaving Portsmouth, and the club had been created not so much to commemorate the year in which Charles II established the corps, as to raise support for a Royal Marines museum in the Victorian building in which we stood. I had been granted honorary membership in recognition of the support I had been able to give that cause in my capacity as leader of Portsmouth City Council.

There was a buzz of excitement as we drank champagne and waited for the guest of honour in the opulent dining room, with its intricate gold-leaf ceilings, two splendid Italian marble fireplaces, glittering chandeliers and impressive paintings. Finally, he arrived: Lord Louis Mountbatten, life colonel-commandant of the Royal Marines, former chief of the Defence Staff, the last viceroy of India, who had overseen the granting of independence to India and Pakistan, and former commander-in-chief, Allied Forces South-East Asia (1943–45). As a great-grandson of Queen Victoria, he was related to generations of royalty, and had been closely associated with the greatest figures in political life – Churchill, Gandhi, Nehru, Roosevelt and Eisenhower among them.

The conversation became hushed as a tall figure with patrician features and erect bearing entered the room in glittering uniform mess dress, the aiguillettes shining with gold. He was introduced to the assembly by General Sir Peter Whitely, the presiding officer and commandant general of the Royal Marines.

Summoned to dinner, we moved up the grand staircase to the Minstrels' Gallery. The table was dazzlingly set with the corps' silver and glassware. The dinner proceeded through its courses, each accompanied by fine wines. I was sitting just four places away from Lord Mountbatten, and when the small talk gave way for a moment I caught his eye for long enough to put a question. How confident was he, I asked, that Anna Anderson, who claimed to be the Russian grand-duchess Anastasia and so heir to the Romanov fortune, was in fact an impostor?

Lord Mountbatten seemed delighted to talk about this part of his family history, which was in the news at that time. He looked me in the eye and answered with complete certainty: 'Absolutely no doubt. I have spent a great deal of time and not a little money on the legal case against this impostor. In my childhood, before the Great War, I was sent over to play with my cousins in the Tsar's summer residence in Russia. I knew them all very well. Anastasia was murdered in Ekaterinburg with the others.' (He was proved correct when the family's bodies were found in two mineshafts close to Ekaterinburg in 1991 and identified through DNA.) Warming to his subject, Lord Mountbatten jabbed his finger at me and said, 'You have to remember that, in my youth, European affairs were family business.'

At the time, I thought this statement rather arrogant. But as I researched this book, I realised that he was speaking the literal truth. In the early twentieth century, the Tsarina of Russia, the Kaiser of Germany, the monarchs of Greece, Denmark, Norway, Portugal, Spain, Belgium, Sweden, Romania, Bulgaria, Yugoslavia and, of course, Great Britain were all his relations.

How had this monopoly of monarchical power and influence been accumulated by one family – and one that had ruled a fairly obscure German principality, without fortune or political influence – in such a short space of time? Like Lord Mountbatten himself, almost all the heirs to the European monarchies were the offspring of Prince Albert and Queen Victoria. Their marriage was pivotal to the spread of the family's influence.

Was it by chance or design? Who among the Saxe-Coburg-Gotha

family (it was only in 1917, in the wake of anti-German feeling, that the British royal family changed their name to 'Windsor') had had such monarchical ambitions? What contributions did they make to the economic, political and cultural life of the palatinates and principalities of Germany? And what influence did they have on the unification of Germany in 1871?

In 1837, at the start of Victoria's reign, Britain was pre-eminent among nations. It was the most experienced and balanced of the democratic countries, particularly since the widening of the franchise in the Reform Act of 1832, giving many more people the right to vote, and the first to embrace industrialisation on a large scale. Its public-school system – in fact, private and expensive – and excellent universities guaranteed an educated leadership class for the administration of both Britain's burgeoning empire and her international trading interests. Although polite society still disdained 'trade' in principle, it could be overlooked if it happened outside Britain – so a director of the East India Company could move in the highest circles, whereas a Lancashire mill owner could not. Since the Royal Navy's victories in the Napoleonic Wars, culminating in the Battle of Trafalgar, few countries had dared challenge its role in protecting Britain's global trade routes and foreign policy.

France had not recovered from the trauma of Napoleon's defeat and its subsequent occupation by the Allies: Prussia, Russia and Britain. Germany, despite its growing nationalism, remained divided into fiercely traditional palatinates and principalities. Russia was still a feudal autocracy, and the Italian lands were a collection of warring states.

There was social unrest in England, too, as industrialisation gathered pace. Poverty, the radical political movement known as Chartism and the plight of the growing urban underclass all held dangers for both government and monarchy. But after the excesses and scandals of the Hanoverian dynasty, the British welcomed their young queen with pride. The country, despite its transitional problems, was substantially at peace with itself.

In this context, Victoria's marriage to Albert seems surprising. She was queen of a great empire, he the second son of the ruler of a small German dukedom, who brought little to the union in terms of prestige or finance – in fact, he would have to be 'kept' financially for the rest of his life. Moreover, Albert's parents had been divorced, publicly, at a time when divorce was rare and, in Britain, frowned upon. There was even some question about his legitimacy. But, extraordinarily, none of these issues seems to have been considered at the time. Certainly this apparent omission needs to be examined more fully, since the integrity of bloodline to royalty is paramount.

Evidence from contemporary journals, letters and reports shows that the arrangements for this marriage were made exclusively by the family: the state merely observed the formalities on being informed of Victoria's decision. Was this marriage – which brought no obvious advantages to Britain, and might actually have weakened Victoria's position – a love match? Or could Albert's close blood relationship to Victoria have been part of a Coburg conspiracy to spread the family's sphere of influence across Europe? This book will attempt to answer these questions.

The family

With the marriage of Victoria to Albert on 10 February 1840, monarchical control in Great Britain passed from the Hanoverians to the Saxe-Coburg-Gotha family. That control continues to this day. But who were the Coburgs and where did they come from?

In AD 962, Otto I, King of Aachen, was crowned emperor of the Holy Roman Empire by Pope John XII, in succession to the emperors of ancient Rome. It was an empty title: Charlemagne, who had also been awarded the accolade, preferred to style himself 'King of the Franks', which recognised his hegemony over France as well as Germany, and many centuries later Voltaire famously derided the title as 'neither holy, nor Roman, nor an empire'. In fact, Otto presided over a loose and quarrelsome alliance of kings, electors, princes and dukes, controlling their territories in feudal style, and supported by varying degrees of nobility.

The empire, known later as the First Reich, lasted until 1806, when after his defeat by Napoleon at Austerlitz Emperor Francis I was forced to agree to its dissolution. Napoleon then set up the Confederation of the Rhine to protect France's eastern front. From 1807, its thirty-five members, ranging from large kingdoms and duchies to smaller principalities and city states, included Saxe-Coburg-Saalfeld.

The dukes of Coburg were descended from the ruling house of Wettin, one of the oldest and, at one time, most powerful, of the German families. Their male line could be traced back unbroken as far as the first century AD. The name itself is taken from the town on the River Saale in Saalkreis in Saxony-Anholt, the original home of the Wettin dynasty, which ruled what is today's German state of

Saxony from 1034 for more than 800 years.

The family first came to prominence with their appointment as margraves of Meissen in 1089. A margrave was a military governor of a border province, which was then important to the security of the central realms of kings and princes. Over time, these border provinces became larger than those closer to the centre of the realm, and the powers of the margraves increased accordingly.

The Golden Bull of 1356 raised the Duke of Saxe-Wittenberg to the rank of Elector of Saxony, a post that remained in the hands of the family until 1918. However, in 1485 the brothers Ernst and Albrecht, who had ruled jointly, concluded what became known as 'the great Wettin land division'. Ernst, the elder, retained the title Elector of Saxony and established his seat at Wittenberg, controlling northern Meissen and Thuringia – this line became known as the Ernestine Wettins. Albrecht became Duke of Saxony, ruling his lands from Dresden as head of the Albertine Wettins.

In 1547, the Ernestine branch lost the electorship to the Albertines, who retained most of Saxony, thereby maintaining itself as a significant power in the region, and also ruled as kings of Poland (1692–1763) and Saxony (1806–1918). The Ernestine Wettins, on the other hand, repeatedly subdivided their territory, creating a patchwork of ever-smaller duchies and counties in Thuringia. As a result, the Duchy of Coburg became independent under Duke Johann Casimir in 1572. He died heirless, and the Duchy was subsequently ruled by various families of the Ernestine line until 1680, when it became the independent Duchy of Saxe-Coburg, which in 1735 was united with Saxe-Saalfeld as Saxe-Coburg-Saalfeld.

In 1825, when the Gotha-Altenburg line expired following the death of Duke Frederick IV without a male heir, there were five Ernestine duchies: Gotha-Altenburg, Coburg-Saalfeld, Weimar-Eisenach, Meiningen and Hildburghausen. The resulting rearrangement of family property was disputed by Meiningen and Hildburghausen, but these disputes were settled in 1826 by the Emperor, whose arbitrary judgement was final. The Duke of Hildburghausen received Altenburg; the Duke of Saxe-Coburg-Saalfeld received Gotha but had to give up Saalfeld to the Duke of Meiningen.

The Ernestines were sovereign princes of the German Confederation, but this constant division and subdivision meant that they had no influence on German affairs, unlike larger principalities such as Hanover and Saxony. According to the 1812 census, Ernst I ruled over 17.75 square miles with 57,266 inhabitants – yet, despite this, within the space of some thirty years Coburgs had been established on the thrones of Belgium, Portugal and Great Britain, as king and consorts respectively. And much more was to follow.

This astonishing change in the Coburgs' political fortunes began on 2 May 1816, with the marriage of Leopold to Princess Charlotte, heiress presumptive to the British throne. The change in their financial security came with the marriage on 31 July 1817 of Ernst I to Luise, the only daughter of Frederick August, younger brother of Duke Frederick IV of Saxe-Gotha-Altenburg. As her uncle the Duke was childless, Luise was the heiress to his fortune. Yet on 12 May 1823, she was prevailed upon by her husband to give full powers over her future inheritance of Gotha to Lotz, Counsellor of the Regency. When Duke Frederick died on 11 February 1825, Lotz, in accordance with the rules of the ducal house of Saxe-Coburg-Saalfeld, was empowered to examine and settle the issue of Gotha. He took possession of the estate in trust for Ernst I and Luise's children Ernst and Albert; except for personal bequests, Luise received nothing.

Luise's elder son Ernst succeeded to the dukedom of Saxe-Coburg-Gotha following his father's death on 29 January 1844, and ruled as Ernst II until his death, also childless, in 1893. But his brother Albert, who had married Queen Victoria, had nine children. Their second son, Alfred, Duke of Edinburgh, inherited the duchy, but he too died without an heir, and it passed to his brother, the Duke of Connaught, who waived his claim in favour of his next brother Leopold, Duke of Albany. But before he could collect his prize, Leopold died, and in 1905 the duchy passed to his son Carl Edward. With Carl's abdication at the end of the Great War in November 1918, the Duchy of Saxe-Coburg-Gotha came to an end. In 1920, the burghers of Coburg were allowed to vote whether they wished to remain in Thuringia or join the state of Bavaria. Fortunately for their successors, the electors chose Bavaria – which in 1945, after the

Second World War, remained in the West, whereas Gotha, some fifty miles to the north-west in Thuringia, was submerged into the Eastern bloc.

To present a case for a Coburg conspiracy to gain a dominant influence in European affairs, one must look at the personalities behind such a remarkable achievement. Their marriage strategy was so successful that Bismarck observed: 'Coburg is the stud farm of Europe.' But this story is about more than marriage policy: the people who propelled a provincial family to such dizzy heights are all-important. History is essentially made by the acts of individuals and, therefore, is influenced by their characters – for example, we couldn't understand the origins of the First World War without a sense of the character of Kaiser Wilhelm II or Bismarck's influence on him in his youth, nor follow the steps towards the Second World War without studying the background and character of Hitler.

In the late nineteenth century, the Vanderbilts and Rockefellers would carve out huge financial empires across the Atlantic, giving them enormous economic power and political influence. At an earlier stage, the Saxe-Coburg-Gotha family achieved substantial political influence and accompanying riches, but much more subtly. Those playing a major role in this drama include: Augusta, the Dowager Duchess of Coburg; her sons Ernst I and Leopold; Baron Christian Stockmar; Duchess Luise and her second son Albert – and, of course, Albert's first cousin and wife Queen Victoria.

CHAPTER 3

The Dowager Duchess Augusta

While the marriage of Albert and Victoria was pivotal to the Coburg family fortunes, the policy of advancement through strategic marriage began much earlier, with the Dowager Duchess Augusta, mother of Duke Ernst I. If anyone can claim the credit for the Coburg pre-eminence in late nineteenth-century Europe, it is this matriarch, whose ambitions became her children's, who arranged their marriages and played a critical role in establishing the family's financial stability and influence.

Augusta von Reuss zu Ebersdorf was a formidable woman, who set the family on course for dynastic hegemony of European thrones. Born on 19 January 1757 in Ebersdorf, daughter of *Graf* Heinrich XXIV Reuss zu Ebersdorf and *Gräfin* Karoline Ernestine zu Erbach Schoenberg, she married Franz Friedrich (later Duke Franz I) on 13 June 1777. A painting of her at the age of eighteen by Johann Heinrich Tischbein, known as the Kasseler, shows a good-looking young woman with classic features in Grecian dress, pouring wine from a carved wooden urn (*see plate section between pp. 40 and 41*). Her bare left arm and her hand holding the wineglass are the focal points of the painting, and her young face, with intelligent eyes, sculpted cheekbones and firm chin, exudes charm and vivacity. The artist has perfectly captured her expression of deep concentration.

Fortunately, as was then the custom among aristocratic ladies, Augusta kept a journal. Although her handwriting is sometimes difficult to read, being in typical Gothic script, there are enough legible entries to give a good insight into her thinking and actions.

She had already had the bitter experience of her father-in-law's inadequate control of the Coburg court budget, soon to be repeated by her husband. Sophia Antoinette, wife of her father-in-law Duke

Ernst Friedrich, a princess of the House of Brunswick and a sister of the Queen of Prussia and Denmark, had run the *Schloss* and court in the royal style to which she was bred. Her indulgences had led to debts of over one million *Thaler* (£150,000 at that time – very roughly, some £20 million today) and had given the ducal family some anxious moments – even the fear of bankruptcy. Matters became so bad that Emperor Franz II insisted on the appointment of an independent court administrator, who enforced swingeing cuts in their expenditure. However, Ernst Friedrich could not maintain his court within the sum allocated to him, and Baron Christian Stockmar's grandfather, from whom the Duke constantly borrowed money, financed their high social life, receiving back neither interest nor capital. The glittering lifestyle that Augusta could normally have expected was drastically curtailed.

Her husband Duke Franz I ruled Coburg from 1800 until his death in 1806, at the age of fifty-six. He had inherited a bad economy, and the war with France had made it worse. He could not control events, nor was it in him to live quietly at home – he was a flagrantly unfaithful husband.

Augusta's original motive for enhancing the family's fortunes was the security of the House of Coburg. During the Napoleonic Wars, the ducal estates were further impoverished by the continual foraging of armies across their lands, with cattle, fodder and agricultural produce being systematically taken by the passing military. Moreover, by installing an occupying army in the area, the French also reduced the political power of the Duke in his duchy. However, Augusta found the resolve to survive the war, expecting better times ahead. Her weapons were her children: with them, she could aim at higher targets, offering both wealth and political influence. In this, the able Dowager Duchess was to succeed admirably.

There is no evidence in her journals that Augusta had a specific plan for European monarchical dominance for her family – it would have been inconceivable before 1816, given their economic plight and lack of political influence. But Augusta was the founder of the future security of the Coburgs. Having created the all-important buttress of strict economy for their immediate protection, her aristocratic background had taught her to recognise the absolute authority of her son, now the Duke. He *was* the House of Coburg, as this feudal, provincial duchy duly acknowledged and fully accepted. It knew little else. There were no urgings towards a democratic state; little or no unrest against the existing order. Augusta saw it as her duty to give the Duke all her loyalty, and the Coburgs owed her a great debt for her quiet strength behind the scenes. She never publicly criticised the Duke, even over the international scandals, dealt with later in this history, that could have ruined their reputation. She was also loyal to her daughter-in-law Luise until that loyalty clashed with the higher interest of the House of Coburg.

Her first act immediately following her son's succession as Ernst I in 1806 was to encourage him and his brother Leopold to visit Napoleon in Paris and plead for the restoration of ducal rule. In 1807, they completed this visit successfully, at the cost of joining the French Confederation of the Rhine.

Augusta also inculcated in her children a belief in the tight ducal control of affairs, a belief continually reinforced in her correspondence with them after their marriages. She was an arch-conservative: new ideas and independent thought were anathema to her. When her daughter-in-law Luise introduced social liberal ideas to help the poor in the town, Augusta was appalled, considering this to be treachery against the Duke. In her mind, Luise's charitable notions would only give the people ideas that could weaken the authority of the ducal government.

Augusta encouraged her children to seek kingdoms and authority abroad, but once they achieved these, they followed their own perceptions of good government, free from the Dowager Duchess's strict hierarchical ideas. In their new circumstances, her offspring and subsequent descendants were able to accept – and even embrace – 'enlightened rule' as a measure for the greater stability of the Crown.

Augusta's reactionary caution should not be despised. She had had to secure the duchy against the economic instability that she had experienced over a long period, and well understood how that could have led to the downfall of the House of Coburg. In the early nineteenth century, German society was accustomed to reactionary politics, and it would have been perverse for her to have deviated from the norm. The enlightened liberalism of Beethoven, Schiller and Goethe during this period was struggling against the tradition of German autocracy. It certainly bypassed the government of the dukes of Coburg.

However, a form of enlightened government would eventually evolve in Belgium under Leopold and would later be encouraged by Victoria and Albert in Britain and, through their children, abroad. It would be the great hope of both Victoria and Albert that their daughter Vicky and her husband, the German emperor, would bring about liberal enlightenment in a united Germany, which could only enhance the security of the Coburg dynasty. In this respect, they were far ahead of their contemporaries.

Augusta's quest to encourage her family to seek their ambitions abroad was helped by the fact that other German ducal houses were generally so nationalistic and provincial that they scorned 'foreign acquisitions'. Her children all found material success, if not happiness, in their marriages. The eldest son Ernst I inherited the dukedom of Coburg – his character and marriage to Luise, the heiress to the wealth of Gotha, is much discussed later. The second son Ferdinand married Antoinette (Toni), heiress of the immensely rich Prince Joseph of Koháry, Chancellor of Hungary, whereupon the Koháry family immediately settled large estates in Hungary on the Coburg descendants of the marriage. Ferdinand and Toni's eldest son, also called Ferdinand, became husband to Queen Maria da Gloria of Portugal in 1836. The third son Leopold first married Charlotte, daughter of the Prince Regent (later George IV) and heiress presumptive to the British Crown. Following her death and that of their child at birth, and after he had become King of the Belgians, he married Louise Marie, the daughter of Louis Philippe, King of France. The marriage proved happy, despite Leopold's typical Coburg infidelity.

The eldest daughter, Sophia, married Emmanuel, Count Mensdorff-Pouilly, who had fled France after the Revolution, and gained the rank of general and much distinction in the Austrian army; her sons became great friends of their cousin Albert, son of her brother Ernst. In 1795, Tsarina Catherine II invited Augusta to bring her three remaining unmarried daughters to the Russian imperial court, with the objective of one of them marrying her grandson Grand Duke

Constantine. This was despite the fact, recorded in her memoirs by Caroline Bauer, a close friend of Augusta's son Leopold, that 'Constantine had told his grandmother he had no desire to marry any of the Coburg princesses, as they were too shy and dull to suit him. But Catherine was a woman of decision, and Julia at the age of fourteen was bizarrely chosen by her for her grandson.' Caroline wrote that Catherine's decision was made when the family first arrived by coach: the Tsarina saw that Julia left the coach gracefully, whereas her elder sisters stumbled or even crawled out.

This would have been an advantageous marriage for any Coburg daughter had Constantine not been – even at sixteen – sadistic, coarse and brutal. Not surprisingly, the marriage was never a success. Soon after the death of the Tsarina Catherine, some eight years after the marriage, Julia – whose Russian name was Anna Federovna – could no longer suffer the cruel beatings and humiliation she received from her husband, and she left Constantine and moved to Elfenau, near Berne in Switzerland. Her brother Leopold remained in correspondence with Constantine, and twelve years after the separation, Constantine, in the company of Leopold, met his wife in Berne and tried to persuade her to return to him. The Dowager Duchess Augusta wrote in her journal: 'Julia amiably declined all his advances. I cannot blame her for refusing to resume a life of brilliant misery.'

The next daughter Antoinette married the Duke of Württemberg, maternal uncle to emperors Alexander and Nicholas of Russia. This, too, was an unhappy marriage – apparently the duke was avaricious and a glutton and was shockingly ugly – but Antoinette did not leave him.

Finally, the youngest daughter Mary Louise Victoire first married Prince Emich Charles of Leiningen-Dachsburg-Hedenburg, a childless widower twenty-eight years her senior. He died in 1814, leaving her with a ten-year-old son Charles and a seven-year-old daughter Feodore. In 1818, Victoire married Edward, Duke of Kent, and in May 1819 gave birth to Victoria.

Augusta died, aged 74, on 16 November 1831. But during her lifetime, she was a continuing influence on her family and the way they conducted their affairs. The comments in her journals on the personalities she came across – particularly Luise, her daughter-in-law – and on the current events of the day illuminate the thinking behind the governance of Coburg, and are important evidence of the progress made in, and limitations to, the ruling of the duchy.

CHAPTER 4

Leopold and Charlotte

Leopold of Saxe-Coburg-Saalfeld was born in Coburg on 16 December 1790, the youngest child of Duke Franz and Duchess Augusta, and grew up during the tumultuous events following the French Revolution and Napoleon's rise to power. He was just sixteen when his father died and the French invaded the duchy, expropriating the family's possessions. At the prompting of the Dowager Duchess Augusta (and with the assistance of the Tsar, whose brother was married to his sister Julia), he accompanied his brother Duke Ernst I to Paris in 1807 to obtain from Napoleon the return of the family's ducal powers and possessions.

Leopold never forgot that family fortunes could depend on a well-connected marriage, and his stay in Paris was important in other respects too. His charm, good looks and demeanour won him admiration on a world stage, and his entry into the centre of European politics and society taught him discretion and diplomacy, and gave him a polish that he could not have acquired in provincial Coburg.

As a child in 1795, Leopold had been granted the honorary title of colonel of the Ismailovski Imperial Regiment, and now, in late 1807, he accepted the offer of the Tsar – one of whose favourites he now was – of the post of major-general of cavalry in Russia. It was in this capacity that he successfully led his regiment at the battle of Kulm on 30 August 1813. He was in the Tsar's entourage at the Allies' triumphal entry into Paris, and also attended the Congress of Vienna with Ernst, where he showed considerable diplomatic skill.[1]

There are many paintings of Leopold, but perhaps the one by Winterhalter that hangs above the grand staircase in the City Hall in Brussels is the finest. Standing in a commanding pose, resplendent in uniform, his left arm extended holding the hilt of his sword, whose point is touching the ground, this handsome figure exudes grace, dignity, breeding, charm, leadership qualities, determination and ambition. He looks like a man who has not only succeeded but could never contemplate *not* succeeding. It is Leopold, through his life, care and devotion to the cause of the Saxe-Coburgs, whom his family can thank more than anyone else for its direction and purpose, exercised well beyond the limited bounds of that small dukedom. More particularly, Leopold's conduct in his public life, and through his utterances and letters – although not always his actions – ensured that he always held the high moral ground.

Furthermore, Leopold was different, culturally and intellectually, from both his father and his eldest brother. Opportunist he may have been – he was fully aware that, as a third son, he would have to make his own place in the world – but his wish to raise himself to a higher station was understandable. Realising that the arrogant style of his brother would not win him friends or influence events, he distanced himself from Ernst and honed his personal charm and diplomacy with the aim of constructing an advantageous future. Leopold had the clarity of mind to know what he wanted and how to achieve it, was prepared to bide his time – and was a master of the timing that was paramount in public life. His strategy and tactics remained unseen, and therefore unobstructed, by those who might have opposed them; and if on occasion he found he was in danger of alarming persons of influence, he had the wisdom to recognise this and reduce sail for a moment and wait for a more favourable wind. His long-term view held him in good stead, since in due course he was able to assert himself as a role model for moral enlightenment and good government.

Leopold used his leadership qualities not only for his own fulfilment, but also in developing his influence with his family and, specifically, with his young niece Princess Victoria, daughter of his sister Victoire. Victoria greatly admired him, and they corresponded voluminously for decades. Similarly, he developed a close relationship with his nephews Ernst and, more particularly, Albert. From the earliest moments, Leopold schooled Albert with a view to his betrothal to Victoria, the liaison that would eventually see the Coburg family at the top of the royal houses in Europe.

In this quest, Leopold sought the help and lifelong services of Christian Stockmar, first for a short period as his private physician, then as his trusted envoy. Stockmar served him loyally and with the greatest integrity in every task he was given in this unique pivotal role: perhaps the nearest equivalent would be that of *consigliere* to Leopold's Mafia *don* – the quiet adviser in the shadows and, consequently, the more effective to his master.

Despite his probity in public, Leopold had not escaped the amorous habits of the Coburgs; his life was enlivened by many mistresses, though he was more socially selective in his choice of them than either his father or his brother Ernst. Caroline Bauer, a beautiful actress and a cousin of Stockmar's, depicts him in her memoirs as a person who certainly did not lead a virtuous life, but she had reason to write bitterly of Leopold. Many years after the death of his wife Princess Charlotte, Leopold brought Caroline to England to live with him and, on 2 July 1829, participated in a form of marriage ceremony with her. The ceremony was no more than a private agreement between them and was never legally recognised, but she still resented the ending of their relationship in 1831 when Leopold became King of the Belgians. (Caroline was created Countess of Montgomery, and died by her own hand from an overdose of sleeping pills in 1877.)

Leopold's eye for an opportunity to cause a dramatic change in his and his family's position was first seen in action in London in 1816, when dash, a certain bravado and lucky timing led him to meet Princess Charlotte. It was a key moment in the rise of the Coburgs.

Princess Charlotte, daughter of George, Prince of Wales and Prince Regent, and Princess Caroline of Brunswick, was born on 7 January 1796. Her parents had an acrimonious relationship, and on his accession George IV notoriously had his queen locked out of the coronation ceremony at Westminster Abbey, leaving her beating vainly on the doors. Charlotte's parents cared almost as little for her as for each other: as she later expressed to Stockmar: 'My mother was bad, but she would not have become as bad as she was had my father not been infinitely worse.' [2]

Moreover, the Prince Regent was also on bad terms with both his father George III and his mother Queen Charlotte, and Princess

Caroline could not bear either of them. Brought up amidst violent family quarrels and a distinct lack of respect between her parents, Charlotte, not surprisingly, grew into a rebellious and strong-willed personality, clearly a handful for any would-be suitor.

But Charlotte was heiress presumptive to the throne. At first, she was left in the care of her mother, whom George III protected from the excesses of her husband's conduct, but Caroline lost this protection in 1810, when the King became so mentally ill that the Prince of Wales was able to assume the regency. Charlotte was taken away from her mother and placed in the care of her grandmother Queen Charlotte at Windsor, so the heiress presumptive of Great Britain and its ever-widening empire grew up isolated from close friends of her own age. The Princess of Wales was only allowed to see her daughter once a week, further limited to once a fortnight in 1812. Fortunately for Charlotte, her governess and 'lady companion' Cornelia Knight was wholly supportive and loyal towards her – and is also an important witness to the events leading to Leopold's introduction into the royal family.

Cornelia Knight (1757–1837) recorded her personal reminiscences and historical observations in her autobiography. Born into an upper-class family, her father a rear admiral, she was educated from the age of five in Switzerland, and as a child travelled in France and Italy with her mother (whose friendships with Thomas Gainsborough and Sir Joshua Reynolds Cornelia records, along with her own memories of Samuel Johnson). In 1812 she entered the service of Princess Charlotte at Warwick House as lady companion. Given the enmity between the Prince Regent and Princess Caroline, the birth of a son who would take precedence over Charlotte was acknowledged as beyond probability. Thus at this crucial point in history, following the loss of the American colonies and the French Revolution and their consequences, the British royal family was as dysfunctional as it could be, and a husband must therefore be found for Charlotte.

The tragicomedy of the proposed marriage began when Charlotte was sixteen, in 1813. Cornelia Knight relates that on 11 December the hereditary prince of Holland, the Prince of Orange, arrived in London and met Charlotte for the first time at the home of her father, the Prince Regent.[3] On 12 December the Prince Regent took his daughter aside and asked: 'Well, it will not do, I suppose?' Charlotte replied, 'I do not say that: I like his manner very well. He is by no means as disagreeable as I expected.' Upon which the Prince of Wales took Charlotte's hands and declared that, as from that moment, she was engaged to the Prince of Orange.

Despite its perfunctory manner, and the fact that no discussion with ministers or family had taken place, the marriage was deemed to be politically sound: Great Britain and the United Netherlands would be an effective bulwark against France. So in January 1814, the intended marriage was confidentially communicated to a number of foreign sovereigns,[4] and in March Faigel, the Dutch ambassador to the Court of St James, along with Count Van der Duyn de Maasdon, formally requested the hand of the Princess for their Prince, and received her assent. The sovereign of the Netherlands officially announced the approaching marriage to the States General and Plenipotentiaries, and both sides drew up a draft treaty of marriage.

However, in June 1814 Charlotte broke off the engagement. Her mother had put into her head the thought that the Prince Regent wanted to get Charlotte out of the country and, once she was abroad, would do his utmost to prevent her return and so annul her right of succession. Country and accession were very dear to Charlotte, and her experiences in childhood – in particular, the low opinion she had formed of her father's character – led her readily to believe these insinuations.

She wrote to her father on 15 April 1814, asking for confirmation about her future residence since, when the marriage had been first proposed, she had never considered that she would not continue to live in England. The Prince Regent sent for Cornelia Knight to express his displeasure at the letter. The confirmation demanded by the Princess, he said, was impossible and contrary to the duty of a wife. If she insisted on maintaining her stance, the engagement must be broken off and he would never give his consent to any other marriage.

Cornelia reported back and, on 19 April, returned to the Prince Regent with a letter from Charlotte saying that she couldn't withdraw a word. Preparations were being made for a residence in

Holland, but none for one in England, even though the Prince of Orange had, on 9 February, put in writing his wish that Parliament might stipulate that they should reside in England for at least six months a year. The Prince of Wales, finding it demeaning to enter into further personal discussion on this matter with his daughter, asked his brother, the Duke of York, to intervene as a mediator.

The Duke of York arrived accompanied by William Adam, the Chancellor of the Duchy of Cornwall, an uncle of Charlotte's former governess Miss Mercer Elphinstone. They repeated the Prince Regent's arguments, and added that 'the magnitude of the annuity which in case of her marriage would be asked from Parliament was the best proof of the intention to allow her to reside chiefly in England'. But after the interview, Charlotte wrote to her uncle that she must insist on the stipulations that she had first sent to the Prince Regent.

The Duke of York tried to set up another interview, but Charlotte declined. Several letters were exchanged, with the Duke writing that the Princess had bound herself too far to withdraw now: the Dutch envoys had made a formal offer and she had given consent in a state audience; the Prince of Orange had sent money for the purchase of jewels; and she had already placed several orders for those. She should, he wrote, reflect on what sort of light all this would show her in. Charlotte replied that she thought herself in no way bound; the audience of the envoys and the purchase of the jewels were preliminary steps of minor importance.

On 30 April, the Prince of Orange called on Charlotte. She was in bed with a light fever, but rose, dressed and exchanged assurances of unaltered affection for him. He went straight to the Prince Regent, and then returned to Charlotte with the news that her father would see them together, that there had been a misunderstanding, and that it had never entered his mind that the Princess should live chiefly abroad. Charlotte excused herself on the grounds of her health: in fact, she couldn't trust her own fortitude face to face with her father.

On 8 May, the prime minister Lord Liverpool visited Charlotte, explained that there was no suggestion that she should permanently reside out of England, and proposed articles to be incorporated into the marriage contract to safeguard her position. Charlotte responded that this did not ensure her perfect freedom of choice as to her residence and, throughout the rest of May, remained resolute against all persuasion. Finally, on 10 June, after further correspondence and jockeying, Charlotte acceded to the amended articles. All seemed settled for the marriage to proceed.

Now, however, as they occasionally do at key moments in history, events took over. On 7 June 1814, the Allied sovereigns and victorious generals arrived in London to celebrate what was then thought to be the final victory over Napoleon. The visit caused a new family quarrel when the Prince Regent ordered his wife and daughter to be excluded from court during the festivities. This was understandable from his viewpoint: he was not prepared to risk a public scene with Caroline among such internationally important visitors and, furthermore, was by now seething at the public humiliation that Charlotte was causing him through her antics over her marriage. The issue was compounded by the fact that the Prince Regent had ensured that the Prince of Orange *was* included in the invitation lists.

Cornelia Knight comments that, at this point, Charlotte had met and fallen in love with Prince Frederick, the King of Prussia's nineteen-year-old nephew, whom she had met at a dinner party at Carlton House. Cornelia had subsequently helped her to meet him clandestinely at the princess's home, Warwick House. It was also in June 1814 that Leopold arrived in London. Aware of the situation between Charlotte and the Prince of Orange, he considered it perfectly reasonable to do his best to meet Charlotte and influence her towards himself. Cornelia Knight notes that, due no doubt to her new passion for Prince Frederick, Charlotte remained uninterested in Leopold's attempts to gain her attention.

In a personal interview on 16 June, Charlotte told her fiancé, the Prince of Orange, that it would be impossible for her to leave England immediately after the marriage, and also demanded that the marital home should always be open to her mother, the Princess of Wales. As the Prince of Orange would not agree to this, Charlotte told him that the marriage was impossible, repeating this in writing the same day, and leaving him to explain it to the Prince Regent. Since the Prince of Orange declined to do this, Charlotte was obliged to do so herself and, on 18 June, wrote her father a letter in which she tried to blame the Prince of Orange.

In a brief reply on 19 June, the Prince Regent expressed 'deep concern'. He received no response from Charlotte by 12 July, by which time, as Cornelia Knight records, he had got wind of the fact that Charlotte was having secret meetings with a man whom he mistakenly thought was his disreputable thirty-five-year-old cousin Prince Augustus of Prussia. Outraged at his defeat by his daughter over the matter of the Prince of Orange, and in the belief that Charlotte was engaged in secret dealings with his cousin Augustus, the Prince Regent could contain himself no longer. He appeared suddenly at Warwick House, summarily dismissed all her household as evident accomplices in her insubordination, and sentenced her to strict seclusion in Cranbourne Lodge in Windsor Great Park.

The headstrong Charlotte ran down the back stairs of Warwick House and hailed a passing cab, which drove her to her mother's house in Connaught Street. She was pursued, and finally, at two in the morning, her uncles, the dukes of York and Sussex, and the Bishop of Salisbury persuaded her to return. The next morning, she reluctantly but dutifully went to Cranbourne Lodge. No more was heard of the Prince of Orange. Charlotte did, however, manage to carry on a secret correspondence with Frederick.

But Frederick, having got in over his head and not wishing to involve himself further with the boisterous Charlotte, whom he realised was beyond his control, finally broke off the relationship in January 1815. Now that the Prussian had left the scene, the way was at last open for Leopold to press his case. As part of the Tsar's retinue, dressed in an attractive uniform, he cut a handsome figure. His timing was impeccable. His eye for an opening was even better.

There had been long months of battles between Charlotte, her father, her uncle the Duke of York, advisers and even the prime minister, not forgetting the Prince of Orange and the Dutch envoys. It took remarkable staying power for a girl of eighteen to stand alone, except for her lady companion, and argue her position with such eminent and practised forces arrayed against her. It was later said that Victoria had a similar wilful persistence at the same age, but few could compete with Charlotte's resilience between April and July 1814, which, in fact, lasted until May 1816.

With the final withering of her relationships with the Prince of

Orange and Prince Frederick, Charlotte announced that she wanted to become better acquainted with Leopold. She prevailed upon her aunt, the Duchess of York, to hold a ball for her, which was a great success for both the Princess and Leopold. Each had wanted to meet the other, and it was not long before Charlotte succumbed to Leopold's charms and became infatuated with him.

By now, he was internationally experienced in diplomacy and respected for his military record. He went out of his way to impress the British ministers and, while on duty with the Tsar's forces in Paris, made a point of creating a lasting friendship with Charlotte's uncle, the Duke of Kent. In the early days of their courtship, before the Prince Regent finally gave up the struggle to control his daughter, Leopold could only communicate with Charlotte through the Duke: his ability to see her regularly was limited and their meetings were substantially clandestine. However, his good looks and charming manners were sufficient to secure her affection, which his absences in Paris only strengthened. She told her father and everyone she encountered that Leopold was necessary for her happiness.

A wedding to the Prince of Orange would have been a state marriage, but Leopold, a third son, could bring neither wealth nor status to the match. Coming from Coburg, with its population of fewer than 60,000, neither could he bring political influence to a marriage with the heiress presumptive to the British Crown. The Prince Regent did what he could to pour scorn on any association between his daughter and Leopold, but after the miserable saga of the Prince of Orange he was in no mood to enter the lists again and, after some resistance, withdrew. If his daughter wanted to throw herself away on a nonentity, so be it.

Charlotte and Leopold were married on the evening of 2 May 1816 in the crimson room at Carlton House in the presence of some fifty guests. Her wedding dress was silver lamé on net, over a silver tissue slip, its elbow-length sleeves trimmed with Brussels point lace. Leopold, who had been granted a commission as field marshal of the British army, wore a general's embroidered uniform coat, white waistcoat and white breeches. The honeymoon was spent at the Duke of York's country seat, Oatlands in Surrey; then the newly-weds took up residence at Claremont House, a mile south-west of Esher, which had been purchased for them by the government. Parliament had voted Charlotte a dowry of £60,000 and a joint annuity of £50,000, with an additional £10,000 for the couple's household, plus the grant of Camelford House in Oxford Street as their town house.

Leopold's character – a cool and formal manner, slow in speech and careful in action – contrasted starkly with that of the headstrong Charlotte, who had little of the dignity and self-containment necessary for a queen. Yet he soon controlled Charlotte's wildness and brought out her natural good-heartedness. As Leopold explained much later to Victoria:

> There was friction, but standing before me like a rebellious boy in petticoats, her body pushed forward, her hands behind her back, with flaming cheeks and sparkling eyes, she would declare: 'If you wish it, I will do it. I want nothing for myself.' I would reply: 'When I press something on you, it is from a conviction that it is for your interest and for your good.' [5]

Certainly to England Leopold was a welcome change from the Hanovers, who had exhausted the public's goodwill with their financial extravagances, their amoral relationships with countless women of all orders, and their notorious inability to present a united family front. It was a surprise to many that Leopold and Charlotte led a scandal-free life, given the examples set by their respective parents and relatives. But Leopold knew how to handle his wife, and Charlotte, for the first time, was really happy, having found sympathy, support and love. Years later, in May 1845, Leopold wrote to Victoria a great eulogy of Charlotte enclosing a gift of Charlotte's portrait, which included these words:

> Her constancy in wishing to marry me, which she maintained under difficulties of every description, has been the foundation of all that touched the family afterwards. You know, I believe, that your poor father was the chief promoter, though also the Yorks were, but our correspondence from 1814 'til 1816 was entirely

carried on through his kind intervention. It would otherwise have been impossible, as she was really treated as a sort of prisoner.

So the Coburgs had made their first key move, and the stage was set for them to consolidate their gains. The tool for that was already to hand: just over a month before the royal wedding, Christian Stockmar had arrived in England to enter Leopold's service.

CHAPTER 5

Stockmar

Leopold needed an unassuming administrator to act as a front for him, a man who could receive the confidence of ministers and those close to power, so that he himself could keep a dignified distance from any detailed discussions affecting the Coburg family. Christian Frederick Stockmar was that man. He has gone down in history as the epitome of loyalty, discretion and selfless devotion – not only to his prince, but also to the whole House of Coburg as well as to Princess Charlotte, Queen Victoria and Prince Albert.

Stockmar was born in Coburg on 22 August 1787, grandson to the Stockmar who had so generously funded Leopold's father, and the second child and first son of Ernst Stockmar, a successful lawyer who rose to become a magistrate of the town. He was educated at the Coburg Gymnasium and subsequently studied medicine at the universities of Würtzburg, Erlangen and Jena, where he was known as a serious student but also a wit – an attribute he seems not to have retained, since according to Lytton Strachey, he was 'dyspeptic by constitution and melancholic by temperament'.[1]

His interest in politics developed at university. He dreamed, like many of his fellow students, of a united Germany under the leadership of Prussia, yearned for unity, power and greatness for the Fatherland, and held Napoleon's Confederation of the Rhine in contempt. Stockmar particularly despised the smaller German states, the principalities and duchies that had remained stubbornly feudal in style and had no interest in developing constitutional democracy, being intent only on maintaining their lands to provide their personal revenue. He was much influenced by the ideals behind the French Revolution and the sense of enlightenment pervading Continental Europe, and was aware of the rising power of Britain, which he attributed to its comparatively liberal constitutional monarchy that had evolved since the Civil War of the seventeenth century. When he was in a position to influence princes, he always instilled in them the benefits of moral leadership, arguing that it cost them no personal power but rather gained the affection of the people they were destined to rule and consequently ensured the security of the Crown.

Stockmar qualified as a doctor in 1812, and began work at the military hospital in Coburg when the Napoleonic Wars were still raging. In 1814, with the conflict at its height, he was transferred to Worms, where he first met Leopold. The hospital was full of wounded French troops when a large number of German wounded arrived, and the senior medical officer ordered Stockmar to give priority to the Germans. Stockmar refused, saying that he would deal with all wounded in strict medical priority. A fierce argument ensued, but Stockmar gained his point. Leopold heard of this and, deeply impressed, asked to meet him: so began a relationship that was to last until Stockmar's death on 9 July 1863.

In 1815, at the end of the Napoleonic Wars, Stockmar returned to Coburg to practise as a physician, while Leopold was courting Princess Charlotte in London. The next spring, Leopold summoned him to come to London as his physician, and Stockmar accepted with alacrity. On 29 March he landed at Dover, full of excitement at his new position in this powerful constitutional country he so admired. He wrote in his diary: 'The country, the houses, their arrangement, everything, especially in the neighbourhood of London, delighted me and so raised my spirits.'

He had anxieties. He had given up a settled life in the small but comfortable surroundings of his own country for an uncertain future in a country whose language and customs he did not know. However, it didn't take Stockmar long to gain the complete trust of Leopold, who was impressed by the way Charlotte took to him. He wrote in his diary: 'My master is the best of all husbands in all the five [sic] quarters of the globe; and his wife bears him such love as can only be compared with the English national debt.'[2]

The happy marriage was, however, sadly brief. Charlotte died shortly after the birth of her stillborn son at 2am on 6 November 1817. Despite Charlotte's pleas to 'Stockie' to be her *accoucheur*, he had consistently refused to care for her: he didn't trust what the English doctors would say about him if anything went wrong. In a letter of 10 February 1818, he wrote: 'I can only thank God that I never allowed myself to be blinded by vanity, but always kept in view the danger … if I arrogantly pushed myself into a place in which a foreigner could never expect to reap honour, but possibly plenty of blame.'

His ambitions and happiness so quickly destroyed, Leopold turned to Stockmar. 'I am now desolate,' he wrote. 'Promise always to stay with me.' Stockmar subsequently wrote, 'I did not hesitate to promise,' and now acted as Leopold's private secretary and political adviser, as well as controller of the household. In this new position, he became not just a legal, political and diplomatic adviser with the aim of expanding the Coburg power base, but set about his own, much greater and far-seeing mission to establish a moral leadership that would be respected worldwide. That would truly place the Coburgs on the map.

Stockmar soon realised that he could only succeed if he were seen to be without ambition beyond his allotted position, so that he intruded into no one else's sphere of influence and could be accepted by all sides. His discretion reassured the influential, who felt secure in discussing their confidential thoughts with him. He thrived on passing unobserved. Consequently, in a comparatively short time, he built up a wide-ranging network of those who held influence, both in government and in opposition, and quickly gained a reputation as a man of sound judgement. It was a unique situation for a foreigner. Only a very few people, in very high places and exceptionally well-informed, knew how important Stockmar was. For Stockmar, that was enough.[3] Later, in 1839, Lord Melbourne said to Queen Victoria, 'Stockmar is not only an excellent man but also one of the most sensible I have ever met with.'[4] Even Lord Palmerston, who on good authority disliked Stockmar, said of him: 'I have never but once met a perfectly disinterested man of this kind, and that is Stockmar.'[5] And Lord Aberdeen, Palmerston's predecessor as prime minister, stated: 'I have known men as clever, as discreet, as good, and with as much judgement; but I have never known anyone who united all these qualities as he did. He is a most remarkable man!'[6]

Perhaps the key to Stockmar can be found in words he wrote shortly before he died:

> Were I now to be asked by any young man just entering into life, 'What is the chief good for which it behoves a man to strive?' my only answer would be 'Love and friendship'. Were he to ask me, 'What is man's priceless possession?' I must answer: 'The consciousness of having loved and sought the truth; of having yearned for the truth for its own sake. All else is either mere vanity or a sick man's dream.'

Stockmar had two political ideals. First, he wanted to see Germany united under Prussia, and second, he wanted to establish a unity of purpose between England and Germany. In particular, he yearned for the unity, power and greatness of the Fatherland to his last breath.

In 1821, Prince Leopold granted him a patent of Saxon nobility, and in 1832 he was raised to the rank of baron in Bavaria, to which an Austrian barony was added in 1840. In August 1821, Stockmar married his cousin Fanny Sommer in Coburg, and founded a home and family there. They had three children: Ernst, born in 1823, Marie in 1827 and Karl in 1836. In their thirty-six years of marriage, he only spent, on average, six months a year at home; sometimes several years passed without him seeing his wife and children.

His married life was not successful: his priorities were Leopold, Victoria and Albert, and his constant absences deprived Fanny of the love and companionship she craved. When Stockmar eventually retired, he was met with a sullen and bitter woman who was to plague him to his death. He wrote to Leopold: 'I confess I was not prepared for so comfortless an old age. Often, very often, I am in despair.' During his lengthy illness in late life, he could not 'obtain in his own house a bowl of broth'. Frau Stockmar was even fined in the Coburg Court for giving her servant food unfit for human consumption.

Caroline Bauer recorded Stockmar's sister's account of his death on 9 June 1863. 'His last hour was terrible. When he lay at the point of death, his hard wife took off his back his flannel jacket and shirt so that after his death, according to Coburg custom, the undertaker might not claim them.'

But that was in the future. Following Charlotte's death, Prince Leopold's friends and relations in Coburg urged him to return there, but Stockmar advised him to spend an appropriate time of mourning in England, and Leopold took his advice.[7] It was the late summer of 1818 before he returned to Coburg, where he met up with his mother Augusta, his brother Ernst I and, significantly, Ernst's young, attractive and flirtatious wife Luise.

CHAPTER 6

The Greek affair and victory in Belgium

Leopold returned from his stay in Coburg to Claremont Lodge in June 1819. He liked England, where he was accepted in society as the widower of the late heiress presumptive, and there was enormous sympathy for the grievous loss of his wife and stillborn child. He was much admired for his calmness and propriety, maintained his charisma, was good at networking, kept aloof from controversies and generally maintained a dignified royal presence. With the annuity of £50,000 granted by Parliament on his marriage, his life interest in Claremont Lodge and his town house in London, he was no longer an impecunious scion of a faraway minor dukedom. With acceptable discretion he took Stockmar's cousin, Caroline Bauer, as his mistress, and the couple were welcomed in the country houses of the aristocracy and influential politicians.

When the Duke of Kent died suddenly and unexpectedly from pneumonia in January 1820, leaving substantial debts, Leopold stepped in to assist the destitute widow, his sister Victoire, and her daughter Victoria. Much later, on 12 December 1842, Leopold wrote to Victoria: 'The Regent's great wish was to get you and your Mama out of the country, and I must say without my assistance you could not have remained ... I know not what would have come of you and your Mama, if I had not then existed.'[1]

Leopold was not someone who could be content with a hedonistic life. He had a sense of duty and responsibility, inculcated by his military service and familial ambitions, from which he had no wish to deviate. Biding his time, he watched for opportunities to achieve such ambitions. And in 1829, Greece beckoned.

The Ottoman Empire had ruled all of Greece, except for the Ionian islands, since its conquest of the Byzantine Empire in the mid-fifteenth century. But during the late eighteenth and early nineteenth centuries, the influences of the Enlightenment and nationalism, accentuated by the example of the French Revolution, began to be felt there. The Ottoman Empire was by then in decline, and Greek nationalism received support from France, England and Russia. It was encouraged within Greece itself by Rigas Feraios, who published a Greek-language newspaper in Vienna in 1795, proposing a Greek republican constitution. He and his colleagues were arrested in Trieste by Austrian agents in June 1798, and handed over to the Ottoman authorities: they were all strangled and their bodies thrown into the Danube, their martyrdom further fanning the flames of independence.

In 1814, Greek nationalists in Odessa formed a secret organisation called the *Filiki Eteria* ('Friendly Society'), which won support from Greek exile communities in England and the United States, together with covert assistance from Russia. On 23 March of that year there were uprisings both in the southern isthmus of the Peloponnese and in central Greece, and eight years later, in January 1822, Greece's first National Assembly declared the country's independence.

The Ottomans retaliated brutally: civilian populations were massacred, and the Sultan dangerously escalated the conflict by bringing in his most powerful vassal, Egypt. Its ruler Mehemet Ali soon took command of the Aegean, while on land, Tripolis, the administrative centre of the Peloponnese, was captured by his son Ibrahim Pasha.

In Europe, there was widespread sympathy for the Greeks' courageous resistance against the odds: the sight of a Christian nation attempting to cast off the rule of a Muslim empire – especially the nation that was seen as the cradle of Western civilisation – appealed to the public. The poet Byron, in particular, imbued the cause with a spirit of romanticism; when in 1824 he died from fever in Messolonghi in central Greece, sympathy for the Greek cause rose to greater heights in England.

In 1827, France, Britain and Russia intervened directly, and on 20 October 1827 their combined fleets destroyed the Ottoman navy at Navarino, while on land the Greeks seized as much territory as possible before the powers imposed a ceasefire. Finally, on 12 December 1828, the ambassadors of Russia, France and Britain that were accredited to the Ottoman Empire agreed at a conference at Poros that Greece was to be made independent of Turkey and to have a Christian hereditary monarchy.

At this stage, Leopold began to canvass support for his taking the crown. It is not clear from the records whether either he or Stockmar appreciated the extreme volatility of Greece's recent history, but for Leopold the prospect of its crown was too enticing to ignore: it was a prize to be seized. He took the initiative by visiting Greece and holding discussions with Ioannis Kapodistrias, the President of the Greek Assembly, with whom he put his easy charm to work to good effect. By the end of his visit, Kapodistrias felt that Leopold was a person he could work with. When, in 1829, the ambassadors asked Kapodistrias whom he recommended as sovereign, he unhesitatingly supported Leopold.

Both France and Russia favoured this choice too, but George IV fought it, influenced by the Duke of Cumberland, who wanted his wife's brother Duke Charles of Mecklenburg to secure the position. The British government only forced the King to accept Leopold's candidature by threatening to resign. But negotiations over international financial support and acceptable frontiers were confusing and lengthy. From time to time, agreement appeared to have been reached, only for the Greek National Assembly to object, and Kapodistrias always played a duplicitous game.

However, on 30 January 1830 Leopold made a grave mistake when he told the Tory foreign secretary Lord Aberdeen that he was not inclined to accept the throne unless the powers were ready to add Crete, then known as Candia, to the territory already granted. Aberdeen wrote curtly the next day:

Of Candia there has not hitherto on any occasion been a question. Your Royal Highness is free, notwithstanding all that has passed, to decline the sovereignty of Greece but the exclusion of Candia cannot offer any satisfactory explanation of such a decision. Your Royal Highness must consider how little such a course would be compatible with the real dignity and consistency of your own character. The powers have no intention whatever of negotiating with your Royal Highness. They expect a simple acceptance of their proposal and would consider a conditional acceptance as a virtual refusal.[2]

One reason for Aberdeen's hardline stance was that Leopold had inherited from his wife acquaintanceships and friendships among the leaders of the Whig opposition. His contacts with Earl Grey and Charles Greville had not gone unnoticed, and Wellington's Tory Ministry distrusted Leopold's new stance, believing it to be mischief-making by the Whigs. In his letter of 31 January, Aberdeen clearly considered that Leopold had been acting on the advice of persons hostile to his ministry, since his letter goes on: 'However these sentiments may accord with the political objects of persons in this country by whom your Royal Highness may have been advised.'[3]

Nevertheless, the Protocol of 3 February 1830 officially offered Leopold the Greek crown. On 11 February, Leopold sent a written answer to the ambassadors, laying down five conditions. They would not hear of conditions, and Leopold, humiliated, had to withdraw them. In a letter of 10 April 1830 to Baron Stein (a Prussian states-man who had been with Tsar Alexander when Napoleon had occupied the Kremlin, and had strongly encouraged the Tsar to refuse to listen to any overtures of peace from the French emperor), his bitter-ness showed. He wrote of the 'hard struggle carried on for months against ill will and a mistaken policy so that one's very soul is chilled within one ... of the vain and obstinate men with whom I had to negotiate'.

Kapodistrias, ever manipulative, wrote to Leopold in early May 1830 that the Greeks had been told that they were allowed no voice in the settlement of their own destiny. He also passed on the many comments hostile to Leopold, referred to the almost insurmountable difficulties that he would find, and called the provisions in the Protocol respecting frontiers disastrous. Leopold passed these com-munications on to the ambassadors, and in a letter of 21 May 1830 finally declined the offer of the crown, on the grounds that Greece was irrevocably hostile to the conditions laid down by the powers.

The comments on Leopold's handling of the Greek position were substantially hostile. Prince Lieven, the Russian ambassador in London, wrote: 'Prince Leopold had accepted decisions of the

Conference unconditionally and had abandoned all his original objections.' Baron Stein added more trenchant criticism in a letter to the Archbishop of Cologne:

> Instead of conquering difficulties, completing the work he had undertaken, he withdraws like a coward his hand from the plough and calculates the possible chances which the approaching death of George IV may throw his way. A man of weak character is totally unfit to play a bold part in life. He has no colour.

To place Leopold's position in a fairer light, his withdrawal had taken place a whole month before the illness of George IV might have led him to hope for the regency, and Stockmar had spoken even earlier of the possible breaking off of the negotiations because of practical difficulties. As for Lieven's comments, the Duke of Wellington considered his wife a mischievous intriguer who would 'betray everybody in turn if it should suit her purpose'.[4] During the Iron Duke's time as ambassador to Russia, Madame Lieven and her husband had, he wrote, 'taken pains to represent my conduct in the most unfavourable light in St Petersburg. They note all the evil that they thought and much more than they knew.'[5] English political circles generally saw Leopold as a man of honour, however disappointed they may have been at his refusal of the Greek chalice – which certainly turned out to be thoroughly poisonous: the wily Kapodistrias was himself assassinated on 9 October 1831 and anarchy took over.

Leopold's nephew Ernst II, brother of Albert, later wrote in his memoirs:

> It had been suggested that Leopold was relieved not to have succeeded to the Greek throne because of Greek volatility. It is true that personal inclination was not in this case entirely without influence on my Uncle. I can still perfectly remember my grandmother's [Augusta] angry complaints and outbursts of grief over the fact that her beloved son, Leopold, was forced to look to an uncertain fate. She tried as well as she could to warn him against it … But he really felt the deepest interest in the Greek question; and has done so all his life. That the throne of the wavering

descendants of the ancient Hellenes was denied the House of Coburg, he considered up to the last years of his life as a piece of ill luck which he felt himself bound to make up for.

The final episode of the Greek saga saw Leopold recommending his brother Ernst I, the reigning Duke of Coburg, as the new King. Inevitably, negotiations were drawn out, and by the time Ernst I sent his final conditions to Leopold, King Louis of Bavaria had already completed an agreement on behalf of his son Otto. At the London Conference in May 1832, Britain, France and Russia offered the throne to Prince Otto with the proviso that the thrones of Bavaria and Greece would never be joined. The final protocol, signed on 7 May 1832, created Greece as an independent kingdom with a loan of £2,400,000; the Ottoman Empire was indemnified the sum of 40,000,000 piastres for the loss of the territory. And within a year of his refusal of the Greek crown, Leopold was offered another kingdom.

In 1815, following the defeat of Napoleon, the Congress of Vienna created a kingdom for the House of Orange-Nassau, combining the United Provinces of the Netherlands with the former 'Southern Provinces' (later Belgium), to be known as the 'United Kingdom of the Netherlands'. The intention was to create a strong buffer state north of France, and also to compensate the Dutch for their loss of Ceylon and the Cape Colony, which the British had seized when Holland had been an unwilling partner of Napoleon and insisted on retaining.

However, the domination of the Dutch over the economic, political and social institutions of the former Southern Provinces led to unrest. Generally, the Dutch supported free trade while the less-developed industries in Belgium wanted the protection of tariffs. Free trade resulted in a lower price for bread made from wheat imported from the Baltic states through Antwerp, which depressed the grain-growing regions in Belgium. Further, the French of the upper and middle classes became the sole official language there, with Flemish banned in schools.

Unrest grew among both the working people and intellectuals at the dismissive manner in which the king of Holland was treating their historic customs and national identity. Finally, on 25 August 1830, an upsurge of nationalism led to riots, purportedly triggered by a performance of the patriotic opera *La Muette de Portici*. Crowds poured on to the streets afterwards and swiftly took possession of the Hotel de Ville and other government buildings.

Crown Prince William, representing the Dutch monarchy in Brussels, tried hard to obtain a measure of co-operation from the Estates General, but by 1 September he had become convinced that they would only accept a solution that would effectively separate the administrations of the north and south. His father the King rejected the proposal, and tried to restore order by force. But the army under Prince Frederick was unable to retake Brussels in bloody street fighting between 23 and 26 September, and on 4 October a provisional government in Brussels declared the independent state of Belgium.

At first, the European powers had been divided over the Belgian issue. The Napoleonic Wars were still fresh in their memory, and there remained substantial suspicion of French motives. When the French, under the recently installed 'July Monarchy' of Louis-Philippe, supported Belgian independence, Russia, Prussia, Austria and Britain not surprisingly supported the continued union of the Provinces of the Netherlands. None of them, however, sent troops to aid the Dutch government – Russia was then having difficulties with a rebellion in Poland, and Britain was not ready to commit military forces to the Continent so soon after Waterloo.

On 20 December, at the London Conference convened to settle the question, the European powers recognised *de facto* the independence of Belgium. The usual diplomatic card-playing then took place. The National Congress of France supported the Belgian constitution and, on 3 February 1831 nominated Louis, Duc de Nemours, the second son of Louis-Philippe, for the throne of Belgium, a unilateral act wholly unacceptable to the other powers. Two weeks later, the French king declined the crown on behalf of his son.

In Britain, Leopold's name was not mentioned in this connection. He was not in favour with the Wellington government, after its disappointment over the Greek business – and, in any case, the government would not hear of Belgium's independence. However, he was once again lucky with timing: on 16 November 1830, Wellington was defeated in the Commons and resigned.

He had believed that the fright caused by the French and Belgian revolutions would lead his supporters to fight the proposed reforms to extend the franchise in Britain. However, most Tory MPs considered that the mood of the country was in favour of franchise reform and that to take an implacable line against it would be nothing short of political suicide. On 2 November 1830, Wellington's speech in the House of Lords had proved their judgement correct. 'I have never read,' he had said

'or heard of, any measure up to the present moment which could in any degree satisfy my mind that the state of the representation could be improved … The representation of the people at present contains a large body of the property of the country, in which the landed interests have a preponderating influence. Under these circumstances, I am not only not prepared to bring forward any measure [of parliamentary reform], but I will at once declare that as far as I am concerned, as long as I hold any station in the government of this country, I shall always feel it my duty to resist such measures when proposed by others.'[6]

As he had sat down, Wellington had whispered to Lord Aberdeen, his foreign secretary, 'What can I have said which seems to have made so great a disturbance?' to which Aberdeen had replied, 'You have announced the fall of your government, that is all.'

Charles Greville, the Whig diarist and clerk to the Privy Council, astutely noted about Wellington:

He has an overweening opinion of his own all-sufficiency, and that is his besetting sin, and the one which, if anything does, will overturn his government; for if he would be less dictatorial and opinionated, and would call to his assistance such talents and information as the crisis demands, he would be universally voted the best man alive to be at the head of the government.[7]

On 16 November, the new king William IV called upon Earl Grey to form a ministry, one that supported the independence of Belgium and favoured the candidature of Prince Leopold for its throne. The French foreign minister Count Sabastiani angrily observed to a colleague: *'Si Saxe Coburg met un pied en Belgique, nous lui tireons des coups des canons.'* ('If Saxe-Coburg sets foot in Belgium, we shall let fly the cannons on him.')[8]

However, from 17 February 1831, after the candidature of the Duc de Nemours had finally been abandoned, both Britain and France became more and more reconciled to the idea of seeing Leopold on the throne. In April 1831, a deputation of four members of the Belgian National Congress arrived in London to solicit – in confidence – his views in the event of the crown being offered to him. After preliminary conversations with Stockmar, they were received on 22 April by Leopold at Marlborough House.

Leopold accepted on condition that Belgium's borders were accepted by France, Prussia, Austria and Britain, together with a guarantee of financial stability. The deputation urged him to accept the offer unconditionally, since Belgium was exhausted by its revolution and its Congress required an immediate solution; his failure to accept would give rise to threats from French partisans, republicans and Orangists. But Leopold remained steadfast.

On 4 June, the Belgian Congress formally elected him king, and dispatched deputies to London to ask him to accept the crown. They also sent two commissioners, Daraux and Nothomb, to represent them at the London Conference, which had been reconvened by the four powers to bring outstanding matters to a conclusion.

On 26 June, the conference approved the eighteen articles of the protocol, which dealt with territorial matters, the issue of public debt, and guarantees for Belgium's neutrality and independence. On the same day, Leopold met with the commissioners and accepted the crown. The Belgian Congress then debated the articles, which were controversial to many, but were eventually accepted on 9 July. Two days later, a second deputation reached London to notify Leopold of the acceptance of the eighteen articles and to conduct him to Brussels.

On 12 July, Leopold received the ambassadors to the conference and asked them: 'Will all the powers recognise me immediately if, without awaiting the King of Holland's answer, I proceed at once to Brussels?'

'Yes,' said Count Mantuszewicz, 'because in that case we should find the means to force the King of Holland to accept.'[9]

This assurance was unfortunately misguided. The King of Holland refused to accept the eighteen articles, whereupon the Russian, Prussian and Austrian ambassadors declared that their governments must postpone recognition of Leopold. Leopold, however, concluded that he had made a solemn pledge, and departed for Brussels.

The Dutch took matters into their own hands, and invaded Belgium on 2 August, defeating the Belgian forces near Hasselt and Louvain in a ten-day campaign. France, however, came to the support of the Belgians, and the arrival of its army was enough to make the Dutch retreat.

And so in 1831, when Leopold found himself a king at last, Belgium was instantly at war with Holland but protected by France. Britain, although suspicious of French motives, organised yet another conference, which produced twenty-four articles reducing Belgium's territory but bringing recognition and peace. On 3 November, the Belgian National Congress authorised its new king to conclude the formal treaty for the separation of Holland and Belgium on the basis of these. The Treaty of London, signed on 15 November 1831, made Leopold King of the Belgians, recognised *de facto* and *de jure* by the European powers – although King William of the Netherlands was still not prepared to come to terms. It was not until 19 April 1839 that he finally formally acknowledged Belgium as an independent, neutral country.

Ernst II wrote in his memoirs of the adverse reaction in Germany to Leopold's election to the Belgian Crown.

In the princely houses, and particularly at the German court, there was a definite antipathy to this flouting of the rule of law of other sovereign states. They could not and would not understand how a German prince, from one of their oldest families, could allow himself to be chosen king as a result of an open revolution. This was so extreme that in many circles the name of our House was for a time uttered only with a certain aversion in clubs and influential households. Prince Edward of Altenburg was much applauded by the older men for remarking at one such gathering that it was a great pity that one could no longer visit the Coburg Court, because one would always expect to hear the word 'Belgium' spoken there.

He went on: 'I must mention this particularly as this attempt, over thirty years, to exclude our House deeply influenced my and my brother's whole development. We were often sidelined and virtually forced into a stance opposed to the views generally held by our German peers.'

But Leopold had acquired a kingdom of his own, in a strategic area of western Europe, that, however small it was, could never be ignored by its neighbours. So far, his ambition to climb from his comparative lowly position as a third son of an impecunious German duke had met with considerable success – and ambition feeds upon ambition.

CHAPTER 7

The Coburgs' advance

Now that Leopold had his throne, he could turn his attention to wider horizons for the Coburg dynasty – notably for his nephew Albert and niece Victoria, both twelve years old in September 1831. He had carefully watched over Albert when he was a small child, and there was a bond of affection between them. He had also looked after the interests of his sister Victoire and her daughter Victoria, who also adored her Uncle Leopold. With the premature death of Charlotte and his stillborn son, Leopold had lost in one moment his grand future. If he could arrange the marriage of his nephew to his niece, Albert would regain it, and a Coburg dynasty would be achieved for successive generations. As Albert and Victoria grew into adulthood, Leopold and Stockmar planned Albert's education and for their marriage.

Nor did Leopold neglect other opportunities for his family as they presented themselves. Even after his appointment as King of the Belgians, the Saxe-Coburgs were still perceived as from a backwoods German palatinate totally lacking in influence. But this was also a strength, since they were not perceived as a threat by the great powers concerned with keeping a balance of power in Europe. The Coburgs' much more significant competitors, such as the Dutch House of Orange and the Orléans family of Louis-Philippe, often fell by the wayside owing to differences in allegiances of the powers, allowing the Coburgs to slip through the net.

In 1836, a further bizarre opportunity came the way of the Coburgs. Queen Maria II of Portugal, born in 1819, had come to the throne in difficult circumstances. She was the daughter of the heir apparent Pedro, who had been due to become Pedro IV. However, in 1822 he had proclaimed the independence of Portuguese-owned

Brazil and assumed the title Emperor Pedro I of that new nation. His younger brother Miguel had been exiled and barred from the succession after leading a number of uprisings against his father King João VI's liberal regime. When João died in March 1826, the Portuguese recognised Pedro as the heir, but did not want the re-unification of Portugal and Brazil. To avoid a civil war with Miguel's supporters, Pedro agreed to abdicate in favour of his daughter Maria, who was then seven years old. It was also agreed that Miguel would return to act as regent and accept the liberal constitution. However, when he did return to Lisbon, he deposed Maria, proclaimed himself king, and abolished the constitution. During the reign of terror that was required to keep Miguel in office, Maria was taken to various royal courts in Europe, including that of her grandfather, Emperor Franz I of Austria.

In 1831, Pedro abdicated the Brazilian throne in favour of his son Pedro II, then attacked Miguel from his base in the Azores. With the help of the British and French fleets, he forced Miguel to abdicate in 1834, and Maria was restored to the throne. On 26 January 1835, she married Charles, Duke of Leuchtenberg, who died just two months later.

In the early summer of that year, Leopold introduced as a suitor to Maria his nephew Ferdinand, the son of his elder brother Ferdinand and Princess Toni, a rich, Catholic Hungarian noblewoman. To be able to take advantage of his wife's substantial inheritance from the powerful Koháry family, Princess Toni's husband had converted to Catholicism, which made their son acceptable in Portugal. The domestic situation there required stability, and so the marriage was not left to chance. Stockmar had trained Ferdinand in the arts of royal government by introducing him as an attentive observer in London, and had seen to it that he also received advice and learned from the example of his uncle Leopold in Brussels.

Stockmar, in association with the Coburg minister von Carlowitz, was charged with the negotiations for the union and the drawing up of the marriage contract, which was signed on 6 December 1835 in Coburg. There were the usual intrigues among the great powers in respect of this marriage. Stockmar wrote to the foreign secretary Viscount Palmerston on 10 December 1835: 'I know ... that after

Leuchtenberg's death, the English cabinet formally announced to the Portuguese that a marriage with a French Prince would never receive the sanction of England.' Palmerston replied:

> I think the Portuguese and their Queen are very fortunate in the choice that has been made. It is quite certain that some in the pay of Louis-Philippe did carry on an intrigue ... to persuade the Queen to declare in favour of the Duke of Nemours whilst at the same time Louis-Philippe was solemnly assuring Granville [the British ambassador in Paris] that such a proposal, if made, would not be accepted by him.[1]

The marriage took place on 9 April 1836, and from 1837, when the couple's first child, the future Pedro V, was born, Ferdinand bore the title 'King' as Maria's consort, in accordance with the Portuguese constitution. The fact that marriage was in Britain's interest seems to have obscured the point that Stockmar was once again the *eminence grise* working with great subtlety towards this major achievement for the Coburgs. Equally, Leopold had once more demonstrated that he could quickly spot an advantage and needed no prompting to seize it.

Following the Belgian and Portuguese triumphs came a third, one which would lead to the Coburg hegemony of the European royal houses. This remarkable sequence of events had begun with the tragic death of Princess Charlotte and her child. In his memoirs, Stockmar wrote: 'The death of Princess Charlotte, in opening up the prospect of succession to the throne to the younger sons of George III, had inspired them with a desire to marry.'

The fact that Charlotte's father, the Prince Regent (later George IV), was separated from his wife Princess Caroline and therefore incapable of producing a legitimate heir, led to the Ruritanian comedy of his brothers, the royal dukes, competing to produce one that would take the crown of an unenthusiastic Britain. The House of Hanover at this time was seen as politically inept, spiritually impoverished and financially profligate: not one of the brothers was admired, and the Duke of Cumberland was positively reviled.

The Prince Regent's three married brothers, the dukes of York,

Sussex and Cumberland, had no legitimate children, although numerous illegitimate ones from their many illicit relationships. In the Duke of Sussex's case, his first marriage – which had produced two children – was void under the Royal Marriages Act as far as the succession was concerned, since the sovereign had refused his consent to the union; the Duke's second, approved, marriage was childless. Of the three unmarried brothers, the Duke of Clarence, who was fifty-two in 1818, had produced ten illegitimate children by the actress Mrs Jordan, but his attempts to contract a financially advantageous marriage had been unsuccessful. The Duke of Cambridge, the only brother without severe financial problems, lived in Hanover, was known to wear a blonde wig and was thought likely to remain childless. The Duke of Kent, then aged fifty, was living with his mistress of twenty-seven years in Paris.

Regarded as by far the most intelligent of George III's sons, Kent was in desperate financial straits and began to consider marriage with a view to providing an heir to the throne. If it were to be approved under the Royal Marriages Act, it could provide him with an increased parliamentary grant, the only route he could see to some sort of financial security as old age beckoned. In the event, both he and Clarence were disappointed following their subsequent 'royal marriages', as the motions to increase their annuities were defeated in the House of Commons. The Duke of Wellington was not surprised: 'By God, there is a great deal to be said about that. They are the damnedest millstones about the necks of any Government that can be imagined.' However, the Duke of Kent's annuity was subsequently increased by £6,000.

Leopold and Stockmar naturally took an interest in these events. In a race against time, Leopold discreetly introduced Kent to his sister Victoire, the widow of Prince Emich Charles of Leiningen, and Clarence to his cousin Adelaide of Saxe-Meiningen. Any child of Adelaide and Clarence or of Victoire and Kent would be of Coburg stock, and Leopold and Stockmar would be waiting to educate and influence it towards their doctrine of enlightened monarchy.

The Prince Regent made it known that he strongly favoured the marriage of the Duke of Kent, who duly married Victoire. It was with a sense of ambitious duty, but not without some sadness, that he broke up his long and happy liaison with Madame Julie de St Laurent, who retired to a convent.

Victoire, whose first husband had also been some twenty years older than she, was thirty-two when she married Kent. She had certainly known hard times; she had lived through her father's impoverished dukedom and later, as Princess Leiningen, had had to struggle with finances while living in the small town of Amorbach. In an area where the French, Austrian and Russian armies marched and counter-marched and drew military requisitions from the land, poverty remained. At first, she had not wanted to accept Edward, Duke of Kent; she was happy acting as Regent of the tiny principality of Leiningen for her young son Charles, and also looking after her daughter Feodore. In this, she followed the ruling traits of the Coburg family by accepting her responsibilities to serve the people of her constituency, particularly when times were hard, for as her mother the Dowager Duchess had taught her, government was a duty to be cherished and performed. In later life, it was one of Victoire's gravest disappointments that William IV did not die earlier, thus allowing her to take the position of Regent of Britain until her daughter came of age. It would be a double disappointment when Victoria, who had inherited this trait for governance even more strongly, cast Victoire into the background on her accession.

Victoire and Kent were married on 29 May 1818 in the Giants' Hall in Schloss Ehrenburg, the centrepiece of the town of Coburg and the primary residence of the Duke of Coburg, so the natural setting for his sister's wedding. After driving in his coach through Theatre Square to the grand entrance recessed between two outer wings of the building, the Duke of Kent, his adjutant major John Conroy and aides were led up the staircase to the first floor. Passing through the foyer into the Family Room, they would have had a moment to look at the Coburg family portraits before making their entrance into the Small Gallery, with more paintings of eighteenth-century dukes of Coburg, whence it was just a few steps into the Hall of Giants.

This curious baroque hall, dating from the time of Duke Albrecht in 1690, is named after the twenty-eight Atlases that top its columns. Embrasures in the walls feature fifty-six coats of arms of former dominions of the House of Wettin, while the painted ceiling depicts allegories of the arts and sciences, with their protective goddess Minerva in the centre. Here the marriage of Edward, Duke of Kent, resplendent in a British field marshal's uniform, to Victoire was performed. Augusta wrote of Edward in her journal: 'His simple blunt soldier's manner, combined with the refinement of a man of the world, makes his company very agreeable.'

Edward Kent, the fourth son of George III and the father of Victoria, was born on 2 November 1767. When Edward was eighteen in 1785, his father decided that he should have a military career, and sent him to Lüneburg in Hanover to be supervised by Baron Wangenheim. The Baron has been described as 'an arbitrary and inflexible governor ... No community of feeling could exist between [Kent] and the Baron. He had a governor instead of a tutor; a rigid master instead of a kind companion; a morose narrow-minded dictator instead of a considerate and friendly adviser.'[2]

This military education had a lasting effect on Edward's army career. In 1790, unable to bear the Baron's oppression any longer, he returned to London, where he was received secretly by his brothers. But the news soon reached the King, who was furious and refused to see him. When a courtier tried to speak up for the young prince, the King exploded in rage: 'Edward has returned to England without my consent or knowledge; he has left his post without leave. His presence here is an act of most daring and deliberate disobedience; and you call on me to sanction it.'[3] Within a few days, George III sent Edward, under seal, peremptory written orders to proceed within twenty-four hours to Gibraltar, only admitting him to his presence for a few 'cold and curt' minutes on the night before his departure. It had been five years since Edward had last seen his family.[4]

Edward later distinguished himself on active service in the West Indies, but he was a stern disciplinarian, a manner he had learned in his German training, and never understood that such hard tactics were not the solution with British soldiers. When serving subsequently in Canada, in order to put an end to drinking and gambling he would command his men to appear before him on the parade ground at five in the morning in impeccable condition, and punished infringements of his draconian rules with the occasional execution and regular severe floggings – he would frequently order as many as 400 lashes for 'trifling faults in dress', and 999, the maximum permitted, for desertion. Canadian judge Brenton Halliburton of Halifax wrote to one of Edward's friends, Sir John Hervey:

> His Royal Highness's discipline was strict almost to severity. I am sure he acted upon principle; but I think he was somewhat mistaken in supposing such undeviating exactitude essential to good order. Off the parade, he was the affable prince and polished gentleman. At his table everyone felt at ease; but while it was evidently his object to make them so, his dignified manner precluded the possibility of any liberty being taken by the most forward.[5]

In 1802, Edward was once again sent to Gibraltar, this time to restore order to a mutinous garrison. The troops were undoubtedly ill disciplined, and their behaviour had deteriorated further since the departure of the former governor General Elliott: they were drunk and disorderly and had vandalised property belonging to merchants and shopkeepers, who as civilians received no redress or compensation. As soon as he arrived, Kent took matters in hand with his usual draconian style. 'A roll call was established at sunrise, and the men should attend regularly at meals, and ... be in barracks after the firing of the second evening gun.'[6] He also 'insisted on uniformity of the appearance of sentries. All sentries were ordered to don or remove greatcoats at the command of the orderly officer, and not merely when they felt too cold or too hot. At daylight every day each member of a guard or a picket had to wash, untie his hair, comb it, tie it afresh, and brush his clothes to the satisfaction of the orderly officer.'[7] The Duke quickly became popular with the Gibraltarians but, as an inevitable corollary, was feared and reviled by his own troops.

On Christmas Eve 1802, Edward's own regiment, the Royals, having spent their wages on drink, lost control and staged a mutinous demonstration outside his house. His reaction was predictable, and so severe that even his elder brother the Duke of York – who had been appointed commander-in-chief of the army – said that his conduct 'had from first to last been marked by cruelty and oppression'. Although many key officers and civilians were thankful that His Highness had cured the soldiers of their bad habits, York remained 'hostile, adamant, and unapproachable' towards Edward.[8] He was recalled and arrived in London on 26 May 1803 'wounded and insulted'.[9]

The Prince of Wales came to his defence:

> You send a man out to control a garrison all but in a state of open mutiny. You tell him to terminate such a disgraceful state of things. You assure him of an unqualified support of government in his undertaking. He goes out. He finds matters infinitely worse than they were represented. The impending outbreak occurs. He quells it thoroughly. By way of reward you disgrace him! If you want to deter an officer from doing his duty, or desire to encourage a mutinous soldier, your tactics are admirable. They cannot fail to attain such a result. Edward may well complain.[10]

On 5 September 1804, the Duke was promoted to field marshal by George III's command, but he was never again active in the military.

On his departure from Gibraltar, the townspeople, who considered that he had acted in their interests, presented him with silverware to the value of 1,000 guineas. The Duke, who was known for his financial ineptitude and had run up debts of £20,000, an enormous sum in those days, gave his regiment an engraved silver bowl, for which he never paid. The local silversmith was eventually paid by his daughter Victoria, following her accession some forty years later.

At almost the same time as Kent's betrothal, his elder brother the Duke of Clarence (later William IV) married Princess Adelaide, the eldest child of Georg, Duke of Saxe-Meiningen, and also a member of the Saxe-Coburg family. There had been no preliminary courtship before their discreet introduction by Leopold and Stockmar, but they had a happy marriage, albeit without surviving children – they suffered the miscarriage of twins, then produced a daughter who lived only a few hours, and finally another child who died at four months. So it was Kent and Victoire's daughter Victoria, born on 24 May 1819, who became heiress presumptive to the crown of Great Britain and its ever-broadening empire. Adelaide wrote to Victoire: 'My children are dead, but your child lives and she is mine too.'

Victoria was conceived in Amorbach, but Kent was sufficiently astute to realise that the British people would require a future queen to be born in the country where she would reign. His friend Joseph Hume, the radical politician, strongly advised him to return to England for the birth of the child, because he considered the child's legitimacy might 'be challenged ... from the circumstances of the birth taking place on foreign soil'. But Kent, desperately short of money, couldn't afford the journey. The Prince of Wales – now Prince Regent – instructed his private secretary to turn down his requests for funding, suggesting that it would be more sensible for the child to be born on the Continent, thus both saving money and relieving HRH the Duchess from 'the dangers and fatigues of a long journey at this moment'. He continued: 'If you are still bent upon returning and succeed in raising the money to do so, you cannot expect to meet with a cordial reception.'

In the event, Kent raised sufficient sums, with the help of his brother the Duke of Cambridge and various friends. The Duke and Duchess set off from Amorbach to Calais on 28 March 1819 in a caravan of carriages, the Duke himself driving the lead carriage to save costs, followed by the Duchess's lady-in-waiting Baroness Spath and Dr Marianne Heidenreich von Siebold, a skilled obstetrician who had qualified as a surgeon at the University of Göttingen. After them came Princess Feodore, Victoire's daughter by her first husband, her governess and English maidservants, and then the rest of the retinue and the Duke's personal physician, Dr Wilson.

Victoria was born in Kensington Palace in London at quarter past four on the morning of 24 May 1819. Stockmar noted that she was 'as plump as a partridge and a model of strength and beauty combined'.[11] Kent wrote to his mother-in-law Augusta: 'the dear mother and child are doing marvellously well ... it is absolutely impossible for me to do justice to the patience and sweetness with which Victoire behaved.'[12] In her reply, Augusta was ecstatic. 'My

God, how glad I am to hear from you! I cannot find words to express my delight that everything went so smoothly.' Hoping that Victoire was not disappointed that the child was a girl, she added, 'The English like queens.'[13]

Kent's pleasure in the birth was not shared by the rest of the family. Leopold noted that the Prince Regent did not trouble to disguise his hope that Kent, Victoire and the child would soon return to Amorbach: he stipulated that the baptism be strictly private. It took place on 24 June at 3pm in Kensington Palace's Cupola Room, the only people present being the Prince Regent, the Duke of York (representing the absentee godparents), the Duke of Gloucester, the Duchess of York and Leopold, the widower of Princess Charlotte. The godparents were the Prince Regent; Tsar Alexander of Russia; Augusta, Dowager Duchess of Coburg; and Kent's sister Charlotte, the widow of the King of Württemberg.

Kent and Victoire sent, as required, a list of names for the child for the Prince Regent's approval: Victoire, for her mother; Georgina, for the Prince Regent; Alexandrina, for the Tsar; and Charlotte and Augusta, for two of her aunts. On 23 June the Prince Regent declined Georgina, since he could not allow his name to appear either before or after the Tsar's, and also disapproved of Charlotte, the name of his deceased daughter.

At the ceremony, the Archbishop of Canterbury held the child and asked the parents about names. The Prince Regent said: 'Alexandrina.' After a pause, Kent said 'Elizabeth', to which the Prince Regent dissented. Victoire was by then in tears. The Prince Regent told her to give the child her name, but not preceding that of the Tsar, so the child was christened Alexandrina Victoria. Leopold noted that the Prince Regent didn't speak to Kent during the ceremony, nor had he invited his brother the Duke of Sussex to attend, although he was also living in Kensington Palace.

Luise, the wife of Duke Ernst I, produced a second son Albrecht (Albert) on 26 August 1819, some three months after Victoire's Victoria. Dr Siebold, who had helped to deliver Victoria in England, was also the obstetrician for his birth. The following day, Augusta wrote to her daughter Victoire:

The date will of itself make you suspect that I am sitting by
Louischa's [Luise's] bed. She was yesterday morning safely and
quickly delivered of a little boy. Siebold, the *accoucheuse*, had only
been called at 3pm, and at 6pm the little one gave his first cry ...
[Luise] sends you and Edward a thousand kind messages ... how
pretty the Mayflower [Victoria] will be when I see it in a year's
time. Siebold cannot sufficiently describe what a dear little love
it is.

And she noted in her journal: 'The little fellow is the pendant to the
pretty cousin.'

As a child of three, Albert was told by his nurse 'that some day the
little Mayflower would be his wife'[14] – and never thought of marrying anyone else.

CHAPTER 8

Victoria and Albert: Grooming for government

The Coburgs' Greek tragedy, which had begun with Charlotte's unexpected death, continued. Victoria's father, the Duke of Kent, died on holiday in Sidmouth in the cold, damp January of 1820, having shortly before tempted fate by telling Stockmar: 'My brothers are not as strong as I am ... I shall outlive them all. The Crown will come to me and my children.'[1] He went for a walk, got his feet wet and caught a cold that led to pneumonia. Coincidentally Stockmar, who two years earlier had been close to Princess Charlotte's deathbed, was staying with the Duke at the time. He advised that a will be prepared, to ensure that the guardianship of Victoria would be given to her mother. The Duke was just conscious enough to understand and sign the document – his last act before he died the following morning. But Victoire found herself 'friendless in a country that was not her own; endeavouring to speak a language which she had not mastered'.[2]

The prime minister suggested to the King that some provision ought to be made for his fatherless niece Victoria, but the King would not consider it: her Uncle Leopold was quite rich enough, he declared, to take care of both her and her mother. Victoire first had to borrow £6,000 from the banker Thomas Coutts,[3] but Leopold did, in fact, grant his sister an annuity of £2,000, which he soon raised to £3,000.

Brought up in the adult world at Kensington Palace by her mother, who had the single-minded purpose of preparing her for accession to the British throne, Victoria rarely saw children of her own age.[4] 'Morning and evening, day and night, there was no relaxation from maternal vigilance. As a child, then as a young woman, she still slept in her mother's bedroom. She still had no place where she might sit or work by herself.'[5]

In 1824, Louise Lehzen, the daughter of a Hanoverian clergyman in her mid-thirties who had previously had the care of Victoire's first daughter Feodore, was appointed governess to Victoria, and subsequent events show that she had an increasingly strong, and beneficial, influence on the princess's upbringing. Feodore later referred to her as 'very strict, and the Princess has great respect and even awe of her, but with the greatest affection ... The Princess was her only object and thought ... She never, for the thirteen years she was governess to Princess Victoria, once left her.'[6] And when Lehzen first took on her role, she observed that the little girl was extraordinarily truthful; whatever punishment might follow, she never told a lie.[7] In 1827, John Conroy, secretary to Princess Victoire, the Duchess of Kent, gained influence over George IV's sister Princess Sophia, who also had apartments in Kensington Palace. At the prompting of Conroy, whom she had appointed her unofficial comptroller, she persuaded her brother to grant honours to members of the Duchess's household. As a result, Louise Lehzen was created a Hanoverian baroness and Conroy a knight commander of the Hanoverian Order. Eventually, in 1842, Lehzen was removed from her position at Albert's behest and retired to her home in Bückeburg near Hanover, where she died at the age of 86 in 1870.

Victoire's single-minded preparation of Victoria for her accession was gradually recognised. In a House of Commons debate of 27 May 1825 about increasing the annuity paid to her for the education of the young princess, Foreign Secretary George Canning stated:

> There would not be a greater compliment to Her Royal Highness [Victoire] than to state the quiet unobtrusive tenor of her life, and that she has never made herself the object of public gaze, but has devoted herself to the education of her child, whom the House is now called upon to adopt.

In March 1830, when Victoria was ten, the bishops of London and Lincoln were invited by Victoire to assess whether the Princess's education under the watchful eyes of her mother and Lehzen was proceeding satisfactorily.[8] They expressed themselves 'completely satisfied' with the child's answers to comprehensive questioning on subjects that included divinity, foreign languages, history and art.[9]

On 26 June 1830, George IV died at Windsor Castle. The Duke of Clarence ascended the throne, taking the title of William IV, and the Duchess of Kent's parliamentary grant further increased. More importantly, on the advice of Sir John Conroy – her late husband's adjutant – Victoire petitioned Parliament through the Duke of Wellington that, in the event of William's death during Victoria's minority, she, Victoire, should become sole regent. Parliament, conscious of the terrible possibility that the Duke of Cumberland might manoeuvre himself into that position, agreed. When Victoire was told this, she was reduced to tears, saying that it had 'given her more pleasure than anything … since the death of her husband'.[10]

William IV was 64 on his accession, so was unlikely to enjoy a long reign. Victoire, well advised by Leopold and energetically supported by Sir John Conroy, now her secretary, did not wait long before publicly presenting her daughter, the heiress to the throne, to the public. As part of this process, they planned a series of formal visits to the most influential aristocratic families and important towns, to ensure that Victoria became well known and popular with the people over whom she was to reign, and got acquainted with the leading families in the easiest of circumstances – for which of those would not wish to act as host to the future queen on such popular visits?

In September 1830, they visited Stratford-upon-Avon, Kenilworth and Warwick – with Conroy's daughter, also called Victoire, as a companion for Victoria – and stayed with the Duke of Marlborough at Blenheim Palace before going on to Hereford, Gloucester and Stonehenge. On 23 October, Victoria opened the Royal Victoria Park in Bath, then was taken around the porcelain works at Worcester. They stayed at Earl Beauchamp's house, Madresfield Court, at Malvern, and at Badminton House with the Duke of Beaufort. In towns where her visit had previously been well publicised, she met with large, enthusiastic crowds, who seemed delighted that a member of the royal family was taking such an interest in them. Victoria received addresses from lord mayors and other important local businessmen, along with official receptions. These tours, which became known as royal progresses, began to upset the King, who spoke of them with ill humour.

In 1832, one such tour took in the Midlands mining districts on the way to North Wales, and in 1833 Victoria visited towns in the south and west of England – including Portsmouth, to see the *Victory*, Nelson's flagship at Trafalgar, where she ate 'excellent beef, potatoes and grog as a sample of sailors' rations'.[11] In 1835, another tour of the northern and eastern counties was planned, but the King wrote to Victoire strongly disapproving of his niece 'flying about the kingdom as she has been for the last three years'.[12]

Victoire asked Lord Melbourne, who had replaced Earl Grey as prime minister in 1834, 'on what grounds Victoria could be prevented from making these visits'.[13] None could be found. When Victoria told her mother that she didn't want to upset the King, Victoire told her firmly: 'Will you not see that it is of the greatest consequence that you be seen, know your country, and be acquainted with it, and be known by all classes … Turn your thoughts and views to your future station, its duties, and the claims that exist on you.'[14]

The King felt his position was being usurped, derogating his royal dignity, but there was little he could do. However, when he heard that Victoire, while sailing in the Solent, had insisted Victoria be acknowledged with a royal salute by any ship of the line and all the forts, he declared that such acknowledgements should cease. The prime minister and first lord of the Admiralty each privately wrote, at his request, asking Victoria to waive her rights. Sir John Conroy responded: 'As her Royal Highness's confidential adviser, I cannot recommend her to give way on this point.'[15] That same month, the King issued a special order-in-council prohibiting the firing of royal salutes for any ship except those carrying the reigning sovereign or his consort.

Nor did relations improve over time. On 20 August 1836, the day before his birthday, the King was in London to prorogue Parliament. He then paid a visit to Kensington Palace, but found that the Duchess and Victoria had already left for Windsor for his birthday celebrations. He observed that, against his express orders, the Duchess had taken over a large suite of rooms for her own use, and his resentment boiled over. The next evening a remarkable scene took place at the birthday banquet, attended by one hundred guests. With Victoire sitting on his right and Victoria opposite, the King, in reply to the toast to his health, made an extraordinary speech, referring to the Duchess as 'that person', and hinting that she was surrounded by evil advisers – meaning Conroy, whom he detested, and Leopold, whom he considered Victoire's principal accomplice in keeping Victoria for the Coburgs' own family marital ambitions. Determined to use all his influence to thwart them, conscious of his age and the time limit on his reign, he could not contain his anger and frustration. He insisted that the Princess spend time at court – 'that woman' was incompetent to act with propriety in the high station she filled. He hoped to God, he went on, that his life would be spared for six months longer, so that the calamity of a regency might be avoided, and the functions of the crown pass directly to the heiress-presumptive instead of to 'the person now near to him upon whose conduct and capacity no reliance whatever could be placed'.[16]

The Princess, then aged seventeen, burst into tears. The Duchess sat in silence and the guests in horror. Victoire waited until the company had retired and then, scarlet with rage, called for her carriage for an immediate return to Kensington Palace. Only with the greatest persuasion did she agree to put off her withdrawal until the following morning.[17]

Like Charlotte, Victoria was high-spirited and wilful, with strong personal prejudices, yet she also had a strong sense of duty and dignity. She was fond of dancing, concerts, plays and operas, and devoted to open-air exercise, particularly riding. Like Charlotte, she became hostile to her mother, and Charlotte would have agreed that, in essence, both were equally fatherless. Both were also highly emotional and impressionable, poor judges of character, often lacking in gratitude, profoundly self-centred and susceptible to flattery.

Providentially, however, Victoria understood the middle-class point of view. Among many examples of her liberal tolerance, she was to distance herself from the rigorous class hierarchy that was the basis of her family's shameful argument to have the Battenbergs enter into a morganatic marriage. In addition, Victoria showed a complete disregard to the anti-Semitic prejudices of the day. In autumn 1835, on holiday with her mother at Ramsgate, she stayed at Townley

House, which belonged to Moses Montefiore, a man well respected in the City of London. Soon after her accession in 1837, she knighted the London Sheriffs at a ceremony in the Guildhall, and noted in her journal 'one of them was Mr Montefiore, a Jew, an excellent man, and I was very glad that I was the first to do what I think quite right'.[18] In 1837, Jews were not generally accepted in society, but Victoria was refreshingly free from the racial, cultural and religious prejudices prevalent at that time. Later in her life, her relationship with another Jew, Benjamin Disraeli, was perhaps the warmest she had with any of her prime ministers.

That her Uncle Leopold had a strong influence over Victoria's girlhood was undeniable. He was always kind and paternal towards her. She enjoyed her childhood visits to Claremont Lodge, and after he left for Belgium in 1830, he rarely failed to see her when he returned to London. The vast correspondence between them continued until Leopold's death in 1865. Indeed, it would be difficult to overestimate the importance of his closeness to her. He inspired her, by example, with a sense of duty, and from the first instilled in her the necessity of acquainting herself closely with the details of political administration.

Leopold also took pains to maintain the interests of the Coburgs in the forefront of Victoria's mind. In 1836, he ensured that Stockmar was introduced to a new sphere of activity at the British court. His first duty was to give immediate aid and counsel to Victoria as she approached her coming of age, and his second was to afford Leopold every assistance in his plan to marry Albert to Victoria. Leopold felt the time had now arrived to take the first serious step towards the execution of this long-held plan.

Extracts from Stockmar's correspondence show how much forethought and method Leopold put into this work. Some years later, Queen Victoria wrote in a memorandum for the creation of the book *The Early Years of His Royal Highness the Prince Consort*:

The King of the Belgians has latterly given the Queen some of his letters written to Baron Stockmar in the spring of 1836 to read, and it appears from them that he had early formed the highest opinion of his young, handsome, very amiable and highly gifted nephew, Prince Albert; and come to the happy conclusion that no Prince was so well qualified to make his niece happy and fitly [*sic*] to sustain the arduous and difficult position of Consort to the Queen of England.

Stockmar's view was more cautious. 'He must have true ambition and a great strength of will ... If the mere consciousness of filling one of the most influential positions in Europe does not satisfy him, how often will he feel tempted to repent his adventure?' In a further letter, he advises 'a well-planned system of education for his future career, with special reference to the particular land and people where he would be called upon to dwell; and the second is that he should win the affection of the Princess before he asks her hand in marriage.' (Here Stockmar was at fault, being unaware of the proto- col of royal marriages. A queen is not asked for her hand: it is for her to bestow – which, indeed, was what later occurred.)

Both Stockmar and Leopold agreed that Albert should widen his upbringing with 'a stay in Brussels and a grand tour of Italy', aware that his education had been limited in his provincial backwater and that he was not yet 'a man of the world'. On 16 April 1836, Stockmar wrote to Leopold: 'Now is the right moment for the *first* appearance in England. If the first favourable impression is now made, the foun- dation stone is laid for the future edifice.'

After eighteen years of waiting since Charlotte's death, it was time for action. Stockmar therefore advised the acceptance of an invita- tion from the Duchess of Kent to her brother Ernst I and his two sons: 'but it must be a condition *sine qua non* that the real intention of the visit be kept secret from the Princess as well as the Prince, that they may be perfectly at their ease with each other.'

After a stay of four weeks with their aunt the Duchess of Kent, the princes Ernst and Albert left (via Paris) for Brussels. There, in accor- dance with 'the plan', they stayed for ten months. In December 1836, Albert wrote to his former tutor, Dr Seebode, director of the *gymna- sium* at Coburg: 'Our residence at Brussels will last till Easter, when we shall go in search of more wisdom, probably to some German university. Which is still undecided.'

Stockmar and Leopold corresponded at length on Albert's further education. Munich was rejected as 'formal and priggish', Göttingen, Jena, Berlin, Vienna and Heidelberg for similar reasons. Finally, they agreed on the new University of Bonn, which had at that time an enviable complement of intellectual professors. It was decided that both brothers, Ernst and Albert, should commence their university education on 3 May 1837, attended by their tutor Christoph Florschütz, their valet Isaac François Daniel Cart, who had been with them since Ernst was eight and Albert seven, and Baron von Wiechmann, in charge of non-academic matters.

All this was decided by Leopold and Stockmar, with little reference to the princes' father, whose only concern was that university life could reduce his sons' status to that of ordinary Germans, so they were enrolled as noblemen rather than normal students.[19] Indeed, most of Albert's further education, including his grand tour through Switzerland and Italy, was arranged without his father's involvement. He wrote to his father: 'Uncle Leopold has written to me a great deal about England and all that is going on there … [He] advises us to journey to the south of Germany and Switzerland or even to the north of Italy … *I feel that his opinion is* right, *and* am sure you will also agree in thinking his reasons imperative and conclusive.' This cleverly left no room for dissent. Similarly, on 29 November 1836 Albert wrote another carefully composed letter to his father from Brussels:

Dear Papa,
We should be glad to accept your invitation to go to Coburg for a few days and spend Christmas there. But if we are to profit from our stay here, I am afraid we must deny ourselves that pleasure. Such an expedition would require 5 or 6 weeks, and our course of study would be quite disturbed by such an interruption. We told dear Uncle the purport of your letter, and he said he would write to you on the subject.

Victoria turned eighteen on 24 May 1837. Her youth and inexperience led Leopold to fear that others might intrigue to entrap her, as he was effectively doing, hoping thereby to rule the future sovereign. One example is revealed in the correspondence between Lord

William Russell, minister in Berlin, and the Duchess of Kent, in
which Lord Russell asks for an introduction to Victoria for Prince
Adalbert of Prussia, with a view to marriage.

> Berlin, 3rd May 1837
> Madam,
> Would it be agreeable to your Royal Highness that Prince
> Adalbert of Prussia, the son of Prince William, should place him-
> self on the list who pretend to the hand of HRH the Princess
> Victoria?
> Your consent, Madam, would give great satisfaction to the Court
> of Berlin.

Victoire wrote a diplomatic refusal: 'I will candidly tell your lordship
that I am of the opinion that the princess should not marry till she
is much older.' It is clear that Victoire isolated Victoria from any
suitors other than her cousins, and when Leopold spoke to his niece
during a stay at Claremont, they agreed that, following Victoria's
eighteenth birthday, Stockmar should no longer simply visit England
but reside there, as the trusty helper and adviser to the Princess. He
duly arrived on 25 May 1837.

The combined influence of Leopold and Stockmar had not
gone unnoticed in high British circles. Melbourne commented acidly: 'King Leopold and Stockmar are very good and intelligent
people, but I dislike very much to hear it said by my friends that I
am influenced by them. We know it is not true, but still I dislike to
hear it said.'

On 26 April 1836, Victoria wrote to Leopold: 'Uncle Ernst and my
cousins will probably come here in the beginning of next month, I
hear, and will visit you on their return.' She signed the letter in her
usual affectionate way: 'Always, my dearest best uncle.'

But Leopold rightly felt that William IV was trying to thwart his
plans. The King was anxious to see a union between Victoria and the
House of Orange, and on 13 May 1836 gave a ball in honour of the
two princes of Orange, William and Alexander. He also invited
Victoria's eighteen-year-old cousin from the Hanoverian side of the
family, Prince George of Cambridge, who was heir to Augustus

Frederick, George III's seventh son. It must have seemed clear to Leopold that William was fully aware of the Coburg plans for Victoria and that he was intent on stopping them. In exasperation, and fearful of losing the initiative, Leopold wrote to Victoria on 13 May 1836:

> I am really astonished at the conduct of your old uncle the King; this invitation of the Prince of Orange and his sons … is very extraordinary. Only yesterday, I got a half-official communication from England, insinuating that it would be <u>highly</u> desirable that the visit of your relatives <u>should not</u> take place this year – *qu'en dites vous?* … Really and truly, I never heard or saw anything like it, and I hope it will a <u>little rouse your spirit.</u> Now that slavery is abolished in the British colonies, I don't understand <u>why you alone should be kept in a white slavery</u> for the pleasure of the English court, who never even bought you, as I am not aware of their having gone to any expense on that head, or the king's even having <u>spent a sixpence on your maintenance.</u> I expect my visits to England will also be prohibited by an Order in Council. I have no doubt that the King, in his passion for the Oranges, will be <u>excessively rude to your relations.</u> This, however, will not signify much; they are your guests and not his.[20]

The feud between Leopold and William II of the Netherlands, formerly the Prince of Orange, went back a long way, of course: the Prince had been a candidate for Charlotte's hand and effectively engaged to her before Leopold had triumphed, and the Dutch had lost Belgium to him as well. He therefore had no reason to be friendly towards Leopold, of whom he said: '*Voila un homme qui a pris ma femme et mon royaume*' (Here is a man who has taken my wife and my kingdom). The British king William IV also wanted a match between Victoria and a prince of Orange, which he considered politically useful, whereas he could see no benefit to Britain in an alliance with any of the little-known Coburgs. What, he asked, could a second son of an impoverished duke of Coburg offer the British Crown? He could not stand Victoire, was suspicious of Leopold's familial ambitions and seems never to have considered that Victoria might personally prefer a Coburg husband: his mind was set on national duty and political considerations, as against the personal and family indulgences he saw in Leopold and Victoire. But it is also worth noting that William IV's political acumen was not great.

In any case, he stated that no marriage should take place except with the House of Orange, and even proposed that the Duke of Saxe-Coburg and his sons not be allowed to land in England. However, the Coburgs had many advantages over William in their plans for his niece's marriage. Leopold, Stockmar, Victoire and Victoria were able to exchange regular private messages. The Princess was compliant, worshipping as she did the uncle who had assiduously looked after her interests all her life, and Victoire steadfastly refused to allow Victoria out of her sight and control and continued to deny other would-be suitors any access to her. Finally, despite William's continued requests for Victoria to spend time at court, where he could begin to influence her in her duty, as he perceived it, to make a correct marriage of state, he was prevented by Victoire and Conroy, both well aware of the dangers to their charge.

The close Coburg family had successfully, and seemingly without public or private detection, brought about a situation where they – not William IV – were in charge of Victoria's future. Leopold had no reason to worry. Victoria wrote to him on 17 May 1836: 'The [Netherlander] boys are very plain and have a mixture of Kalmuck [Mongol] and Dutch in their faces, moreover they look heavy, dull and frightened and are not at all prepossessing. So much for the Oranges, dear Uncle.' And in later years, Queen Adelaide told Victoria that, if she had told the King that it was her earnest wish to marry her cousin, that her happiness depended upon it, he would have given up his opposition to it at once, as he was very fond of his niece.

On 23 May 1836, Leopold received with elation and relief a letter from his niece:

My dearest Uncle,
Uncle Ernst and my cousins arrived here on Wednesday *sains et sauf* ... my cousins are most delightful young people ... I must say that they are both very amiable, very kind and good and

extremely merry, just as young people should be ... Albert is extremely handsome, which Ernst certainly is not.[21]

It is perfectly clear that Victoria was by now privy to the plan. On 7 June 1836, she wrote to Leopold:

I must thank you, my beloved Uncle, for the prospect of great happiness you have contributed to me in the person of dear Albert. Allow me ... to tell you how delighted I am with him and how much I like him in every way. He possesses every quality that could be desired to render one perfectly happy. He is so sensible, so kind and good, and so amicable too. He has also the most pleasing and delightful exterior and appearance you can possibly see.

I have now only to beg you, my dearest Uncle, to take care of the health of one now so dear to me, and to take him under your special protection. I hope and trust that all will go on prosperously and well, on this subject of so much importance to me.[22]

Indeed, at this moment Victoria was taking the initiative. On 9 August 1836, she wrote: 'Pray, dear Uncle, say something most kind from me to them,' and again in a letter to Leopold from Ramsgate on 14 November 1836, 'Pray, dear Uncle, say everything most kind from me to Ernst and Albert.'[23]

With William's health declining, and the accession clearly close, Leopold wrote to Victoria, subtly underlining his family's loyalty and support. 'You may count upon my faithful good offices in any difficulties, and you have at your command Stockmar, whose judgement, heart and character offer all the guarantees we can wish for ... My object is that you should be no one's tool.'[24] A cynic might have added: 'Except mine!'

And in a letter of 17 June 1837, Leopold wrote in tones that could have come straight from Polonius to his son Laertes: 'Cultivate always a genuine feeling of right and wrong; this gives great strength. I have taken into consideration the advantage or disadvantage of my coming over to you immediately ... I think it is better to visit you later ... People might fancy I come to enslave you, while I glory in the contrary.'[25]

Victoria responded two days later:

Your kind and dear letter containing wholesome, prudent, sound
and excellent advice, was given to me by our good and invaluable
honest friend, Stockmar. Before I say anything else, let me tell you
how happy and thankful I am to have Stockmar here; he has been
and is of the greatest possible use and be assured, dearest Uncle,
that he possesses my most entire confidence. The King's state, I
may fairly say, is hopeless; he may perhaps linger a few days, but he
cannot recover ultimately ... Your advice is most excellent and you
may depend upon it that I shall make use of it and follow it, as
Stockmar also says.[26]

That letter could only confirm to Leopold that his planning for so
many years was about to come to fruition.

CHAPTER 9

Victoria and Albert: The match

Victoria's journal for 20 June 1837, the day of her accession, reads:

> Informed 6am. Letter from Melbourne to see Queen 9am with meeting of Council at Kensington Palace at 11. Breakfasted at 7.30, during which time good faithful Stockmar came and talked to me. Wrote to Leopold at 8.30 and after Melbourne meeting wrote to Adelaide [Victoria always treated the Queen with the utmost consideration and almost daughterly affection]. In the evening wrote my journal. Took my dinner upstairs alone. Went downstairs. Saw Stockmar. At about 9.40 came Lord Melbourne and remained till near 10 ... Saw Stockmar. Went down and said goodnight to Mama etc.

It is interesting to note that, on the most exciting and impressive day of her life to date, the new Queen of the most powerful nation on earth was guided principally by meetings with Stockmar – rather than her mother or prime minister.

On the death of William IV, the ties between Britain and Hanover were loosened. After 123 years, when the Hanoverians had ruled in Britain and the British King, through his family, had ruled in Hanover, the British crown now belonged, *de facto*, to the family of Saxe-Coburg-Gotha. Hanover by its constitution could not accept a woman as its king and elector, so adopted Ernst August, Duke of Cumberland, until his death in 1851.

On 30 June, Leopold sought to consolidate his influence, writing to Victoria: 'I recommend to your kind attention what Stockmar will think it is his duty to tell you: he will never press anything, never plague you with anything, without the thorough conviction that it is indispensable for your welfare.' And five days later, Albert wrote from Bonn to his father:

> The death of the King of England has caused much sensation everywhere. From what Uncle Leopold, as well as Aunt [Victoire] wrote us, the new reign has begun very successfully. Cousin Victoria is said to have shown astonishing self-possession. She undertakes a heavy responsibility, especially at present, when parties are so excited and all rest their hopes on her. Poor Aunt has again been <u>violently</u> attacked in the newspapers; yet she has found good defenders.

Leopold's attention now turned to Albert again. On 13 April 1838, he wrote to Victoria applauding her decision to give Stockmar the assignment of accompanying Albert on his grand tour, as her emissary general. 'Concerning the education of our friend Albert ... Stockmar will make regular reports to you ... Nothing enlarges the mind more than travelling. On one thing you can rely, that it is my great anxiety to see Albert as a very good and distinguished young man, and will think no pains of mine too much to achieve this end.'[1]

Meanwhile, on the grand tour, Stockmar worked at maintaining Victoria's interest. On 16 April 1839, he wrote from Naples of their visits to Florence, Terni and Rome: 'From morning to noon, the Prince was seeing sights, and he made such good use of his time that I don't think anything really remarkable was left unseen ... The music of the Sistine Chapel ... has not failed to make a lasting impression upon a mind so musical as the Prince's.' (In 1864, after Albert's death, Victoria recorded that he had sent her a booklet containing views of almost all the places he visited on his tour – including a scrap of Voltaire's handwriting – which she treasured and assembled in an album annotated with the dates on which each place had been visited.)

The Coburg influence on Victoria was undeniably strong. However, when it came to the interests of her own kingdom, it was not the only factor. Although inexperienced, she had inherited a strong will from her mother, which grew more pronounced as she gained confidence. For example, 2 June 1838 brought a desperate letter from Leopold on the security of Belgium, whose independence Holland was still refusing to recognise. Following discussions with Melbourne, Victoria replied, flattering Leopold's role and the system of government he supported – 'You must be assured, my beloved Uncle, that both Lord Melbourne and Lord Palmerston are most anxious at all times for the prosperity and welfare of Belgium'[2] – but signally failing to offer any concrete support.

When Holland finally did recognise Belgium the next year, and Leopold pressed for amendments to the twenty-four articles that the powers had drawn up, Victoria wrote him (9 April 1839) a friendly letter, but one that was clearly from a powerful head of state to a minnow in the European pool:

> You say that the anger of the Belgians is principally directed against England. Now, I just say that you are very unjust towards us and (if I could) I might even be a little angry with you, dear Uncle. We only <u>pressed</u> Belgium for her <u>own</u> good and <u>not</u> for ours. It may seem hard at first but the time will come when you will see that we were right in urging you not to delay any longer the signature of the treaty.[3]

Leopold was in no mood to accept the *de facto* change of roles from dominant avuncular adviser to subservient applicant. In a rather bitter response, he wrote:

> Physicians will tell you that often an operation which might have been performed at one time, could not without great danger to the patient be undertaken some years later … We have not been listened to, and arrangements forced on us are … in themselves full of seeds of danger. I do not say these things with the remotest hope of bringing about any change, but only because in the high and very responsible position in which Providence has placed you, it is good to tell you the truth, as you ought to have weight and influence on the affairs of Europe.[4]

On top of Leopold's failure to influence Victoria to use her powers for his own national interests, she delivered him a further blow in respect of the long-planned union between herself and Albert. In a powerfully sensitive letter, Victoria made it clear – not least by underlining her points as she was always very fond of doing – that she was not committed in any way to Albert, and should there be no attachment, no blame could be laid at her door:

To mention some feelings of mine upon the subject of my cousins' visit which I am desirous should not transpire. First of all I wish to know if Albert is aware of the wish of his <u>father</u> and <u>you</u> relative to me? Secondly, if he knows that there is no <u>engagement</u> between us? I am anxious that you should acquaint Uncle Ernst that if I should like Albert, that I can make no <u>final promise this year</u>, for, <u>at the very earliest</u>, any such event could not take place till two or three years hence. For, independent of my youth, and my <u>great</u> repugnance to change my present position, there is <u>no anxiety</u> evinced <u>in this country</u> for such an event, and it would be more prudent, in my opinion, to wait till some such demonstration is shown, else if it were hurried it might produce discontent. Though all the reports of Albert are favourable, and although I have little doubt that I shall like him, still one can never answer beforehand for feelings, and I may not have the feeling for him which is requisite to ensure happiness. I may like him as a friend, and as a <u>cousin</u>, and as a <u>brother</u>, but not <u>more</u>; and should this be the case, which is not likely, I am <u>very</u> anxious that it should be understood that I am <u>not</u> guilty of any breach of promise for I <u>never gave any</u>. I am sure you will understand my anxiety for I should otherwise, were this not completely understood, be in a very painful position. As it is, I am rather nervous about the visit, for the subject I allude to is not an agreeable one to me. I have little else to say, dear Uncle, as I have spoken openly to you, which I was very, very anxious to do.

On receipt of this letter, Leopold spoke with Albert and wrote to Stockmar:

I have had a long conversation with Albert … One thing he observed with truth: 'I am ready to submit to this delay if I just have some assurance to go on. But if after waiting, perhaps, for three years I should find the Queen no longer desired the marriage, it would place me in a very ridiculous position and would to a certain extent ruin all the prospects of my future life.'

On 25 September 1839, Victoria wrote to Leopold from Windsor Castle:

> My dear Uncle,
> You will, I think, laugh when you get this letter and will think that I only mean to employ you in <u>stopping</u> my relations in Brussels … In the first place I don't think one can <u>reckon</u> on the Cousins arriving here on 30th. Well, all I want is that <u>you</u> should detain them one or two days longer, in order that they may arrive here on <u>Thursday</u>, the 3rd, if possible <u>early</u>. My reason for this is as follows: a number of Ministers are coming down here on Monday to stay until Thursday, on affairs of great importance … I think if all the Ministers were to be down here when they arrive, people would say it was to <u>settle matters</u>. At all events, it is better to avoid this.

After these letters Albert began to play it cool, not expecting any decisions from Victoria at the proposed meeting. On 1 October, Victoria again wrote to Leopold:

> My dear Uncle,
> … the retard of these young people puts me rather out, but of course cannot be helped. I had a letter from Albert yesterday saying they could not set off, he thought, before the 6th. I think they don't exhibit much *empressement* to come here, which rather shocks me.

But finally, there was good news for Leopold. Victoria wrote to him on 12 October:

My dear Uncle,
The dear cousins arrived at 7.30 on Thursday after a very bad and almost dangerous passage but looking both very well. Having no clothes, they could not appear at dinner but nevertheless debuted after dinner in their *negligée* ... Albert's <u>beauty</u> is <u>most striking</u> and he is so amiable and unaffected, in short very <u>fascinating</u>; he is excessively admired here ... They are passionately fond of music.

And just three days later, Leopold and the House of Coburg triumphed. Victoria wrote:

My dearest Uncle,
This letter, I am sure, will give you pleasure for you have always shown and taken so warm an interest in all that concerns me. My mind is quite made up and I told Albert this morning of it; the warm affection he showed me on learning this gave me <u>great</u> pleasure. He seems <u>perfection</u> and I think that I love him <u>more</u> than I can say ... These last few days have passed like a dream to me and I am so much bewildered by it all that I know hardly how to write; but I <u>do</u> feel <u>very very</u> happy.

It is absolutely necessary that this determination of mine should be known to <u>no one</u> but yourself and Uncle Ernst till the meeting of Parliament – as it would be considered otherwise neglectful on my part not to have assembled Parliament at once to have informed them of it ...
Ever dearest Uncle, your devoted Niece
Victoria

On 16 October 1839, a note from Lord Melbourne makes it clear to Victoria that the intended marriage is private to her and a matter of her happiness only, not a marriage of state: 'Lord Melbourne will be ready to wait upon your Majesty's expression of feeling as your Majesty's happiness must ever be one of Lord Melbourne's first objects and strongest interests.'

On the same day, Albert wrote to Stockmar: 'I write to you on one of the happiest days of my life, to give you the most welcome news possible.' Two weeks later, he wrote again to Stockmar from Windsor:

> Dear Baron Stockmar,
> A thousand thousand thanks for your dear kind letter. I thought you would surely take much interest in an event which is so important for me, and which you yourself prepared. Your prophesy is fulfilled.

On 25 October, Victoria wrote again to Leopold, explaining the constitutional procedures in respect of the marriage, and the ease with which they would be carried through:

> My dearest Uncle,
> Your most kind and most welcome letter of the 24th arrived yesterday and gave me very great pleasure. I was sure you would be satisfied and pleased with our proceedings.
> Before I proceed further, I wish just to mention one or two alterations to the plan of announcing the event. As Parliament has <u>nothing</u> whatever to say respecting the marriage, can neither approve or disapprove it (I mean in a manner which might <u>affect</u> it), it is now proposed that, as soon as the cousins are gone (which they now intend to do on the 12th or 14th November, as time presses), I should assemble all the Privy Counsellors and announce to them my intention …
> Oh! dear Uncle, I do feel so happy! I do so adore Albert! he is quite an angel, and so very very kind to me, and seems so fond of me, which touches me much. I trust and hope I shall be able to make him as happy as he <u>ought</u> to be! I cannot bear to part from him for we spend such happy, delightful hours together …
> Victoria

Nevertheless, Leopold was losing not only an avuncular advantage, but also a more general influence over his niece. Just a few weeks later, on 8 December, Victoria wrote to Albert, then in Coburg attending to his affairs: 'I have received an ungracious letter from Uncle Leopold … I no longer ask for his advice, but dear Uncle is given to believe that he must rule the roost everywhere.'

Stockmar's duties accompanying Albert on his grand tour having finished, he had returned to Coburg for 'matrimonial leave'. However, after only two months, early in the new year of 1840, he was recalled to England, arriving on 9 January. His first official employment was to negotiate, in his capacity as Prince Albert's adviser, the treaty of marriage with Lord Palmerston. In fact, Stockmar held no official position from Duke Ernst I nor indeed from Albert at this time, but only from the King of Belgium, but he was accepted and acknowledged by all parties as Albert's representative for this purpose.

Stockmar recorded the events as follows: 'I called on Lord Palmerston in Carlton Terrace and found him very absent and overworked; yet he congratulated me in the heartiest manner; and assured me that of all the marriages possible, this was one which he most approved of.' He observed that

> ...ultra Tories are filled with prejudices against the Prince in which I can clearly trace the influence of Ernst Augustus of Hanover [the Duke of Cumberland]. They give out that he is a radical and an infidel and say that George of Cambridge or a Prince of Orange ought to have been the Consort to the Queen ... The public is tolerably indifferent as to the person of the bridegroom; but I hear it generally complained that he is too young.

For Leopold, it was the culmination of his long-term plans. He had seen his youngest sister Victoire come out of comparative obscurity as the widow of the Prince of Leiningen to become mother of the British queen, and had taken Albert from the same provincial life in Coburg to join his niece in ruling the greatest country in the world. On 22 November 1839, Victoria wrote to Albert:

> As there is nothing to be settled for me, we require no treaty of marriage; but if you should require anything to be settled, the best will be to send it here. Respecting the Succession, in case Ernst [Albert's brother, heir to the Duchy of Coburg] should die without children, it would not do to stipulate now, but your second son, if you had one, should reside at Coburg. That can easily be

arranged if the thing should happen hereafter, and the English would not like it to be arranged now.

This has the thumbprint of Stockmar's advice, if not dictation! He would certainly have advised Victoria on all the subtleties of the Coburg succession and the importance of clearing up these matters at an early stage.

Leopold had suggested to Victoria that Albert should be appointed a peer so that 'his foreignership should disappear as much as possible. The great object must be to make Albert as English as possible, and nothing will render that more difficult than a foreign name.' Victoria objected, replying on 26 November 1839:

The whole Cabinet agree with me in being strongly of the opinion that Albert should not be a Peer; indeed I see everything against it and nothing for it; the English are very jealous at the idea of Albert's having any political power or meddling with affairs here which I know from himself he will not do.

To Albert, she wrote on the same day:

The English are very jealous of any foreign interference in the Government of the country and have already in some of the papers expressed a hope that you would not interfere – now, tho' I know you never would, still, if you were a peer they would all say the Prince meant to play a political part – I am sure you will understand.[5]

Albert did understand. He responded graciously: 'As regards my peerage and the fears of my playing a political part, dear, beloved Victoria, I have only one anxious wish and one prayer: do not allow it to become a matter of worry to you.'[6]

But Albert could not understand, nor did he wish to accept, the appointment of his personal staff on political grounds, without consultation with him. As a consequence, he was unable to bring with him any of the friends with whom he had grown up, who could have eased his path and in whom he would have had confidence. Victoria disagreed with Albert on this; she well understood the problems that would arise if Albert were to surround himself with his Coburg friends, and wrote to him:

> As to your wish about your Gentlemen, my dear Albert, I must tell you quite honestly that it will not do. You may entirely rely upon me that the people who will be round you will be absolutely pleasant people of high standing and good character ... proper people and not idle and too young and Lord Melbourne has already mentioned several to me who would be very suitable.

There was worse to come. Parliament required guarantees that Albert possessed no vestige of papalism, which in itself could have negated the marriage. Questions were sent to members of the family, in particular to Leopold, to resolve this point, and Leopold replied on 14 December 1839:

> The Ernestine branch of the Saxon family has been, there is no doubt, the real cause of the establishment of Protestantism in Germany, and consequently in great parts of northern Europe. [The Veste stronghold, on the peak overlooking Coburg, had been Martin Luther's refuge when the Catholic world had wanted to destroy him for heresy. Had the papal forces conquered the Veste, the Coburgs' lands and lives would have been forfeit.] This same line became a martyr to that cause, and was deprived of all its possessions in consequence of it. Recently there have been two cases of Catholic marriages. The main branch, however, has remained ... very sincerely Protestant.[7]

Further, Victoria and Albert, together with his close family, had always assumed that Parliament would grant Albert the same annuity as had been granted to Leopold on his betrothal to Charlotte: £50,000 for life. But perhaps feeling it had not had full value from Leopold following Charlotte's premature death, Parliament accepted the amendment of MP Colonel Charles Sibthorpe, carried by 260 votes to 158, to reduce the annuity to £30,000. This also reflected the widespread opinion among the public that Albert was a fortune-seeker. As was not uncommon at the time, rude rhymes were published, such as:

> *He comes the bridegroom of Victoria's choice*
> *The nominee of Lehzen's Voice;*
> *He comes to take for better or for worse*
> *England's fat Queen and England's fatter purse.*[8]

The Parliamentary amendment rankled with Albert, who thought it insulting. On 28 November 1839, he wrote a sharp letter to Victoria showing his fury:

> Those nice Tories have cut half my income ... It is hardly conceivable that anyone could behave as meanly and disgracefully as they have to you and me. It cannot do them much good for it is hardly possible to maintain any respect for them any longer. Everyone here [in Coburg] is indignant about it.[9]

Victoria was also livid about the reduction of Albert's proposed annuity. Beside herself with rage against the Tories, she refused to invite any of them to the wedding – even the Duke of Wellington, who had sided with the amendment. When Melbourne advised her that it would be a national scandal if the victor of Waterloo and former prime minister were not invited, she at first stood her ground, but eventually had to give in. However, she made no attempt to conceal her bitterness, and the Duke himself was well aware of all that had passed. Although present at the wedding, he was not invited to the wedding breakfast. 'Our Gracious was still very much out of temper,' he concluded.

What prompted Victoria to soften her approach was the Duke's change of mind over the precedence to be given to Albert. Originally, Wellington would not consider requiring Victoria's uncles, the Hanoverian dukes, to give way to Albert. 'Oh, give him the same which Prince George of Denmark [the consort to Queen Anne] had: place him next before the Archbishop of Canterbury,' he said to the clerk of the Privy Council, the diarist Charles Greville.

The latter responded: 'That will by no means satisfy her,' to which the Duke arrogantly countered: 'Satisfy her! What does that signify?' When, however, Wellington read Greville's memorandum for the Privy Council on the subject, he declared that 'the Queen had a perfect right to give her husband whatever precedence she pleased'.

While Britain prepared for the wedding, Albert had a sadder preoccupation at home. On 23 January 1840, he wrote to Victoria from Gotha:

> We have had a terrible loss here which has plunged us and the whole country in grief. Herr von Carlowitz, Papa's best and, I may say, only intimate friend, died suddenly of a stroke. He had been First Minister for 18 years and Chancellor of the House, and was a distinguished statesman. He was universally respected and loved.

Nevertheless Victoria and Albert's wedding took place on Monday, 10 February 1840, on a sunny afternoon after a wet and blustery morning. Dressed in white satin adorned with Albert's present of a sapphire and diamond brooch, and her head bedecked with orange-blossom, Victoria was driven to the Chapel Royal at St James's Palace. Still smarting from the insult handed out to Albert and herself by the Tories, she had wanted to hold the wedding in the privacy of Buckingham Palace, with just a few members of her family, Stockmar and other close friends and advisers present, but Melbourne, appreciating the political need for the Queen to be married before a congregation, and not a closed group of personal supporters, had prevailed. However, among the 300 or so guests, Greville reports that, apart from the Duke of Wellington and Lord Liverpool, there were only three other Tories, and then only because of the offices they held or their relationship with Lord Melbourne. Victoria's former governess, the Duchess of Northumberland, and the Duke were not there; nor were the Duke of Rutland and the Marquess of Exeter, both of whom had given her hospitality in their homes. 'Nothing could be more improper and foolish than to make this a mere Whig party,' complained Greville.[10]

Victoria's Hanoverian uncle the Duke of Sussex, shedding tears, gave her away: 'Quite ready as always to give away that which did not belong to him,' Greville commented acidly. Albert waited nervously at the altar, dressed in the uniform of a British field marshal and decorated with the Order of the Garter. Greville reported that 'as she [Victoria] left the Chapel, it was noticed that she paused to kiss her aunt, Queen Adelaide, but that she merely shook hands with her mother.' And he also noted that, on leaving Buckingham Palace after the wedding breakfast at 4pm, the couple went off in 'shabby style. Instead of the new chariot in which most married couples were accustomed to dash along, they were in one of the old travelling coaches, the postillions in undressed liveries.'

Victoria saw it differently. In her journal she wrote:

Our reception was most enthusiastic and hearty and gratifying in every way. There was an immense crowd of people outside the Palace, and which I must say never ceased until we reached Windsor Castle ... the people quite deafening us; and horsemen and gigs etc. driving along with us. We came through Eton where all the boys ... cheered and shouted. Really I was quite touched.[11]

The ordinary people of the country seemed happy to accept Albert, but the aristocracy remained wary of him, and some members of the old royal family were openly antagonistic. The Duke of Cambridge made a terrible fuss when his Garter banner in St George's Chapel was moved a few inches to make way for that of the 'young foreign upstart', and the Duchess of Cambridge went so far as to remain seated when the Prince's health was drunk at a dinner. Victoria exacted her revenge by denying them coveted invitations to Buckingham Palace.

Stockmar had one more major task to perform for Albert. When Victoria became pregnant in early summer, he wrote to Melbourne on 18 June 1840:

As soon as the Doctors can announce to the Ministers the state of the Queen, with a probability bordering on certainty, the latter must lay before Parliament an agency Bill to meet the possibility of the Queen dying and leaving a minor as her heir ... It appears after considering the arguments on which the Regency Bill of the Duchess of Kent was founded that the best course will be that <u>Albert</u> should be appointed <u>sole Regent</u>.[12]

Melbourne, after a conversation with Stockmar, went straight to Wellington and told him that he had decided against anything like a Council of Regency: the idea of dividing executive power among several people was against the spirit of the constitution, and it was his opinion that the father of the child should be constituted sole regent. The Duke agreed. The Bill met no opposition in either House, except from the Duke of Sussex, and Stockmar had reason to be satisfied with the result of his exertions – which the Prince fully recognised. He wrote on 24 July to his father: 'There had been much trouble to carry the matter through, for all sorts of intrigues were at work, and had not Stockmar gained the Opposition for the Ministers, it might well have ended as did the £50,000.'

On 11 July, Stockmar wrote in his journal: 'With this Act [the Regency Bill] my business here is for the present and perhaps for ever at an end. How much or little I have been of use is not for me to determine. But I can at least say that I have not committed a simple blunder, and this is always a satisfaction to a man of my years.'[13]

He left on 3 August, with a pressing invitation to return in November when the Queen expected her confinement. More than a year later, on 7 October 1841, Lord Liverpool wrote to Stockmar from Fife House, commenting 'that your position was a very peculiar one, and that you might be truly said to be the species of second parent to the Queen and the Prince; that your only object was their welfare and your only ambition to be of service to them.' He might more perceptively have added, 'and also to the interests of the House of Coburg from whom, through King Leopold, you have always received your instructions!'

Leopold had come to accept that he could no longer influence Victoria on matters of foreign policy on which she and her Ministers held different views from his. He had soon learned that, despite his personal influence over his niece, Belgium was a small piece on the chessboard of diplomacy, Britain the international player.

Nevertheless, he did not lose the tight Germanic/Coburg relationship Victoria shared with him, which he could still use to his advantage. His aim was to ensure that Albert played a growing part in British affairs within the constitution, and to sow the seeds of Coburg influence in the British line, ready to colonise new European fields in the future. Stockmar had a further influential part to play here, helping Leopold to nurture his long-term aims for the House of Coburg.

Stockmar's relationship with Albert was part adviser, part affectionate father – and Albert was no Leopold. Virtuous and well intentioned, clever and well informed, he had none of his uncle's unswerving ambition for personal greatness and, in his early days as consort, took no interest in politics and showed no signs of any commanding force of character. Left to himself, he would almost certainly have dwindled into a high-minded nonentity, a dilettante occupying himself with cultural matters, without influence or power. But he was not left to himself: Stockmar saw to that. Incessantly, Stockmar harped on two strings, playing on Albert's sense of duty and his personal pride.

There were, of course, obvious early differences between Albert and Victoria. Albert had been brought up in a small provincial court, and then was imbued with high-minded intellectual values quite distinct from those of that court. Victoria, by contrast, had enjoyed a youth of parties, games and merriment. Albert grew bored with spending his evenings playing drawing-room games – he was once noticed nodding off on a sofa at half past ten – and Melbourne commented that he was keen to invite to dinner persons of science and intellect, whose company Victoria did not consider she could necessarily cope with. Country-bred Albert preferred early nights, didn't like London and found court life stifling, whereas Victoria loved London's buzz, being able to dance throughout the night and then watch the sun rise. Victoria's unpredictable temper flashed out from time to time, and both she and Albert could be obstinate in protecting and promoting their own positions. Ernst II, who stayed with the couple for a while, noted these clashes with 'a friendly and startled eye'.

Victoria, however, was madly in love with Albert, which meant that the quarrels and jostling for position never resulted in a total breach. As Albert had not been allowed to have his Coburg friends in his retinue, and since his English was good but not totally fluent, he was sometimes lonely, and homesick for his beloved Rosenau, the house near Coburg where he had been brought up. But his position slowly began to change. He read Sir William Blackstone's *Commentaries* on the laws of England, and took lessons in English constitutional law. At Victoria's request, he began to be present occasionally when the Queen interviewed her ministers, and at Lord Melbourne's suggestion, he was shown all the dispatches relating to foreign affairs.

Albert's opportunity came when the Tories who Victoria so hated won the general election: on 4 September 1841, she presided over the ceremonial change of ministry. Her beloved Melbourne was replaced by Sir Robert Peel, whose resignation she had forced in 1839 (before he could form an administration) over the appointment of the ladies of her bedchamber. It had previously been agreed that the women occupying this ceremonial post had to be chosen by the government, lest the monarch's most intimate associates relay state secrets to the opposition, but the headstrong young Victoria had taken exception to this.

Albert had been told of that earlier difficulty and, on the advice of Stockmar, took a leading position on the issue, which earned him substantial influence in future arrangements between the government and Victoria. Having achieved a preliminary rapprochement with the Tories over the Regency Act, Albert used his private secretary George Anson as an intermediary to open a dialogue with Peel. In a series of quiet interviews, they reached an understanding about the ladies of the bedchamber, and Victoria abandoned her 1839 position. Peel and his new government now saw Albert as a person who could understand the sensitivities of parliamentary politics, and could be trusted to find sensible solutions. Victoria, too, was impressed and grateful. She wrote to Leopold:

> My dearest Angel is indeed a great comfort to me. He takes the
> greatest interest in what goes on, feeling with and for me, and
> yet abstaining as he ought from biasing me either way, though we

talk much on the subject and his judgement is, as you say, good and mild.

Stockmar, who was in England again, watched Melbourne's departure with satisfaction: with Victoria's trusted prime minister replaced by a man with whom she would have, at best, a cool relationship, Albert should now wield more political influence over her. He noted, however, that Melbourne had not yet come to terms with the fact that he was in opposition and, though out of office, continued to advise Victoria, who adored him.

Melbourne recommended Lord Heytesbury as ambassador to Vienna, and the Queen wrote to the foreign secretary urging the appointment. Stockmar then wrote to Melbourne, pointing out the constitutional impropriety of his continuing influence over the Queen and the consequences should Peel come to know of it. Melbourne exploded when he read this: 'God eternal damn it! Flesh and blood cannot stand this.' Stockmar had to send two further missives before Melbourne started to behave as a past prime minister should and restrict his communications with Victoria. Stockmar gained the point in his usual way – advising independently, quietly and persistently – and even convinced a former prime minister of the constitutional incorrectness of his position. The physician from Coburg had come a long way.

Albert's next move was the banishment of Baroness Louise Lehzen, Victoria's former governess, who still had considerable influence over her. He was cautious about this, since Victoria herself did not agree that Lehzen was a bad influence; they had had many quarrels on the subject. But, Anson noted on 21 June 1842, Lehzen was 'constantly misrepresenting the Prince. She exaggerated the Prince's every little fault … [and] tried to undermine him in the Queen's affections.' The quarrel spread to the nursery, which Lehzen proposed should be handed over to her control. Albert confided in a letter to Stockmar: 'All the disagreeableness I suffer comes from the same person [Lehzen] and that is precisely the person whom Victoria chooses for her friend and confidante – she will not hear me out but flies into a rage and overwhelms me with reproaches and suspicions, want of trust, ambition, envy etc. etc.'[14]

For her part, Victoria told Stockmar, 'I felt so forlorn and I have got such a sick headache, after Albert had stormed out of the nursery … I assure you upon my honour that I see her very seldom now and only for a few minutes, often to ask about papers and toilette for which she is the greatest use to me. Albert often … thinks I see her when I don't.'[15]

The nursery was reorganised under Lady Lyttleton, eldest daughter of the second Earl Spencer, whom the Queen described as 'perfection'. Finally, in October 1842, Albert obtained Victoria's consent to send Lehzen home to Bückeburg, near Hanover. Victoria gave her a generous pension of £800 a year, plus a carriage as a leaving present. Stockmar was content, and Albert was now his own master. Moreover, under his influence, Victoria had become much more of a country-lover and had largely given up her 'trivial pursuits' of late-night balls.

Unlike his father and his predecessors, Albert had no vices. The gaming tables were swept out of Windsor's drawing rooms, and male guests no longer sat over the table after dinner, passing round the port and leering over bawdy stories: the Queen would not allow them to stay in the dining room for more than five minutes after the ladies had left. There was no longer any third, fourth or fifth glass of port at the royal table. Albert was essentially a family man. Not having been brought up in a close family atmosphere himself, he was anxious that his children would experience a loving and caring family life.

In this, as in many matters he undertook, he succeeded admirably, presenting the British people with a picture of family life free from the vice and indulgence that had marked previous reigns. Through his intellect, he slowly and surely gained influence over state affairs, and Victoria began to depend on his calm, dispassionate advice. He was a born administrator, able, quietly and diplomatically, to revise the roles of conflicting authorities into that of a single official, the master of the household, who managed the royal houses. Great economies were made, and despite squeals of horror and despair from functionaries, his reforms worked. At the same time, he worked assiduously with Victoria, and imperceptibly became, as Stockmar commented, 'her private secretary, her confidential adviser and her second self'. He was now almost always present when she met her ministers, and as she fell more and more under his intellectual dominance, he became more absorbed in the machinery of high politics. Stockmar noticed the change with exultation. He wrote: 'The Prince had improved much lately. He evidently has a head for politics ... [and] has become far more independent. The relations between husband and wife are all one could desire.'[16] Greville went even further: 'It may be said with certainty that, by the close of Peel's administration, Albert had become, in effect, the King of England.'[17]

Following the departure of Lehzen, Albert brought about a reconciliation between Victoria and her mother, whose relationship had, by the former's eighteenth birthday, deteriorated almost beyond repair largely because of Sir John Conroy's role in it. He wielded great influence over Victoire, and in association with her had arranged Victoria's progresses and helped to limit her social connections. But his true colours showed in November 1835 when he tried to get Victoria, who was very ill with severe tonsillitis and fever, to sign a paper authorising his appointment as her private secretary. She recorded: 'I resisted in spite of my illness and their harshness, my beloved Lehzen supporting me alone.'[18]

On 9 June 1837, Stockmar reported to Leopold:

> She is very jealous of what she considers to be her rights and future power, and therefore not at all inclined to do anything which would put Conroy into a situation to be able to encroach on them. Her feelings seem, moreover, to have been deeply wounded by what she calls 'his impudent and insulting conduct' towards her. Her affection and esteem for her mother seem likewise to have suffered by Mama having tamely allowed Conroy to insult the Princess in her presence ... The Princess continues to refuse firmly to give her Mama her promise that she will make O'Hum [Conroy] her confidential adviser. Whether she will hold out, Heaven only knows, for they plague her, every hour and every day.[19]

In the week before Victoria's accession, Stockmar recorded that the struggle between mother and daughter was still going on, and the

Duchess was 'being pressed by Conroy to bring matters to extremes and force her daughter to do her will by unkindness and severity'. Following the accession, the tables were turned. When Victoria first met her prime minister Lord Melbourne, she received him 'of <u>course</u> quite <u>alone,</u> as I intended always to do'.[20] Her journal that day records that she informed Lord Melbourne that she had told her mother not to come to her whenever she liked. 'I had to remind her who I was,' she said. Lord Melbourne responded: 'Quite right, disagreeable but necessary.'

Soon after this, her mother remonstrated with her because Victoria would not receive Conroy and his family at court. She replied: 'I thought you would not expect me to invite Sir John Conroy after his conduct towards me for some years past, and still more so after the unaccountable manner in which he behaved towards me a short while before I came to the throne.'[21]

The battle lines were laid out, and it was clear that Victoria was winning.

CHAPTER 10

Albert consolidates

Albert's role continued to grow within the limits allowed by the British constitution. Prime Minister Peel, after discussions with Stockmar, privately urged the Prince to take a greater part in public life. In 1843, when Peel set up a royal commission to encourage the fine arts on the occasion of the rebuilding of the Houses of Parliament, he perspicaciously called on Albert to preside over it. The Prince threw himself into the work wholeheartedly, impressing the commission with his detailed questions and general command of the project. They particularly admired his knowledge of fresco painting and his support for a moral theme to them. (The frescoes, however, soon faded. Stockmar recorded that Albert's knowledge of the techniques of fresco painting was incomplete.[1])

Albert was also looking for a house away from London and Windsor. He longed for the peace and tranquillity of the countryside he had known in his childhood at the Rosenau, and wanted a retreat where his increasing family could enjoy some privacy. In 1844, Peel heard that the 200-acre estate of Osborne, east of Cowes on the Isle of Wight, was to be sold, and suggested it to Albert. Negotiations stalled while Albert went to Coburg for his father's funeral and Victoria was pregnant with her second son Alfred, but a price was eventually agreed – £27,814.5d, including the furniture. Certainly Albert and Victoria planned to welcome ministers and foreign guests to Osborne, but it would primarily be their home, as Buckingham Palace and Windsor Castle could never be.

Albert had to enlarge the house substantially to make room for his family and retinue and to provide the necessary guest rooms, so sought the advice of the builder Thomas Cubitt, who had made his reputation and fortune in the development of London's Belgravia. A warm friendship was forged between these two kindred spirits in matters of construction. The cost of buying adjoining land and extending the house, plus the furnishings, was kept with prudent financial management to just £200,000.[2]

Osborne House became the jewel of Victoria and Albert's private homes. It had extensive grounds, which Albert arranged in a series of lawns interspersed with tree-lined walks; most of the trees were gifts from various countries of the empire. The lawns descended from the ornate gardens of the balustraded terrace to the sea, affording the house unrivalled views across the Solent towards Portsmouth. This was the country house that Albert had yearned for, which gave him peace and time for reflection. Victoria, too, became entranced by the simple life at Osborne. She could work on her government papers with her boxes set out on a table on the lawn, or in her study if the weather was inclement. It was comfortable and homely – a place where she and Albert could entertain their friends, visiting relatives and their personal aides. According to Sir Theodore Martin, Albert's official biographer, 'The royal family spent every day there that could be snatched from London and Windsor.'[3]

The aristocrats, who considered Victoria provincial and Albert stiff, formal and Germanic, may have scoffed, but with the public they were both popular. After the scandals of the Hanoverians, the British yearned for a happy royal family, and Victoria and Albert projected an image of dignity and propriety that the middle and working classes could respect and be proud of. Stockmar wrote: 'It was indeed a model court. Not only were its central personages the patterns of propriety, but no breath of scandal, no shadow of indecorum, might approach its utmost boundaries.'[4] Victoria was no longer Melbourne's pupil but Albert's wife: the Victorian age had arrived.

The tranquillity that Victoria and Albert brought to their domestic life spread to the country as a whole. The peace the country enjoyed, after the long years of war in America and against Napoleon, together with the unparalleled economic growth largely brought about by the Industrial Revolution, gave the British people a sense of accomplishment and well-being, in sharp contrast to the revolutions that overtook Continental monarchies in 1848.

After a wretched harvest, economic depression had spread

throughout Europe, resulting in rising food prices. At the same time, the industrial expansion of the early 1840s had slowed to a recession. This combination paralysed governments that were inexperienced in dealing with the growing modern economic problems of industrial and commercial growth, combined with a lack of any real enfranchisement of their populations. Thus, on 3 March 1848, mobs in Paris constructed barricades and took to the streets: the National Guard refused to support Louis-Philippe, who abdicated, and the Second Republic was declared from the steps of the Hôtel de Ville. Louis-Philippe, humiliated and in partial disguise, having shaven off his whiskers, managed to leave the small seaport of Honfleur for Britain only with the assistance of the British consul. On arrival, he threw himself and his family as suppliant fugitives at Victoria's feet. They were given hospitality at Claremont, where Albert went to see them.

On the same day as the French rebellion erupted, revolution broke out in both the Rhineland and Hungary. And in Frankfurt am Main, more than 600 delegates met and called for universal suffrage and the formation of a national assembly to govern a unified Germany; a further meeting of some 800 delegates created a democratic constitution and an executive council for the purpose of setting up this entity. Meanwhile in Budapest, Lajos Kossuth, backed by a large number of supporters in front of the Hungarian Diet, demanded a representative government: when this was refused, they revolted. On 12 March, Vienna succumbed, and three days later, Berlin. Revolution spread to Milan on 18 March, and four days later to Venice, where the Venetian republic was re-established.

In May, Austria granted Hungary a representative government, causing Chancellor Metternich to resign. But a year later, in June 1849, Austria, with aid from Prussian troops, defeated the revolutions in the Rhineland, Saxony and Bavaria, while Russia intervened to enable Austria to recover its position in Hungary. The revolutions were put down with horrific violence, followed by severe repression.

Russia and Britain were spared these upheavals. In Russia, there was no organised middle or proletarian class to instigate a revolution, nor the communications essential to any alliance between such groups. In Britain, as well as the stability of and respect for the

ABOVE: Admiral of the Fleet Lord Mountbatten (1900–1979), in conversation with the author (then political leader of Portsmouth City Council) in 1976. Born Prince Louis of Battenberg, Mountbatten was a great-grandson of Prince Albert and Queen Victoria

RIGHT: Johann Heinrich Tischbein the Elder's 1775 painting of Augusta von Reuss zu Ebersdorf (1757–1831) as Artemisia. As the Dowager Duchess of Coburg and mother of Duke Ernst I and Leopold, King of the Belgians, Augusta played a crucial role in forming her sons' ambitions and establishing the family's eminence

LEFT: Christian Frederick, Baron Stockmar (1787–1863), by John Partridge. Born in Coburg, Stockmar served as private secretary to Leopold, and assiduously promoted the marriage between Albert, Leopold's nephew, and Queen Victoria

BELOW: Princess Charlotte (1796–1817) and Prince Leopold of Saxe-Coburg-Saalfeld (1790–1865) in their box at Covent Garden, 1817 (engraving by W T Fry after George Dawe)

Leopold I, King of the Belgians, by Franz Xaver Winterhalter, 1846. Leopold was elected to the Belgian crown in 1831 after Belgium had asserted its independence from the Netherlands the previous year

The death of Princess Charlotte in 1817 led to a scramble by George IV's unmarried brothers to find wives and produce an heir to the British throne. They are seen here in this 1818 cartoon riding on the back of John Bull (representing England) in the race to succeed

The Giants' Hall, Schloss Ehrenburg, Coburg, where the marriage of Victoire and Edward, Duke of Kent took place in 1818

Princess Victoire, Duchess of Kent, with her daughter Victoria, future Queen of England, in 1823. The Duchess remains in mourning for her husband, the Duke of Kent, who died in 1820

Victoire, Duchess of Kent, by F X Winterhalter, in 1861, the year of her death

The marriage of Queen Victoria and Prince Albert at St James's Palace on 10 February 1840; engraving published in the *Illustrated London News* in 1887

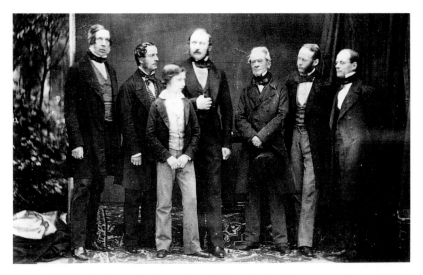

ABOVE: Christian Stockmar played an influential role at the English court as adviser to Prince Albert, promoting Coburg influence on Leopold's behalf. This group photograph shows Stockmar (third from right) with Prince Albert (centre), the young Prince of Wales (front) and others, at Windsor Castle in April 1857 (photograph by Caldesi)

Osborne House, the private home of Victoria and Albert on the Isle of Wight; Albert was closely involved with all aspects of creating the new house and estate

The Opening of the Great Exhibition – the first 'world fair', masterminded by Prince Albert – by Queen Victoria on 1 May 1851

The Royal Albert Hall, which opened after the Prince Consort's death, was Albert's own conception

Schloss Ehrenburg, the centrepiece of the town of Coburg and primary residence of the dukes of Coburg

Luise, Princess of Saxe-Gotha-Altenburg, in 1814 (before her marriage to Duke Ernst), by Josef Grassi

Schloss Friedenstein, where Princess Luise was born on 21 December 1800

This portrait of Duchess Luise by modern artist Johannes Franke is based on portraits by contemporary artists

Nr. 205.

Privi   legirte

Gothaische   Zeitung.

Auf das   Jahr 1816.

52ste Woche, Dienstags den 24. December.

Gotha, vom 22. Dec. -

Am 20sten dieses früh traf Sr. Durchl. der regierende Herzog von S. Coburg-Saalfeld hier ein, und wurde am nämlichen Tage Mittags mit der Prinzessin Louise Durchl. — einzigen Tochter unsers gnädigst regierenden Herzogs Durchl. — in Gegenwart Höchstihrer Durchl. Eltern, des hohen Staats-Ministerii und des ganzen Hofs feyerlichst verlobt. Dieses höchst erfreuliche und rührende Ereigniß, an dem die sämmtlichen Unterthanen des Landes den aufrichtigsten und herzlichsten Antheil nur so ungeheuchelter nehmen, als sie der Höchsten Person der Durchl. Prinzessin mit jener treuen Anhänglichkeit und Liebe zugethan sind, womit sie dem Durchl. Elternpaare ihre tiefste Ehrfurcht stets zu bezeugen bemüht sind, wurde gestern, als am 16jährigen Geburtstage der Durchl. Prinzessin Louise, durch eine am Abend in hiesiger Stadt unaufgefordert veranstaltete glänzende und geschmackvolle Erleuchtung gefeyert. Sprach sich schon früherhin, als die Nachricht von dem glücklichen Abschluß der erhabenen Verbindung im Publicum sich verbreitete, das Gefühl tiefster Rührung, ehrfurchtsvoller Hochachtung und treuer Unterthanenliebe unzweydeutig aus, so äußerte sich jene schöne Stimmung bey diesem erhebenden Feste dann um so unverkennbarer, als unsers gnädigst regierenden Herzogs Durchl. mit dem Höchsten Brautpaare und einem Theile Höchstihres Hofstaats dem froh und zahlreichst versammelten Publicum die Freude gewährte, die einzelnen Straßen der hiesigen Stadt zu durchfahren und von der versammelten Menge den herzlichen und stets wiederholten Lebehoch! Ruf huldreichst aufzunehmen. Schenke der Himmel unsrer gnädigsten und tiefst verehrten Prinzessin Louise Durchl. in dem künftigen Besitze eines der trefflichsten und edelsten Fürsten Deutschlands, zur Freude Ihrer Durchl. Eltern und zum Heil Ihrer künftigen Unterthanen, das irdische Glück, auf welches Höchstdieselbe bey Ihren humanen Gesinnungen und bey Ihren eminenten Geistesfähigkeiten mit Recht Anspruch machen kann!

Wien, vom 14. Dec. -

Der Erzherzog Anton, Bruder Sr. Maj. des Kaisers, von welchem man schon seit einen Jahr erwartete, daß er als Oestereichischer Generalgouverneur im lombardisch-Venetianischen Königreich seine Reise nach Mayland antreten würde, hat, dem Vernehmen nach, diese Bestimmung abgelehnt; es ist aber noch

A report of the celebrations in Gotha following the engagement of Ernst I and Luise of Saxe-Gotha-Altenburg, on the front page of the *Gothaische Zeitung*, 24 December 1816

ABOVE: *Schloss Rosenau, Seat of HRH Prince Albert of Coburg*, 1841, by J M W Turner. Prince Albert was born at the Rosenau

LEFT: Duchess Luise with her children, by Ludwig Döll, 1823–4. Albert, the future Prince Consort, is on the left, and Ernst II on the right. After her separation from Ernst I in 1824, Luise never saw her children again

LEFT: Duke Ernst I of Saxe-Coburg-Gotha as a young man, after a portrait by Ruprecht, the Coburg court painter

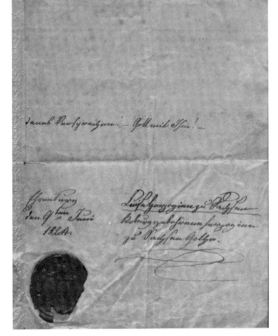

RIGHT: The final page of a letter in Luise's handwriting, apparently signed, sealed and dated by her on 9 June 1824, in which she committed herself to Max von Hanstein and guaranteed his future financial security. It is thought that she backdated the letter to a time when she could not have written it (see Chapter 17)

ABOVE: Duchess Luise's summerhouse at St Wendel in the Rhineland, to which she was exiled in November 1824. St Wendel is some 300 miles from Coburg

LEFT: Ernst II, Duke of Saxe-Coburg-Gotha (1818–1893), elder brother of Prince Albert, in about 1860

Prince Albert *c.* 1860, engraving from a
photograph by O G Rejlander

Nathan Bloom, a descendant of Friedrich
Blum, *c.* 1930; the likeness to Prince Albert in
his later years is striking. Friedrich Blum was
a member of the household at Schloss
Ehrenburg in 1818–19

LEFT: The statue of Prince Albert in the Marktplatz, Coburg

BELOW: Queen Victoria with European royalty at Coburg in 1894. Those present include Kaiser Wilhelm II of Germany, Queen Victoria's grandson (bottom left), and the Tsarevich (on the Kaiser's left), who was married to the Queen's granddaughter Princess Alexandra, and who succeeded his father as Tsar Nicholas II later that year

monarchy, the 1832 Reform Act had defused the case for general enfranchisement, and the repeal of the Corn Laws in 1846, withdrawing the protection of agricultural tariffs, had had a salutary effect on food prices.

The consequences of the 1848 revolutions in Europe were a series of lost opportunities for the bourgeoisie. 'The German bourgeoisie's failure to seize power in 1848 to carry through its own revolution has been described by all shades of opinion as the pivotal non-event for the entire course of German history,' writes David Blackburn in *The Peculiarities of German History.*[5] Similarly, the German historian M R Lepsius refers to the '1848 failures of the German bourgeoisie to generate a combative political liberalism on the model of its counterpart in Britain'. The country 'became saddled with a political system which actively legitimised the arbitrary exercise of bureaucratic and military powers'.[6]

On 28 March 1848, Albert wrote a long memorandum supporting a German federation with a strong sovereign, chancellor and parliament, which would retain the 'states complete in themselves with their dynastic forms that embodied the individualities of these peoples'.[7] He felt sufficiently strongly on the matter to forward copies to Stockmar, his brother Duke Ernst II, King Frederick Augustus II of Saxony, King Ludwig I of Bavaria, Emperor Ferdinand of Austria and King Frederick William of Prussia. His advice supports David Cannadine's opinion that 'the Prince was too close to a backward-looking concept of monarchical power' to have invented with Victoria the concept of constitutional monarchy.[8] Albert wanted to be 'a ruler who was emancipated from the politicians rather than fettered by them, a crown that was influentially, not impotently, above the battle, a sovereign who governed as well as reigned'.[9] For example, when Wellington invited him to become commander-in-chief of the army, he refused on the grounds that 'the husband of the Queen has to be at her service as her adviser'[10] – yet shortly after, he obtained the position for his own candidate Lord Hardinge and continued to interfere in military affairs behind the scenes. Criticism of his conduct simmered, and then, in his struggle to control foreign affairs, the Prince got into even more trouble.

At this point Victoria and Albert found themselves at odds with

the powerful figure of Lord Palmerston, foreign secretary under the
prime ministership of Lord John Russell. Albert thought Palmerston
a coarse, reckless egotist whose combined arrogance and ignorance
must inevitably lead to folly and disaster. Palmerston infuriated
Victoria by ignoring her, which was not unusual – he often ignored
both the Cabinet and even the prime minister as well. He either submitted important Foreign Office dispatches to the Queen so late that
there was no time to correct them, or did not submit them to her at
all. On occasions when he did submit documents and Victoria
suggested alterations to some passages, they were sent off in their
original form. The Queen complained; the Prince complained; it was
all futile. In January 1849, Victoria wrote to Russell, 'No remon-
strance has any effect with Lord Palmerston,'[11] and on another
occasion told him: 'Lord Palmerston has as usual pretended not to
have had time to submit a draft to the Queen before he sent it off.'[12]
When Russell remonstrated with him, Palmerston simply told the
prime minister that 28,000 dispatches passed through the Foreign
Office every year, and if each were subjected to royal scrutiny, the
business of the Foreign Office would grind to a halt.

But Palmerston also failed to communicate his most important
dispatches to Russell. In 1847, for example, he reached the point of
breaking off relations with France without consulting either the
Cabinet or the prime minister,[13] and such incidents constantly
recurred.[14] In 1850, one of them put Palmerston's political life
in jeopardy.

Britain's consul in Athens, Don Pacifico, was a Portuguese Jew
who had been born in Gibraltar and so possessed a British passport.
When his house was burned down by a mob of Greek Orthodox
fanatics, he sent an inflated bill for damages of £80,000 to the King
of Greece. When this was rejected, he sought relief from the British
government. Palmerston – without reference to anyone at all – sent
a fleet to blockade the port of Piraeus and gave the Greek authorities an ultimatum demanding immediate restitution to Don Pacifico,
together with a formal apology. When the ultimatum was not
acknowledged, he instructed the navy to bombard Piraeus.

This high-handed action could have provoked a war with Greece,
which would also have involved France and possibly Russia. Queen

Victoria was beside herself with rage: 'The levity of the man is really inconceivable,' she wrote in her journal, and Lord Stanley raised a motion of censure against the government in the House of Lords. The royal couple were eager to welcome Palmerston's downfall, but the government was keen to repair the political damage and encouraged the energetic MP John Roebuck to lay down a motion of support in the Commons. In the historic debate that followed, Palmerston made perhaps the finest speech of his parliamentary career, lasting over four hours and annihilating his critics. Using, to acclamation, the phrase '*Civis romanus sum*' ('I am a Roman citizen'), he drew on the emotive and jingoistic argument that equated British citizenship with that of the Romans, who during the empire could always appeal to Roman law as the ultimate authority. The motion was carried by forty-six votes. Palmerston was once more the hero of the hour, and 'great was the disappointment of Albert; great was the indignation of Victoria'.[15]

But five months earlier, the prescient Stockmar had drawn up a memorandum for Queen Victoria in case of an emergency. Now it was brought out. The Queen copied out his words and sent them to Russell, requesting him to show her letter to Palmerston:

> She thinks it right in order to prevent any mistake in the future, to explain briefly what she expects from her Foreign Secretary. She requires:
> 1. That he will distinctly state what he proposes in a given case, in order that the Queen may know as distinctly to what she has given her royal sanction.
> 2. Having once given her sanction to a measure, that it not be arbitrarily altered or modified by the Minister. She must consider such an act as failing in sincerity towards the Crown, and justly exercise her constitutional right to dismiss the Minister.

On receiving this, Palmerston was concerned enough to write to the prime minister and acquiesce to the Queen's requirements: 'I have taken a copy of the memorandum of the Queen, and will not fail to attend to the direction which it contains.' He also asked for an interview with Prince Albert, realising that if he were seen to be on bad terms with the monarchy, his ambitions for higher political office would be compromised. Albert immediately invited Palmerston to the palace and, in his memorandum of the meeting, wrote that he was 'astonished to note that when Palmerston entered, he was considerably agitated, shook and had tears in his eyes so as quite to move me, who had never under any circumstances known him but with a bland smile on his face'.

At last, after a long and inconclusive conversation, the Prince said that, in order to give Lord Palmerston 'an example of what the Queen wanted', he would ask him a question point-blank.

> You are aware that the Queen has objected to the protocol about Schleswig, and of the grounds on which she has done so. Her opinion has been overruled, the protocol stating that the Great Powers want to see the integrity of the Danish monarchy preserved has been signed, and the King of Denmark has taken this as an opportunity to invade Schleswig, where war is raging. If Holstein is also attacked, which is likely, the Germans will fly to her assistance; Russia has also indicated that she may intervene militarily if the Schleswigers are successful. What will you do, if this emergency arises, probably provoking a European war, when we are at Balmoral and Lord John in another part of Scotland? The Queen expects you to have considered this possibility, and requires a categorical answer as to what you would do in that event.

Palmerston, who favoured Denmark on the issue, but was well aware that Albert supported the nationalists who wanted to incorporate Schleswig-Holstein into a united Germany, did not want a confrontation on the issue, and so declined to answer this hypothetical question. 'The whole matter,' he said, 'is extremely complicated, and the contingencies mentioned by His Royal Highness are very unlikely to arise.' Albert tried for a full hour to get a categorical answer, to no avail. At length, Palmerston bowed himself out of the room, leaving Albert throwing up his hands in shocked amazement: what could he do with such a man? (Asked much later about the Schleswig-Holstein question, Palmerston said, 'Only three men have understood it. One is dead, one is mad, and I have forgotten.')

In September 1850, shortly after that interview, Palmerston again upset both the Queen and the prime minister. General Haynau, a retired Hungarian general on a European tour, paid a visit to Barclay & Perkins brewery in the City of London. His reputation as a wholesale sadist preceded him. The Habsburg government in Vienna had sent him to Brescia in Italy following the 1848 revolution to exact retribution against the insurgents. There he had ordered countless executions of Italian patriots who had fought for independence, and the flogging of women – including noblewomen – who had aided the insurgents. In Hungary, he had ordered the execution of hundreds of supporters of the insurrection. His deeds were so notorious that they had been published in newspapers and journals across Europe, and he had become known as 'the Hyena of Brescia', a pun on his name. In 1850, when his usefulness had expired and he had become too much of an embarrassment to the Austrian government, he had been retired. Austrian war hero General Joseph Radetsky commented that 'Haynau is like a razor: after it has been used, it should be put back in its case.'

When Haynau appeared at the brewery in London, the draymen, infuriated by his presence and with the apparent acceptance of the authorities, set upon him. He was beaten with broom handles and dragged by his hair along the street before being rescued by the police. Palmerston sent an apology for this degrading treatment to the Emperor's ambassador in London, but commented that it would have been wiser for Haynau not to have come to England since he was not welcome there. The draft was sent to the Queen, who asked for alterations to be made. She was informed that, as in the past, the dispatch had already been sent, but Palmerston, realising that such a bald statement would no longer suffice, added that 'he had good reason to know that General Haynau's ferocious and unmanly treatment of the unfortunate inhabitants of Brescia and of other places and towns in Italy … and his barbarous acts in Hungary excited almost as much disgust in Austria as in England.'[16]

In 1851, Lajos Kossuth, the Hungarian radical leader and orator of sparkling quality, arrived in London to address a number of mass meetings in his excellent English. Palmerston reluctantly bowed to his prime minister's instruction not to meet him, but did meet a deputation of radicals, who thanked him for his support of Kossuth. Despite these provocations, Lord John knew Palmerston had the public on his side, and it was not the right time to dismiss him.

However, Palmerston eventually ran out of time and luck over the affair of Louis-Napoleon. This nephew of Napoleon I, educated in Switzerland and Germany, originally supported liberal causes against the Habsburg Empire; he then entered France illegally to incite a revolt in support of his claim to the imperial throne. He was imprisoned but escaped to England. After the forced abdication of Louis-Philippe in March 1848 and the creation of the Second Republic, he was free to return to France, where he stood for the presidency and, on 10 December 1848, won by a landslide, with more than 5,450,000 votes – some 75 per cent of the total.

In 1851, he asked the National Assembly to amend the constitution to enable him to stand for a further four-year term, since he felt he had not had time to implement his political and economic reforms. (The constitution was fixed at one term, to prevent the abuse of power or a return to dictatorship, and ensure the retention of the republic.) The monarchists, who preferred the return of the Bourbon dynasty, were in the majority in the National Assembly, and accordingly refused all Louis-Napoleon's attempts to obtain this amendment. But on 2 December 1851, confident of his position, he staged a *coup d'état* and seized dictatorial powers. The date had been carefully chosen: it was the anniversary of both the crowning of his uncle, Napoleon I, as emperor, and the victory at the Battle of Austerlitz, which all French people celebrated. He then sought confirmation of his action in a national referendum, which he won convincingly. Exactly a year later, the Second Republic became the Second Empire, and Louis-Napoleon became Emperor Napoleon III.

On 3 December 1851, the day after Louis-Napoleon's coup, Palmerston, without consulting anyone, told the French ambassador that he approved of it. Two days later, he was instructed by the prime minister, in accordance with a letter from the Queen, that the British government's policy was to maintain strict neutrality towards the affairs of France. Nevertheless, in an official dispatch to the British ambassador in Paris – submitted to neither the Queen nor the prime minister – Palmerston repeated his approval of the *coup d'état*, which he had already given verbally to the French ambassador. Lord John Russell's patience was, as he said himself, 'drained to the last drop', and on 23 December 1851 he finally dismissed Lord Palmerston. Charles Greville recorded in his diary:

> Palmerston is out! Actually and irretrievably out. I nearly dropped off my chair yesterday afternoon when at five o'clock, a few moments after the Cabinet had broken up, Lord Granville rushed into my room and said, 'Pam is out, the offer of the FO goes to Clarendon tonight, and if he refuses, it is to be offered to me.'[17]

The next day, he duly recorded: 'To my unspeakable astonishment ... Clarendon did refuse it ... and [Granville] accepted it.'

Queen Victoria wrote in her journal: 'Our relief was great and we felt quite excited by the news, for our anxiety and worry during the last five years and a half, which were indescribable, was mainly, if not entirely, caused by Lord Palmerston. It is a great and unexpected mercy.'[18]

Even then, Palmerston's dismissal might not have happened but for the intrigues of both Victoria and Albert. They were so desperate to rid themselves of their foreign secretary that they resorted to exploiting publicly a sexual scandal some ten years old. In a memorandum on Palmerston's 'worthless private character', Albert wrote to Russell: 'The Foreign Secretary (at Windsor Castle) marched late at night into the bedroom of Mrs Brand (one of the Queen's Ladies of the Bedchamber).' How could the Queen, he asked, treat as her chief adviser and confidential counsellor in all matters of state a man who had committed a brutal attack on one of her ladies under her roof? He had introduced himself into her apartment by stealth, barricaded the door, and would have consummated his fiendish scheme by violence had not his victim's screams saved her.

Russell replied that 'he unfortunately knew another lady in society upon whom he had tried the same thing,'[19] though it was said in mitigation that Palmerston had mixed up the bedrooms: another lady, who normally occupied that room, had allegedly been expecting him!

Out of office, Palmerston used the press to his advantage whenever possible. In an article, he indicated that Coburg interests had influenced the Queen's decisions on foreign affairs.[20] Albert commented:

> There was no interest of the House of Commons involved in any questions upon which we quarrelled with Lord Palmerston; not on Greece, nor Italy, Sicily, Holstein, Hungary etc. Why are princes alone denied the credit of having political opinions based on a concern for the national interest and honour, and the welfare of mankind? Are they not more independently placed than any other politician?[21]

Yet Palmerston's point was close to the mark. The extent to which Albert was torn between dynastic loyalties and patriotism for his adopted country is shown in a memorandum written by his brother, Duke Ernst II, on 'family networking'. This twenty-five-page document was intended for the family's eyes only, and would have fuelled the British public's worst fears of a Coburg conspiracy. It is undated, but must have been written after Ernst II succeeded in 1844. He calls members of the family '*Glieder*' – that is, 'links': ancestors, current and future members of the family, existing outside the conventions of space and time. The family and its glory was, according to Ernst, central to the thinking of every 'link'.[22]

This concept of a strong international dynasty taking an active part in political affairs at home and abroad clashed with British nationalism, and also collided with the idea of the political impartiality of the Crown. Albert's political ideas, as shown in his advice on German federation, had not fully matured. At this stage of his life, he remained too close to his Coburg roots fully to accept the meaning of constitutional monarchy. But politics was not his main goal. Wider horizons beckoned, which would give a fuller meaning to the doctrine of enlightened monarchy.

Albert's enlightened monarchy

At the time of Palmerston's (albeit brief) political demise, Albert had certainly come a long way from the young man who had married the sovereign. After some nine years as Queen Victoria's consort, he was now experienced in public life and confidently managed Victoria's battles on her behalf. Without a formal role in Britain's political life, he also wanted to express his ideals in more tangible form He felt strongly about higher education and about promoting the achievements of his adopted country, particularly its industrial and commercial growth. Thus was born the vision for the Great Exhibition of 1851.

Henry Cole, who was shortly to become chairman of the Royal Society of Arts, had discussed the idea of an international exhibition with Albert in June 1849. Albert liked the idea of a landmark cultural event in London to celebrate the virtues of peace, progress and prosperity, which he considered to be inherently British qualities. He summoned a small committee to Buckingham Palace, including Henry Cole and his friend Thomas Cubitt, the builder of the extension to Osborne House, and laid an outline of his scheme before them. The committee approved the plan in principle, and the great undertaking was set in train without delay.

In January 1850, Victoria set up a royal commission of twenty-four members, with Albert as chairman, to assume responsibility for all matters in respect of the proposed Great Exhibition. A budget of £230,000 was agreed. Albert worked with extraordinary energy, the leading manufacturers warmly took up the idea, the East India Company was supportive and the great foreign nations were eager to send in contributions.

The problem of settling on a suitable site for this huge national venture was a source of great argument and stress for Albert. Battersea Park, Regent's Park, Primrose Hill and the Isle of Dogs were all considered and turned down for one reason or another. Finally, the commission sought parliamentary approval to use a twenty-six-acre site in Hyde Park. However, there was resistance among the Conservatives in Parliament, since the funding was deemed insecure and the outline designs threatened numerous highly valued trees. Furthermore, the idea of having the exhibition in Hyde Park was greeted with a great many objections by wealthy home-owners nearby. *The Times* wrote that the whole park would become a bivouac of vagabonds.

> Kensington and Belgravia would be uninhabitable and the Season would be ruined. The annoyance inflicted upon the neighbourhood will be indescribable ... We can scarcely bring ourselves to believe that the advisers to the Prince cared to connect his name with such an outrage to the feelings and wishes of the inhabitants of the metropolis.[1]

Both these issues were resolved by the commission. First, a sum of £200,000 – a large proportion of the project's budget – was subscribed as a guarantee, and then the plans of Joseph Paxton were selected from the 234 submitted. Paxton was known as a designer of gigantic conservatories. He had built one for the sixth Duke of Devonshire that had impressed the commission for a number of reasons, among them the effect of natural light shining in through the glass roof. A dome would be built to include the taller trees in Hyde Park and resolve that problem. Furthermore, the iron-and-glass construction would be substantially less expensive than the solid buildings offered by engineers such as Brunel.

On 6 July 1850, the *Illustrated London News* published an engraving of the planned structure, which received immediate public and political support. The House of Commons approved the exhibition and the development of the Hyde Park site, based on Paxton's design, by a large majority, and by the end of the month Fox and Henderson, the London builders and contractors, were given the contract for construction.

Then, as so often occurs with great imaginative plans, the detractors and cynics made their pitch. As the enormous glass edifice rose higher and higher, the fury of the critics reached a climax. It was said that the exhibition would serve as a rallying point for all the ruffians in England and all the malcontents in Europe, and that on the opening day there would be a riot and probably a revolution. It was asserted that the glass roof was porous, and the droppings of 50 million sparrows would utterly destroy every object beneath it. Colonel Charles Sibthorpe MP, he of the amendment to reduce Albert's annuity from £50,000 to £30,000, prayed 'that hail and lightning might descend from heaven on the accursed thing'. He declared to the House that it was 'the greatest trash, the greatest fraud, and the greatest imposition ever attempted to be palmed upon the people of this country'.[2]

All this took a toll on Albert's health. He suffered from constant sleeplessness, but he remembered Stockmar's injunctions and never took his eye from his objective. He toiled at committees, presided over public meetings, made speeches and communicated with every corner of the civilised world. And he was rewarded on 1 May 1851, when the Great Exhibition was opened by Victoria before enormous crowds amid scenes of dazzling brilliance and triumphant enthusiasm.

She left Buckingham Palace shortly after eleven o'clock in a procession of nine state carriages, reportedly in a state of excitement bordering on delirium, and performed her duties in a trance of joy, gratitude and amazement. After prayers led by the Archbishop of Canterbury, there was a rendering of Handel's 'Hallelujah Chorus', then Albert, as chairman of the royal commission, made an opening speech. In it he described the exhibition as 'the fertile promotion of all branches of human diligence and the strengthening of the hands of peace amongst all the nations of the earth'. Victoria, accompanied by Albert and followed by courtiers and members of the commission, then paraded through the building among the privileged ticket holders for this opening day before returning to her throne, set up for the occasion. From here, following fanfares, she declared the 'Great Exhibition of the Works of Industry of all Nations' open. She wrote in her journal that evening:

The Green Park and Hyde Park were one mass of densely crowded human beings in the highest good humour and most enthusiastic. I never saw Hyde Park look as it did, being filled with crowds as far as the eye could reach. Mr Paxton, who might be justly proud, and rose from being a common gardener's boy, Sir George Grey in tears, and everybody astonished and delighted.[3]

A few days later, Victoria wrote to Leopold:

The first of May was the greatest day in our history, the most beautiful and imposing and touching spectacle ever seen, and the triumph of my beloved Albert … It was the happiest, proudest day in my life and I can think of nothing else. Albert's dearest name is immortalised with this great conception, his own, and my own dear country showed she was worthy of it.

The triumph was immense, the enthusiasm universal, and even the bitterest critics were converted and joined the chorus of praise. Congratulations from public bodies poured in; the city of Paris treated the exhibition committee to a great fête, and the Queen and the Prince made a triumphal progress through the north of England. The total profit made by the exhibition amounted to £165,000, which was used to buy land in South Kensington for the development of museums and university buildings – everything close to Albert's heart.

What became known after his death as the Royal Albert Hall was Albert's own conception, with Henry Cole's final design including seating for 5,500. His vision for the university and museum complex in the same Kensington area also came together. All this was the consequence of the success of the Great Exhibition, and a grand memorial to Albert's energy, foresight and determination. In its majesty, its nobility of thought, intellectualism and cultural aims, the exhibition brought to fruition everything Leopold and Stockmar had planned all those years ago, when, as a boy in the Rosenau, Albert had first been trained for his position.

Nor should Albert's many other achievements be forgotten. They include the spectacular revival of Cambridge University leading to worldwide eminence during his chancellorship; the laying of the foundations for Imperial College; the Landseer lions at the base of Nelson's Column; the extension to the National Gallery, and its collection of early Renaissance paintings, twenty-two of which he donated and the purchase of the remainder of which he inspired; the idea of the royal balcony at Buckingham Palace; and the inspiration for granting the Victoria Cross to all ranks. His acquisition of both Osborne House and Balmoral, his close interest in foreign affairs and his handling of ministers also added greatly to the purpose, respect and stability of the British monarchy during his lifetime.

In the eight months of its existence, more than six million people visited the Great Exhibition. The day of its closure, 10 February 1852, was the twelfth anniversary of Victoria and Albert's wedding. In such a short time, Albert had stamped his influence on the throne of England.

CHAPTER 12

Marriage: Influence and domination

Victoria and Albert had nine children. The eldest, Victoria, known to her family as Vicki, was born in 1840, and the heir apparent, Albert Edward, in 1841. It was after this birth that Victoria acknowledged Leopold's long-term planning for the marriage in her letter of 6 December 1841:

> My dearest Uncle,
> I am sure if you knew how happy, how blessed I feel, and how proud in possessing such a perfect being as my husband, and if you think that you have been instrumental in bringing about this union, it must gladden your heart.

Alice followed in 1843; Alfred, who subsequently became the Duke of Saxe-Coburg-Gotha, in 1844; Helena in 1846; Louise in 1848; Arthur in 1850; Leopold in 1853; and finally Beatrice in 1857. As the children grew, Victoria and Albert took pleasure in noting their assumption of royal duties, which would take them all over the world in support of the interests of the British Empire. In a speech at Trinity House in London in June 1860, Albert noted the

> curious coincidence that nearly at the same time – a few weeks hence – though almost at opposite poles, the Prince of Wales will inaugurate in the Queen's name that stupendous work, the great bridge over the St Lawrence river in Canada, while Prince Alfred will lay the foundation stone of the breakwater for the harbour of Cape Town ... How important and beneficent is the role given to the Royal Family of England to act in the development of distant and rising countries, who recognise in the British Crown and their

allegiance to it, their supreme bond of union with the mother country, and with each other?[1]

Leopold and Stockmar had supported a united Germany under the leadership of a constitutional Prussian monarchy, and Albert had moved on since his memorandum of 28 March 1848, now accepting Stockmar's argument that Germany could only advance as a unified nation under Prussia's leadership. So in 1855, Victoria and Albert pursued the opportunity for the marriage of Vicki, the Princess Royal, to Prussian Crown Prince Frederick. Here was their dream of uniting the royal houses of Britain and Prussia, the chance to achieve a unified Germany allied to Britain, one that followed a similar path of enlightened constitutional monarchy, which would endure for centuries.

Palmerston, whose dismissal as foreign secretary Victoria and Albert had celebrated in December 1851, had regained office the following year, and when Lord Aberdeen's government fell in 1855, he was the popular choice to succeed him. So Victoria and Albert had to deal with their old enemy as prime minister. But on the issue of Germany, Palmerston agreed to the royal proposal, and the policy was set, even though the Princess Royal was only fourteen, ten years younger than Frederick.

The question of a possible marriage was discussed in correspondence between the two royal houses, and on 29 August 1855 Albert wrote to his mother-in-law the Duchess of Kent: 'We shall probably have Fritz [Prince Frederick's family nickname] visiting us ... for a few days ... He wishes to see Scotland.' Prince Frederick duly arrived at Balmoral on 18 September, and two days later, Albert wrote to Stockmar:

> The event you are interested in reached an active stage this morning after breakfast. The young man, with the permission of his parents, and of the King [of Prussia], accepted the proposal and asked for the hand of Vicki. We accepted for ourselves, but requested him to hold it in suspense till after her Confirmation ... in the spring. The young man wished to make his offer to her himself.

Despite her youth, Vicki was intellectually advanced beyond her years; she also spoke German fluently, whereas Frederick's English was limited. The couple became engaged on 19 May 1857, and the marriage was celebrated on 25 January 1858 in the Chapel Royal of St James's Palace. A minor power struggle between the Prussian officials and the Queen was played out when the Prussian ambassador pointed out that it was customary for princes of the blood to be married in Berlin. Victoria emphatically instructed the foreign secretary to tell him 'not to entertain the possibility of such a question ... Whatever may be the usual practice of Prussian Princes, it is not every day that one marries the eldest daughter of the Queen of England. The question must therefore be considered as settled and closed.'

Vicki had the most engaging personality and was the most intelligent of all the royal children, and Albert, despite the importance to him of the union, was much affected by the marriage. He was losing his favourite child, with whom he had so much in common and whose company he so much enjoyed, with her interest in the arts and sciences, her enquiring mind and her conversation.

Unfortunately, Edward, Prince of Wales, called 'Bertie' by his family, did not share his eldest sister's qualities. When he was seven, Albert set out an educational programme for him under the supervision of several tutors, designed to ensure that he would be thoroughly prepared for constitutional monarchy. Bertie tried to meet parental expectations, but he was not a diligent student, having none of Vicki's capacity for or real interest in studying. His talents, as they were to develop, were charm, sociability and tact. In October 1859, he matriculated as an undergraduate at Christ Church, Oxford, and, two years later, transferred to Trinity College, Cambridge, but he never received a degree – although he quickly gained a reputation as a playboy. Two weeks before Albert died from typhoid, he had visited Bertie in Cambridge on a cold December day to remonstrate with him over his scandalous affair with an actress, which had been the subject of newspaper gossip. As a result, Victoria always held Bertie responsible for Albert's death.

Despite his personal loss, Albert saw Vicki's marriage as symbolising all that he wanted. His daughter would be on the throne supporting her husband, the liberal and constitutionally minded Frederick, towards the development of a united Germany under the leadership of Prussia. Albert had every reason to hope for, and indeed to expect, such a consequence. However, the fates decreed otherwise. In 1858, Frederick's uncle, Friedrich William IV of Prussia, suffered a serious stroke, making it necessary for Frederick's father, the King's brother, first to act as regent, and then, in 1861, to succeed to the throne as Wilhelm I. He was soon in difficulties with the liberal Prussian parliament, which refused to sanction his budget for the army, so he recalled Otto von Bismarck from his position as ambassador in Paris to become *Ministerpräsident* (prime minister) and foreign minister. So in 1861 the name of Bismarck, which was to dominate the European stage for three decades and bring about major changes in the balance of power, first entered the lexicon of international diplomacy.

Bismarck was born in Brandenburg in 1815, into the élite *Junkers* social class, and educated at Göttingen University and at Friedrich-Wilhelm (now Humboldt) University in Berlin. Soon after his appointment by Wilhelm I, he dissolved the hostile liberal-dominated Landtag (parliament) but continued to collect taxes to pay for the modernisation of the army under the leadership of von Moltke, all in violation of the constitution.

He knew that, to resolve the issue of German unity under the leadership of Prussia, he would have to carry the various states and principalities on a wave of German patriotism. He first extricated Austria from the equation, following the second Schleswig-Holstein war against Denmark in 1865, which the Austrian-Prussian alliance won. It had been agreed between the victors at the Gastein Convention that Austria would administer Holstein and Prussia would administer Schleswig, but in 1866, Bismarck precipitated war with Austria on the weak contention that it had violated the convention. Within seven weeks, von Moltke's new army had defeated Austria at the Battle of Sadowa (Königgrätz), and Bismarck was then able to exclude Austria from the North German Confederation, which was formed in 1867 under the aegis of Prussia. This nationalist war made Bismarck popular, and the liberals suffered a major defeat in the Landtag, where the conservatives now formed the majority. Bismarck took the opportunity to have retrospective legislation passed to approve the budgets of the previous four years, which had been primarily designed to support the army's requirements.

His next step was to win the southern German states round to joining the confederation, by means of a popular nationalist war against the French, which Bismarck skilfully brought about in 1870. He induced France to declare war on Prussia – thereby making it appear the aggressor – following his publication of what became known as the *Ems Dispatch*, which referred to a conversation between Wilhelm I and the French ambassador about France's refusal to have a Hohenzollern (i.e. Prussian) prince on the Spanish throne. Following what has become known as the Franco-Prussian War, in which the French were humiliated on the battlefield, Prussia exacted a substantial indemnity and Alsace and Lorraine were ceded to the North German Confederation. As Bismarck had anticipated, all the German states now rallied to the flag, and the new German empire (*Kaiserreich*) was confirmed when Wilhelm I was crowned emperor on 18 January 1871 in the Hall of Mirrors at Versailles – a further humiliation for France. Bismarck was created a prince (*Fürst*) for his successes, and his system of alliances leading to the Three Emperors' League (*Dreikaiserbund*) – Germany, Austria/Hungary and Russia – established him as the leading statesman in Europe.

Bismarck detested both Frederick and Vicki for their liberalism, declaring that the Englishwoman and her mother were a menace to the Prussian state. (Even today, it is accepted in Coburg that Vicki was an English spy.) The feud continued when Crown Prince Frederick succeeded to the throne in 1888, and a family entanglement brought about a new crisis. Vicki's second daughter, Princess Victoria, known to the family as Moretta, was engaged to Prince Alexander of Battenberg, who had recently been ejected from the throne of Bulgaria owing to the hostility of Tsar Alexander III. Queen Victoria, Vicki and her husband Frederick all approved the match, as there were already family connections – the prince's elder brother Louis had married a granddaughter of Queen Victoria, and his younger brother had married her daughter Princess Beatrice. But Bismarck opposed the marriage, which he perceived might endanger the friendship between Germany and Russia so integral to his foreign policy, and a fierce struggle ensued. It did not help that Vicki and Frederick's 29-year-old son Wilhelm (later Kaiser Wilhelm II) set himself against the marriage in alliance with Bismarck.

Painfully for Vicki and her husband, the issue became public. Victoria, whose hatred of her daughter's enemy knew no bounds, travelled to Charlottenburg in Berlin to support them. Bismarck sought and obtained a private interview with her, and the man of blood and iron won the day: the engagement was broken off. Little is known of the conversation, but Victoria found Bismarck friendly and reasonable, whereas he, according to the Queen's secretary Arthur Bigge, stated on leaving her room: '*Mein Gott*! That was a woman. One could do business with her.'[2]

Wilhelm I died in March 1888 and Frederick III succeeded as German Kaiser, but he and Vicki only had a few unhappy months in power. In early 1887, after Frederick's German doctors had diagnosed cancer of the larynx, Vicki had turned to the British doctor Morell Mackenzie, an acknowledged authority on diseases of the throat, for a second opinion. Following several biopsies, Mackenzie opined that any tumour in Frederick's throat was benign. As he accompanied his patient and Vicki as they visited health spas around Europe, he continued to feel confident of his diagnosis, in appreciation of which Vicki induced her mother to grant him a knighthood. Unfortunately, all too soon the diagnosis of the German doctors proved correct, and Frederick died in June 1888.

Vicki's son Wilhelm II, who couldn't abide his parents' liberal views, immediately took over, with the solid support of Bismarck. 'Kaiser Bill', as he became known in Britain, was to change the face of Europe, though not as the Coburgs had hoped. Rather, he would bring down many of the pillars of the edifice of European royalty that Albert and Victoria – and, before them, Leopold, Stockmar and the prescient Augusta – had taken such pains to erect.

Following her years of solitary mourning, Victoria regained her vitality with the arrival of Disraeli's second premiership and, on 12 May 1876, assumed the title of 'Empress of India', reigning over a fifth of the world's population. Her grandson, Kaiser Wilhelm II, was on the throne of Germany, her daughter Alice was married to the Grand Duke Louis IV of Hesse and the Rhine, and Alice's daughter, Princess Alexandra, to Tsar Nicholas II of Russia. Sophie, Vicki's daughter and Wilhelm's sister, married Constantine I and became

Queen Sophie of Greece – so the Coburgs finally attained the crown that Leopold had cast aside.

Princess Beatrice's daughter Victoria married King Alfonso XIII of Spain, whose family rules Spain today. Victoria's son Alfred, who inherited the dukedom of Saxe-Coburg-Gotha when Albert's brother Ernst died childless, married Grand Duchess Marie, the only daughter of Alexander II of Russia. Margaret, Victoria's granddaughter by her son Arthur, Duke of Connaught, married Gustav Adolf, the future king of Sweden, and Edward VII's daughter Maud married King Haaken VII of Norway. Alfred's daughter Marie married Ferdinand, King of Romania, and their son Carol later inherited the throne, and Victoria's great-granddaughter Ingrid married Frederick IX of Denmark. In more recent times, Simeon II, the deposed King Bulgaria, returned to that country in 1996 following the collapse of Communism, and was popularly elected its first prime minister in 2001. Simeon is directly descended from Ferdinand, the brother of Victoire, mother of Queen Victoria, and so is a distant cousin of the latter. When he became prime minister of Bulgaria, it was as Mr Saxe-Coburg ('Gotha' is forgotten nowadays) that he took the oath of loyalty to the republic and the president.[3] It is no wonder that Bismarck called the Coburgs 'the stud farm of Europe', and it was with justification that a disgruntled Habsburg archduke complained that 'the Coburgs gain throne after throne, and spread their growing power over the whole earth'.

Bloodline remained an important issue for the Coburgs. Victoria, who was much more liberal than her German relatives in her views on the subject, was outraged when both Vicki and Wilhelm II wrote expressing their concern that the two Battenberg brothers, Louis and Henry, whom Victoria had admitted into her family were not '*Geblut*' (pure blood) because of the morganatic marriage (one between a person of high rank and someone of lower rank, in which the latter retains his or her station and their children have no claim on the higher-ranked parent's possessions or titles) between their father, Prince Alexander of Battenberg, and their mother, Julia Theresa von Hauche.

Imagine the horror and humiliation of these *Geblut*-obsessed snobs had they suspected that their own lineage might not be what they supposed …

CHAPTER 13

Ernst

If, as I propose to demonstrate, Albert was illegitimate, that fact was known only to the natural father, his assumed father Ernst and his mother Luise. Others, such as the Dowager Duchess Augusta and Stockmar, may have suspected the truth – and understood that it was essential to keep it hidden. The reputation of the Coburgs, with all their sexual indiscretions, might not have survived such public knowledge. It would certainly have destroyed Albert's future, and changed the history of Britain and most of Europe. So I contend that the Coburgs, understandably and very effectively, created a conspiracy of silence on the issue.

To expose this conspiracy, it is essential to move the story over to Coburg, Gotha and St Wendel, where the evidence lies. The lifestyles of Ernst and Luise and the people surrounding them during the years 1815–1831 have to be examined in some detail. Nothing may be conclusive in itself, but an accumulation of circumstantial evidence carries weight. Anecdotal evidence passed down through the generations has to be taken into account, as does the law affecting such evidence – which letters and state documents in the archives in Coburg and Gotha corroborate. But in the last resort, only a DNA study will prove the position conclusively (as in the case of Anna Anderson/Anastasia mentioned in Chapter 1) – and it seems unlikely that any of Albert's many royal descendants would care to co-operate in such a venture!

The town of Coburg is charming. Proud of its heritage, untouched by two world wars, it has changed little over the centuries. Dominating the town is the Veste, a typical walled and turreted Germanic fairy-tale castle set atop a steep wooded hill, which for centuries has stood guard over the town: in the Thirty Years' War, the

Catholic leader von Wallenstein laid siege to the Veste in vain. The Dukes of Coburg lived there from 1353 until 1549, when they moved down to the vast, Gothic-style Schloss Ehrenburg in the town, whose grand staircases front on to the street – even in the eighteenth and nineteenth centuries, the ducal family was very much part of Coburg's community. A statue of Ernst I on horseback overlooks the entrance to the *Schloss* from the hill, while Ernst II's statue stands in the forecourt of the *Schloss*, at the entrance to Theatre Square. In the busy marketplace in front of the Rathaus there is a dignified statue of 'Albert, husband of Queen Victoria'.

Johann Ernst began to construct the *Schloss* in 1543, and after the turmoil of the Thirty Years' War and a catastrophic fire in 1690, Duke Albrecht transformed it into a baroque residence comprising the palace, the church, and the splendid Hall of Giants in which Edward, Duke of Kent, married Victoire. It was here that the tragedy of Albert's mother Luise took place, and Victoria and Albert later visited the place on many occasions.

Ernst I (1784–1844), following the family tradition, was 'a great friend of the ladies, with whom he did not always experience the most honourable adventures', according to Leopold's mistress Caroline Bauer. His lifestyle was centred on his own interests, rather than the responsibilities that he inherited on his birth. He never considered extending his subjects' franchise, and spent most of his time hunting and visiting friends in other states.

Following the French victories at Jena and Auerstadt in 1806, Ernst lost his domains when the French took over his territory – Coburg had earned the hatred of the French during the Revolution, when French *emigrés* had settled there and had been given a warm reception. So when the Napoleonic forces marched into Coburg in 1806, the French governor considered he was dealing with a nest of reactionaries. The Duke was made to forfeit all rights of government, and the governor took over.

Fortunately for Ernst, Napoleon was ready to bribe many of the German princes and dukes by reinstating their former powers if they joined the Confederation of the Rhine – which, under his presidency, was designed as a balance against Prussia and Austria and to unite and manage the many and diverse German principalities. So when, in 1807, Ernst and Leopold visited Paris to meet Napoleon, they had no problem in agreeing to join the confederation in return for the restoration of governance – and their dignity.

During that visit, Ernst met the fourteen-year-old Pauline Panam, and became infatuated with her: in spring 1808, she accompanied him back to Coburg, dressed as a boy. His mother, Augusta, refused to receive her or have her among her ladies – which in view of the war was not unreasonable. That summer, Pauline, still only fifteen, became pregnant: Ernst sent her away to Amorbach in Leiningen, under the watchful eye of his sister Victoire. The Dowager Duchess Augusta stated her terms: Pauline and the child would be provided for, on condition that Pauline promised she would never attempt to become Ernst's recognised mistress. Pauline, who was destitute, had to agree. In Frankfurt in March 1809 – 'on a solitary bed of straw,' she later wrote, 'and without one *Thaler* to prepare the requisite linen' – she bore a son.

Six months later, Pauline and her child appeared unexpectedly in Coburg, with a view to obtaining better terms. After some bargaining, a document was drawn up and signed on 25 April 1810 by order of Maximilian von Szymborski, Ernst's adjutant. Pauline was to receive 3,000 francs every two months, her debts were to be paid off, her expenses defrayed and 200 francs paid for furniture – but all this would be invalid unless she quit the duchy immediately and never returned. She had been successfully bought off. Ernst, under his mother's continued pressure to surrender his interest in Pauline and look positively for a suitable marriage, gave her no support, only encouraging her to accept the best terms available.

In 1812, he became engaged to Grand Duchess Anna Paulovna, sister of Tsar Alexander I, but lost the chance of this advantageous marriage because of the scandal of his affair with Pauline Panam. Yet he found it too difficult to give up his obsession with the French girl. In 1813, he went to Dresden to see her, and undertook to educate the boy, who despite Augusta's commands and Ernst's own wish had been named Ernst after his father. The latter persuaded Pauline to return to Frankfurt, but they soon quarrelled over their future. Ernst's brother-in-law Grand Duke Constantine took Pauline's part, more from perversity than chivalry. Ernst slightingly remarked of her protector: 'He reigns over six peasants and the village surgeon.'

'Repeated efforts were made to kill me,' Pauline later alleged, 'and, when these failed, to kill my son.' After hair-raising escapades she eventually reached Vienna, where the Prince de Ligne espoused her cause, describing her as an angel and 'one of the most beautiful women in the world'. Her son Ernst continued to call himself a prince of Coburg, to the annoyance of the Coburg family, until his premature death at the age of thirty.

Although Ernst's intimate relationship with Pauline did not last beyond their final troubled meeting in 1813 in Dresden, there was a lasting memento of it in a painting he commissioned in Paris to furnish the Rosenau. Years later, Luise would notice that it was 'of a knight who has discovered that his page is really a beautiful girl'. No doubt this was why, as history records, Ernst was reluctant to take his bride to the Rosenau – Luise had to press him to do so several times.

In November 1813, Ernst opened negotiations for a marriage with Hermione Princessin von Anholt-Bernburg-Schaumburg-Hoym, but she declined, later marrying the Archduke Joseph Palatine of Hungary. Ernst had failed to keep secret the scandal of his liaison with Pauline. In aristocratic circles of the early nineteenth century, openly keeping a lower-class mistress with a child was a barrier to a good marriage, and Ernst, having also been turned down by Anna Paulovna, was damaged goods.

Ernst as the ruling Duke of Coburg was not accountable to any parliament, nor was he subject to public scrutiny. The detail of government was left to the chancellor and the *Oberhofmarschall* (head of staff at court) and his advisers, who took care of the Duke's programmes and matters of state, leaving him free to travel, hunt and socialise. As the tide turned against Napoleon on his defeat at the Battle of Leipzig in 1813, Coburg joined with the Prussians and Russians, but as Leopold affirmed in his notes at the Congress of Vienna in 1814, Ernst had embittered both the Prussian king and his own advisers because of his partisanship in the Saxon question. No diplomat, he was arrogant, claiming to know everything and understanding nothing. He had insisted on opposing the Prussians' interests in Saxony, not understanding that, in doing so, he was tacitly admitting the Russians' entry to German soil.

The disposition of the lands freed from French control following Napoleon's fall was subject to substantial negotiations between the four powers – Russia, Prussia, Austria and Britain. Castlereagh, Britain's foreign minister, was anxious not to allow Russia a foothold in Saxony, which had sided with Napoleon: he considered that the future peace of Europe would be compromised should Russian boundaries extend into the heartland of Germany. Following months of protracted negotiations, and the near collapse of the alliance, it was finally accepted that, despite Ernst's objections, Prussia would receive less than half of Saxony, but be compensated with large territories in the Rhineland, which would also act as a bulwark against a possible future resurgent France. Most of Saxony was granted to Austria, and Austria and Prussia retained their former Polish dominions, while Russia incorporated the rest of Poland into its domain.

Given his unhelpful contributions, Ernst lost nearly every bargaining counter. The House of Coburg was granted only a slight enlargement of territory for being on the winning side at the end of the war: the small principality of Lichtenberg, the chief town of which was St Wendel. And despite Leopold's charm and diplomacy, this was obtained only with the greatest effort. The acquisition doubtless satisfied Ernst I's pride, but he soon found it a financial and political millstone – the cost of its upkeep far outweighed the advantage of its accrual.

Soon after the conclusion of peace in Paris in 1815, the three brothers, Ernst, Ferdinand and Leopold, married almost at the same time. Ferdinand married Toni Koháry, and Leopold married Princess Charlotte in the same year. The Dowager Duchess Augusta now wanted her wayward son Ernst to marry; his character, waywardness and life of excess would, she knew, lead to disaster unless he could settle into a stable domestic environment. Moreover, it was important for the impecunious state that he should marry money. Following his mother's promptings, Ernst alighted on the innocent fifteen-year-old Luise, heiress to the Gotha-Altenburg title.

CHAPTER 14

Luise

Luise was born on 21 December 1800 in Schloss Friedenstein in Gotha. Her mother Luise Charlotte, a princess of Mecklenburg-Schwerin, died following her confinement. Her father, Duke Emil Leopold Augustus Saxe-Gotha-Altenburg, married again on 24 April 1802 to Princess Caroline Amalia von Hesse-Cassel. That marriage was childless, but Caroline considered it her duty to bring up Luise properly, and proved a good and reliable stepmother. Emil was by all accounts interested in literature, and considered wise, but he often used his biting wit inconsiderately on his subjects, who could not easily respond to it, and he was undoubtedly selfish and eccentric. On one occasion, after he had arrived at his daughter and Ernst's home at 4am, Ernst's mother, the Dowager Augusta, commented tersely in her journal: 'This lack of consideration is typical.'

But Emil Leopold was a patron of the arts and an enthusiastic admirer of Napoleon. Much as he loved his daughter, his only child, he was always somewhat detached from her. Despite this, Luise loved him greatly, and his influence on her intellectual training was strong. Her close friend Julie von Zerzog, who was with Luise during the last months of her life and produced a revealing document based on Luise's confidences to her, wrote: 'Her lively sensitive nature, and her preoccupation with romantic poetic literature, gave her a certain acting ability, which sometimes led people to accuse her of deceit.' She later observed that had Luise's father not been a prince but a private man, he would have been more aware of the many misjudgements in her upbringing.[1]

This memoir came to light through a handwritten letter from Edmund Lotz in the Staatsarchiv at Coburg, dated 12 November 1913, which translates as follows:

To the Archivist *Coburg, 12 Nov. 1913*

By chance I came across a manuscript by Frau Julie von Zerzog, born von Thon Dittmar, a friend of the Duchess Luise, born Princess of Saxe-Gotha-Altenburg and later Countess of Polzig, entitled *Memories from the Life* [...]. This unique document is written with a friend's love, but is free from all obsequiousness, and claims to be truly impartial.

I am allowed to keep it till 18/11, when I have to send it back to the owner in Saalfeld. Should you wish to read this – and I believe it would also interest the Duke, since it is about his great-grandmother and bears the stamp of authenticity – I can put it at your disposal until 18 Nov. It contains many personal comments by the lady about her father, Duke Emil of Saxe-Gotha-Altenburg, about her love for her children Ernst and Albert, about Herr von Szymborski and the State Minister von Lindenau, her adviser, and last but not least, about Herr von Hanstein, later Count Polzig, her second husband.

This *Denkwürdigkeiten* ('Memories'), now lodged in the Coburg Staatsarchiv,[2] provides corroboration of Luise's thoughts and actions – and crucially, because it is based on her comments when she was dying and therefore had nothing to gain by dissembling, we, like the 1913 letter-writer, can accept it as 'truly impartial'.

On 26 August 1815, a lady at the Gotha court described Luise at her confirmation as a 'young woman lively of spirit, playful, small in build, glowing complexion and cheerful'. She was also described as having 'a striving for independence and a strong will, a carefree openness in the company of men'. These were to prove prophetic words.[3] Charlotte von Bock, Luise's teacher from the age of twelve, had a less positive opinion of her. In a letter to Ernst, she wrote: 'Luise may be vain and proud. She has romantic ideas' – a judgement that was also prescient. These traits, noticed by her friends at Gotha, stayed with her.

Schloss Friedenstein, where Luise was largely brought up, stands on the top of the hill overlooking the town of Gotha. It is a huge, menacing building, with a large central parade ground surrounded by colonnaded walkways. It was more of a military fortress than a home, and there were regular parades combined with strict court etiquette and customs. Luise later wrote to her friend Augusta von Studnitz from Schloss Ehrenburg in Coburg: 'When the Lord High Marshal decrees it, the court is obliged to hold a ceremony; as you well know, since you are the daughter of a lady-in-waiting and were brought up in the Gotha court, where etiquette is the cornerstone of all souls and hearts. It governs everything. It consoles us for lost children, for pleasure and for happiness.'

Ernst first visited Gotha in November 1815, when Tsarina Elizabeth of Russia, the German wife of Alexander I, stayed there. He came again in May 1816 when, worldly wise at thirty-two, he looked at Luise, then fifteen, with an eye to the future. Pressed by his mother Augusta, concerned about the increasing likelihood of a public humiliation over the Panam affair, and conscious of his approaching middle age, his mind was concentrated on marriage. Luise was attractive and vivacious, of good rank and an heiress. She spoke with confidence and intelligence, but given her tender age, Ernst could see that his lifestyle need not necessarily change, and he should have no problems in controlling her.

In September 1816, Ernst again stayed at Schloss Friedenstein. But in November Augusta recorded in her journal a setback in their plans:

> This afternoon the court chamberlain, Count Salisch, arrived from Gotha to see Ernst and explain to him with many excuses that for now the discussions about the betrothal could not proceed further. The state of the Duchess's health has prevented her from leaving Jena earlier, and for some reason there will be no celebrations of the Duke's birthday.

Not all of the Gotha family agreed on a marriage between Ernst and Luise. There is no record of her father's opinion – but he was always aloof from such family 'details' and allowed matters to take their natural course. However, Luise's stepmother, Caroline Amalie, opposed the marriage because of the difference in age – Ernst was then more than twice as old as Luise. This criticism found its way to the ear of the Dowager Duchess, and made her feel sufficiently uncertain for her to write to her son Ferdinand on 2 June 1816: 'Will a cheerful, clever young girl of fifteen years be unfaithful?'

But in this same letter, she commented that Ernst had reported to her, following his visit to Gotha in September, that 'the *Gothaische* business had gone well.' Caroline Amalie finally gave up her opposition when she realised that Luise had fallen in love with Ernst, and by December 1816 all was back on track. On 18 December, Ernst – accompanied by his *Hofmarschall* Ferdinand von Wangenheim, his gentlemen including his adjutant, Colonel Maximilian von Szymborski, and his friend Alexander Graf (count, the equivalent of a marquis in Britain) zu Solms – rode to Gotha with the express purpose of becoming engaged. On 20 December 1816, the betrothal was announced – one day before Luise's sixteenth birthday.

The *Gothaische Zeitung* of 24 December 1816 published on its front page a report of the grand celebrations of the engagement, held at noon on 22 December in Gotha. A court ball was held in Ernst's honour at Schloss Friedenstein, and another was given by Count Salisch, the *Oberhofmarschall*. Finally, the Duke of Gotha, knowing of Ernst's passion for stalking, shooting birds and hunting wild boar, set aside two further days for these activities.

Luise, the mother-in-law of Queen Victoria and great-great-great-grandmother of Elizabeth II, was married at 6pm on 31 July 1817. She was just sixteen. As the couple exchanged rings, a salute of sixty-three cannon shots echoed one after the other. Gotha was *en fête* for a week. On 2 August 1817 there was another great court ball, a public holiday and a thanksgiving service in the chapel of the Friedenstein. Another evening there was a public dinner for 2,000 people chosen from all walks of life. With the celebrations there was also a sadness in the thought that their princess, the sole surviving descendant of the ducal house, was soon to leave them.

On their arrival in Coburg, the newly married couple were greeted by a salute of thirty-six guns. Townspeople unharnessed the horses from the couple's coach and four and, in a traditional demonstration of enthusiasm, pulled the carriage the rest of the way to Schloss Ehrenburg. In her journal, the Dowager Duchess Augusta described in detail Luise's first entry into Schloss Ehrenburg:

The Guard of Honour was drawn up on the Pelonse, and people
of all classes stood in the open *Platz*. She is a sweet little thing, not
beautiful but very pretty through her charm and vivacity ... She
has a pleasant voice, speaks well and is at the same time so friendly and intelligent that one must like her. I hope she is still
growing, as she is very small.

Caroline Bauer wrote an interesting commentary on the marriage:

In Rodach, Ernst's hunting lodge, the illustrious party dined and I
had the pleasure of sitting beside the young princess ... She is the
most natural and amiable creature. In Coburg, however, they will
put her into the polishing mill ... till she is as flat and smooth as
the rest.[4]

In this, her usually perceptive comments were proved wrong, with
disastrous results.

At first, Luise, so young and without true friends, felt lonely; miss-
ing her father and the comfort of her known surroundings in Schloss
Friedenstein, she was homesick and weepy. The Dowager Duchess
wrote in her journal: 'The poor little woman stepped into the room,
so exhausted that she could not talk for crying.' Luise wrote to her
childhood friend Augusta, eldest daughter of August von Studnitz, a
lord in the Duke of Gotha's governing council: 'Excuse the great
length of this letter, but I wanted you to know everything, everything' and 'Only a few words, my dearly beloved Augusta, to tell you
how much I love you and how much my parting from you affected
me. I cried the whole night.'

Gradually Luise began to notice her new world, writing an accurate thumbnail sketch of her sister-in-law Victoire, who would
become the mother of her son's bride Victoria: 'Victoire Leiningen
is very beautiful, tall and big, very pale with black eyes and black hair;
and very charming and unaffected. She gave me a lovely bracelet
with her name set in diamonds.'

Luise also wrote to her friend about her impatience to be taken by
Ernst to the Rosenau:

With infinite longing and impatience, I had awaited the moment when my beloved Ernst would drive me to the long desired and lauded Rosenau. I earnestly entreated him to take me, but his answer was always no, until at last I positively demanded it. We drove there. I saw it; gazed and was enchanted! Its loveliness and charm and everything about it, I will describe in my next letter.

In that next letter, Luise duly describes the Rosenau:

Alongside the *Schloss* are a stone balustrade and stone seats, where Ernst and I often sit in the evening ... Nobody disturbs us and we can talk privately together. Beside the *Schloss* flows the Itz ... a little further away, a large waterfall tumbles into the grotto, in which seats have been built.

Her description remains accurate today. The Rosenau originally belonged to the von Rosenau family, which became extinct in 1662, the last survivor being the childless Adam Alexander von Rosenau. In 1805, it came into the possession of the House of Saxe-Coburg-Saalfeld; it was restored by Ernst I, and the wilderness of its park was returned to its present beauty.

Luise's letters in this early period of her marriage – rather like those of Victoria about Albert – were studded with references to Ernst as an angel and to his perfection. In a letter to her friend Augusta, she wrote: 'If one loves somebody as greatly as I do my Ernst, it is so sweet to tell it to a childhood friend, to repeat it a hundred times because one trusts she will not find it tedious.'

Yet in a remarkable prescient letter to Augusta, Luise relates the story of Anna, a former duchess of Coburg (wife of John Casimir), who was imprisoned with her lover Ulrich von Lichenstein in the early seventeenth century.

I thought I could still hear the weeping of the unhappy Anna, and see the flowing blood of the perfidious Lichenstein. I gripped the Duke's arm and looked anxiously to see whether there was any likeness in his beautiful dark-brown eyes to those of his terrible ancestor. But I don't believe it. Anna was unhappy because she was unfaithful. Posterity will never be able to say that of me.

Luise's early married life with Ernst was certainly blissful, despite the fact that his passion for hunting and sport always took priority. She wrote to Augusta: 'In the mornings, Ernst hunts and I write. In the afternoons, I drive to Jagersruck, a hunting lodge in the middle of an enormous forest. We usually eat there, then Ernst takes us for a drive. In the evenings, he reads us the latest romantics. You see it is a very agreeable life.'

And again: 'Every day is for me one of joy and happiness. The delightful charm of my Ernst increases as much as my love; and in getting to know him better, I find him more perfect every moment.'

The Duchess Augusta also felt a warmth towards her daughter-in-law. In her journal of 21 December 1817, Luise's seventeenth birthday, she wrote: 'I often feel sorry for her that so young, hardly out of childhood, she came from a girl's happy life into the restricted circumstances of wifehood. I would give my own life to ensure the dear child's happiness, for I love her as if she were my own daughter.'

Luise had many qualities, but she required constant support, love and affection, which inevitably led to conflict with Ernst, who was incapable of supplying them. As his sister Sophia von Mensdorff-Pouilly wrote to their brother Ferdinand on 19 May 1835, Ernst had 'no patience, could not give way; and would have to direct his wife in everything'.[5] With all their contradictions of character and personality, a union between Ernst and Luise could only succeed if they came to a mutual arrangement about the conduct of their private lives – but this didn't happen.

CHAPTER 15

Ernst and Luise: Disillusion

In his memoirs, Ernst II, the eldest son of Ernst and Luise, wrote: 'It appeared as if my parents' marriage must turn out very happily, and the universal joy came to a height when, in the course of two years, two sons [himself and Albert] appeared as securities for the future of the House.'

But, in fact, the honeymoon did not last long. In the first year of marriage, during Luise's pregnancy with Ernst II, tensions arose between husband and wife. Luise — still just seventeen — began to complain of loneliness as Ernst left her more and more, and the court staff did not help by feeding her tales of his past scandals: she mentions confidential comments made to her, making her 'very afraid and worried'. Her letters bemoaned the fact that she had no intimate friends at court, since her ladies-in-waiting were constantly replaced by Ernst and his court officers. Her former tutor Charlotte von Bock, who had come with Luise to Coburg for a time before returning to become a lady-in-waiting to her stepmother in Gotha, not only gave her little support, but actively undermined her: for example, she claimed that Luise had been keeping company with a young girl at court, 'a dreadful person, who sadly influenced her completely'.

Cheered by the attention and kind words following Ernst's birth, and the celebration of her first wedding anniversary, Luise wrote to her friend Augusta: '... and I can assure you that I now love Ernst [her husband] more than ever.' But the shadows had not gone away. The carefree Luise, naturally receptive to court gossip, was 'confidentially' informed that her husband was deceiving her. In an undated letter of about this time, she wrote to Ernst, who was about to leave Coburg again:

You will laugh, my dearest darling, when you receive this note, written even before your departure, and consider me quite mad, but I'm sure you will forgive me, since I write it only out of true love. You know my affection for you, and the terrible fears I have. So let me first remind you of your marriage vow. The promise of a true knight is sacred, particularly when he gives it to his lady: and I may consider you a true knight in this respect, mayn't I? So please, please, keep to the old German faith and let your oath prevail.

Pleasuring yourself with another cannot truly please you, since it is sinful. Think just a little of me, and my boundless sorrow in your absence – and think too of my heartfelt pleasure at your return, and my joyful trust in your promise, which I am sure you will keep.

I add another request: take care of your health. Be careful not to catch a cold. Come back to my arms rosy and well. I dread your taking ill far away from me.

Return soon, and look kindly at me. Don't let yourself be blinded by easy beauties, and don't undervalue me. I shall spend the interim, according to custom, in thinking of my beloved lord with longing and humility, spend my days in prayer and work, and wait impatiently for his return.

Now a little kiss, my dear beloved. If only I could give it to you in person!

Forever, your old faithful wife,

Luise, also known as your little woman.[1]

In the summer of 1818, Luise was again complaining of loneliness. But this time it was not sport, but talks at Eger with the Austrian chancellor Prince Metternich that took Ernst away. The two had plenty to discuss. Ernst owned lands in Austria – but more importantly, the Panam affair had come back to haunt him.

In May, Metternich had agreed to meet with Pauline Panam (now known as Pauline Alexandre). At that meeting, he had promised to educate her son and provide him with an estate in Austria, on condition that Pauline did not publish her memoirs or have any account of her liaison with Duke Ernst printed. With political

unrest throughout the empire, the chancellor did not need a public
scandal involving a leading member of the aristocracy who owned
lands in Austria.

Metternich's pledge suggests that Ernst had reneged on his earlier
promise to pay for his son's education. It is well documented that the
Coburgs – like most of their aristocratic contemporaries – took a
relaxed attitude to illegitimate children. For example, in 1828
Augusta wrote to her son Ferdinand, after the death of the President
of Lichtenburg, Baron Ludwig Friedrich Emil von Coburg, that
Emil (whom she had largely brought up) 'was an illegitimate son of
Field Marshal Prince Ludwig von Sachsen Coburg'. So Ernst's
defaulting may have been due more to his chronic impoverishment,
and consequent tight-fistedness, than to any other motive.

For three years, Pauline was silent. And then, in 1821, Ernst
received a letter addressed:

Madame Alexandre to the Duke of Coburg:
I owe all the misfortunes of my life to you. After dishonouring me,
you abandoned me to misery. Were I the only victim of such cruel
neglect, I would die in silence and leave it to divine justice to pun-
ish you. But I have a son, who requires an accounting from you
for the life you gave him and the miseries you heap upon it …
Having exhausted all other means to ensure your son's survival, I
pause at the last: that of publishing my memoirs. They are ready for
press, and so designed that they cannot fail to draw all Europe's
attention to you.

I am sure public opinion will pardon me for a fault committed
in my extreme youth, and already more than expiated by the
untold miseries to which I have been subjected. You, Prince, will
find judges more severe. The seduction of a girl; the dishonouring
of a woman guilty of no other offence than unbounded love and
confidence; the abandonment of your child; and the repeated
attempts on your son's mother by assassination and poison – these
are crimes the public will not pardon, even though perpetrated
by princes.

Before I deliver these memoirs to be published – several book-
sellers have already offered me large sums for them, and as

authentication I have shown them your letters, those of your
agents, and of the Princess your Mother – I thought it wise to give
you timely warning. The manuscript is deposited with M.
Damaisoin, the King's notary in Paris, along with all the original
documents. You may, if you wish, have it inspected at his office.

   Your reply or your silence within the month will determine my
course of action.

I am, with respect, Sir,

Your Serene Highness's most humble and unfortunate servant,

Pauline Alexandre

No lawyer could have drafted this letter better: Pauline's use of the
French king's notary alone suggests that she had the help of powerful friends. Today's media would have made a field day of it, with all
the elements of sleaze at the highest level: under-age sex, criminal
activities and moral degradation, combined with the arrogance common to all establishments in every age. With their usual hypocrisy, the
salons of Europe hummed with the gossip. Since such affairs were so
commonplace at the time, it was Pauline's orchestration of widespread publicity that is remarkable – and it is clear from her letter
that she hoped to destroy Ernst's reputation.

   A great deal of scurrying around by Ernst and his friends succeeded in delaying publication by eighteen months. In January 1823, his
agent Javon offered Pauline an annuity of £200 – not a small sum at
the time – but Pauline refused it, and within a few weeks the
manuscript was published in Paris in two volumes, entitled *Mémoires
d'une jeune greque: Madame Pauline Adelaide Alexandre Panam, contre
SAS le Prince Regnant de Saxe Coburg* ('Memoirs of a Young Greek:
Madame Pauline Adelaide Alexandre Panan against HRH the
Reigning Prince of Saxe Coburg'). A London edition followed, with
W H Ireland, a respected member of the Athenaeum of Sciences and
Arts at Paris, assuming responsibility for the translation. The first page
quoted from the Bible:

   The mighty have stained my forehead with blood. From the depth
   of my misery, O Eternal One, I have invoked Thy Head against
   their injustice.

Given the quality of her writing, and its salacious subject matter, it was no surprise that the book was bought in large numbers. At least Ernst managed to lean on the publishers in the German states to suppress publication there, so the damage in his homeland was limited. But, as usual, the courtiers and their ladies at Coburg made sure that Luise knew the contents of the Panam memoirs – and were also already directing their gossip against Luise herself.

There are many unanswered questions about Ernst's concern to cover up this affair. Given the mores of the time, such a liaison was not unusual, nor does Ernst seem to have worried about damaging his family's reputation or prospects with any of his other amours – and, in fact, Albert's courtship with Victoria was unaffected. Maybe the problem with Pauline was his stinginess rather than his promiscuity: the done thing would have been to provide generously for any illegitimate offspring, and Ernst was far from generous. Also, Meternich had become involved, with disapproval, and Ernst needed Metternich's favour, since he held lands in Austria.

And why did Pauline decide two years later to publish anyway? Between them, Metternich and Ernst had offered a fair price, and judging from the circles in which she was moving, Ernst had not ruined her life socially either. Her letter, complete with her unsupported claim that Ernst was trying to have her and her son murdered, smacks of personal revenge, and her anger almost scorches the page, so perhaps Ernst had yet again reneged on some part of their agreement. It is even conceivable, bearing in mind the French king's notary, that she was encouraged by influential contacts who wanted the Coburgs brought down – though given the Coburgs' relative obscurity at the time it seems unlikely. We will probably never know, but these remain intriguing questions in the tortuous saga of the Saxe-Coburg-Gothas.

At first, the marital infidelities were all on Ernst's side. However, perhaps as a result of the information being fed to her by the courtiers of Coburg, but more probably due to her volatile and flirtatious demeanour, Luise brought problems on herself. In 1818, the seventeen-year-old paid a visit to Dresden where, according to

Frau von Senft, a member of her retinue, she flirted disgracefully. It is easy to see how an attractive, intelligent but immature young woman, whose absent husband's womanising had established in her mind a loose moral culture, might fall prey to admiring looks and flattery served up by graceful and handsome men.

Much more damagingly, in early 1819, before the birth of Albert that August, Charlotte von Bock started to disseminate a rumour that had far-reaching effects. 'Luise,' she stated, 'has fallen in love with Alexander Graf zu Solms.'

The charge was serious, since zu Solms was a childhood friend of Ernst's and in his service. After all, he had accompanied Ernst to Gotha in December 1816 for the Duke's proposal of marriage to Luise. In a letter to her friend Augusta, Luise expressed her outrage that Charlotte von Bock had reported gossip as fact to Ernst who had reacted with fury. Luise noted that Ernst was now misinterpreting and placing the worst construction on everything she did or said. And matters got worse. Ernst, beside himself with rage at the idea that the child Luise was bearing might not be his, immediately exiled zu Solms to St Wendel, where there was no useful position for him, and instigated an investigation that dragged on for several years. The relationship between Ernst and Luise never recovered.

Charlotte von Bock had been busy writing warnings about Luise to Ernst even before their marriage. As Luise's former governess, one might have expected her to show some empathy for her former charge. But for whatever reason – jealousy, self-importance or hope of advancement, perhaps – rather than try to repair any damage, she actively fuelled the rumours, allying herself indisputably with authority in general and the Duke in particular.

However, not everyone accepted her appraisal of Luise, and she came in for considerable criticism from the court, and also from Ernst's sister and brother-in-law, the von Mensdorff-Pouillys. Ernst took note of this, although not enough to change his actions against zu Solms.

On 24 March 1819, von Bock found it necessary to write Ernst a grovelling defence of her actions in response to the attacks on her, in a letter that shows her character clearly.

Your Highness, Gracious Duke,

You wish to bury a matter which is and was unpleasant for you; but allow me just a few objections. Grant me your gracious ear this once, and I promise then to be silent for ever and never to touch on the matter again.

First, I vow that it never occurred to me for a minute to want to undermine your trust in your charming Princess bride; that would have been very stupid. I only wanted to make the Princess herself think harder about her actions, no more than that ... My 'accusations' were just communication. What could have been more honest and open than to bring things to light without reservation, and how could this honesty cause suspicion?

Yet all my warnings about our dear angel's childish, imprudent remarks denigrating others have caused you to mistrust me instead. Things I chanced to notice, and had mentioned earlier to Your Highness, gave me the courage to break my silence, as I thought justly. I never suspected that affection of an old friend would arouse your anger and your mistrust. Moreover, I do not want to go into what I am supposed to have said and done to Count Mensdorff, as I know nothing about it. Enough, my Gracious Duke: I only know that I wanted to do good, and evil has come of it ... May your open-mindedness pass sentence on me. Here are all my thoughts revealed to testify for me as in a court of law; I now leave it to you to judge whether the best-intentioned trust deserves such a wealth of immediate suspicions ... The incredible pain with which I saw myself so speedily and unexpectedly abandoned, the anguish I suffered at being doubted and so coldly treated, I can only feel, not express. I thought I deserved at least some benefit of the doubt, since I know myself to be free of all bad intentions.

I beg your pardon for displeasing you, and hope that the charming married couple will in the end realise how respectfully devoted I am, and always will be.

Charlotte von Bock

PS. I entreat your Highness to accept these lines merely as comments I felt I must make in my own defence, but which need no reply. In any case we shall soon have the pleasure of seeing your Highness.[2]

Following this letter the Duke softened his attitude towards von Bock, but the relations between him and his 'charming Princess' were never the same. Luise acknowledged this later in her comments to her friend Julie von Zerzog as she lay dying from cancer, as Julie faithfully recorded:

Where once the seed of discord has been sown it grows so easily, and nowhere faster and more damagingly than at court ... Luise's inner peace was gone, and despite all her efforts to hide her sorrow through apparent distractions, she felt her situation deeply.[3]

Albert's christening at the Rosenau, with water from the River Itz that flowed just below the castle, may have been the last happy event in the doomed marriage, as Julie von Zerzog corroborates:

Soon after the confinement, after which she was ill for a long time, the widespread gossip about the Duke's changed attitude [to Luise] shook her affection for him ... She [Luise] often confessed to me that it had been a huge, though innocent, mistake to listen to anything at all against the Duke. Later she deeply regretted this, and probably realised that she should have turned a deaf ear to what others wanted to report to her about her husband. People were no less busy in informing the Duke of everything that could harm his wife.[4]

There is no evidence that Ernst punished Luise physically for her alleged misdemeanours: had he done so, she would surely have told Julie von Zerzog when she detailed her relationship with Ernst on her deathbed, but neither Julie's *Denkwürdigkeiten* nor Caroline Bauer's *Memoirs* suggests any such thing. Luise did, however, suffer a gross humiliation that was not far different from a public spanking. In March 1821, Ernst 'returned' her – aged twenty and the mother of two children – alone to her family at Schloss Friedenstein in Gotha in disgrace, accompanied only by Fräulein von Wangenheim, the *Obermarschall*'s daughter.

On 3 March 1821, Luise wrote him a long, loving letter of

Shakespearean quality, robustly defending both herself and zu Solms, in which she discloses her knowledge of Ernst's own weakness for beautiful women. Written in very difficult circumstances, it remains a classic of style and argument:

Following my promise, dear Ernst, I write to you by first post to announce my safe arrival at my father's house. I hope that will please you, and that these lines will remind you of me.

Despite the sad reason for this journey, and a hurt finger, there were nevertheless cheerful moments. We had a few adventures. At the first halt I lost my work basket. In Meiningen, the Duke came to my carriage as I was just biting heartily into a chicken leg. In Schmeihaltung, the *Obermarschallin* discovered her suitcase was lost. In Jumberg, we learned of the death of the Elector of Hesse – you will readily understand how this saddened me for my beloved mother's sake ... And the roads were so bad something in our carriage broke.

Here, my dear friend, I was received with uncommon friendliness and love, which did my heart enormous good. You know how much I need love, and what balm a friendly look is to any pain. My poor mother is very unhappy, but gentle and mild, and it was a great consolation to me to help cheer her up and calm her. She sends her respects to you, and is convinced of your sympathy with her sorrow. My father is also kind and friendly, and has uttered no complaint or reproach. Mother gave me gentle motherly advice, warning me not to make myself and you unhappy. It has never been – as God is my witness – my intention to deceive you: I would far rather know that you are truly happy. But, my friend, forgive me, we cannot both be happy this way. Let me speak my mind to you, and don't be angry. I make mistakes, but correct me kindly. Over-severity does not lead children back to the right path. I may have been wrong to honour too publicly a man who loved me in a way not to your liking. I may have been imprudent from lack of experience and a nature more passionate than the world condones. I admit that, freely and openly, but I maintain that I have always been, and always will be, faithful and true to you.

He [zu Solms] only acted according to my will, and may in his innocence have appeared too publicly pleased and proud of my friendship. Those are our mistakes. Do they deserve to be judged so severely? Must you therefore lose all faith in me, and place more belief in others who judge by appearance, my darling? Did you have to watch my every move, my every word, as if I were planning to deceive you? Oh! Trust is always the greatest virtue one can have – and I know from experience how mistrust tortures one.

You say your honour is impugned. That was never the case. Graf [zu] Solms did not forget the duties he owed you as your servant, and I owed you as your wife. Is your wife's honour not also yours? Didn't you have a duty, as master, husband, prince and knight, to defend your lady's honour in the eyes of the world?

And tell me, honestly, what happiness has your severity brought you? Will your advisers and friends learn about my loving heart? Can people who, for fear of losing their livelihoods, only ever echo their Prince's views, make you happy? You have such noble ideas, and so much understanding – do you want to throw all that away?

Oh, please don't do that. Show openly that you love and respect me, and pardon the Graf, for he is truly innocent of anything except perhaps flattered vanity. Treat your measures to date as a warning, and reinstate him: let no one pay for my guilt except my poor self. In future I will keep a proper distance.

I hope to hear from you soon, and learn that you and the little ones – whom I must ask after – are well, and that you, my friend, do not forget me, and remain faithful … Write to me. I really long for your letters. Now goodbye, my dear friend. Don't forget me completely amidst the beauties of Coburg, and believe that I am your faithful friend and worthy wife,
Luise[5]

Luise's subtle reference to Ernst's many infidelities with 'the beauties of Coburg', while simultaneously declaring her own faithfulness, is brilliant. Although clearly a spontaneous outpouring of emotion, the eloquence of her letter comprises a masterly rebuttal of the criticisms against her. And in fact her exile lasted less than three weeks. Fräulein von Wangenheim, who had orders to report on Luise's behaviour to Ernst, wrote to him that March:

Your most revered Highness, Duke,
We will follow your command, but depart a day earlier: since the 18th falls on a Sunday, the Duchess prefers to leave on the Saturday, for religious reasons I don't wish to disrupt. So we will arrive in Coburg on the evening of the 17th – in, I dare promise Your Highness, a more rational state. The Duchess recognises her fault, and promises restitution. She does not want to see the Graf again, and is content with his transfer to St Wendel. I am delighted to inform Your Highness that the Duchess seems pliant in all respects but one, and set to remain so, so harmony and domestic peace can be restored. In respect of the person who sowed the seed of discord, making her aware of imaginary or unavoidable lack of attention from you – may God forgive them! – she is persistently silent, because she doesn't want to cause trouble for anybody. I can't get anything out of her, but in time it will inevitably come out, and whoever it was will get their just deserts.

My young mistress does not look in the best of health: I mention that to warn Your Highness that you will find her paler than usual. I hope your joy at seeing your beloved wife again will also have a beneficial effect on your own health, and that the tooth- and headaches will be over.

Her mother spends time with her, but only at tea does the Duchess have the opportunity to speak to some of the townswomen. All this is very salutary, and Luise is now beginning to pine for her husband and children. The cure isn't complete, but I don't fear any setbacks.
Frl. von Wangenheim[6]

Meanwhile, Ernst dealt with Graf zu Solms slowly, as if to prolong his agony. There was no formal hearing of evidence until spring 1821, a report of which was duly made by the president of the hearing:

According to Your Highness's solemn instructions, I summoned

Graf zu Solms to me this afternoon and began proceedings in this matter ... I pointed out that everything Your Highness knew had convinced you that his behaviour towards the reigning Duchess had not been as was expected of him. This was the more painful for Your Highness since you had always endeavoured to look after him, and to provide him with a pleasant existence. His behaviour, however, could have cast the young and inexperienced Princess in an unjust light, and therefore it had been his duty to moderate it.

The Graf responded that he had, as always, powerful enemies, but he was still waiting for the man who could in justice speak ill of his manner to the Duchess, and prove it. He did not deny that he had enjoyed the favour the Duchess had shown him, but at the same time, he pointed out that he had never actually wanted to serve in Coburg, but in Russia, and had asked Your Highness to support his application. But His Highness your father had declared that he wanted to retain him in his service and would look after him. Your Highness had also retained him in service here, but he had been neglected severely for years and kept lower in rank than other courtiers, which had hurt him deeply. The Duchess, however, had always preferred him, and made no secret of it to Your Highness: saying to you in open court: 'I give him preference,' which had been very agreeable to him. I remarked that this did not justify anything, and that my principal instruction was to warn him that, if his behaviour went too far, complete dismissal from service here would follow, and he was to keep away from court until Your Highness decided otherwise.

The Graf replied that he would submit to this, but that he would have to consider an invitation from the *Württembergischen* rulers which had been mooted a few days ago, and if he were to receive such an invitation from Her Highness the Duchess of Württemberg, he would not be able to refuse such a dignity. I pointed out to him that his promotion to another position [in your service] was still possible, and therefore advised him to keep his offers of appointment open, which he promised to do.

Graf zu Solms was required to sign a document drawn up by the court of enquiry, as follows:

I assert herewith that I have handed over or destroyed, without the least exception, all effects, jewellery, gifts, letters and written communications received in the past or kept in my possession from Her Highness the ruling Duchess of Saxe-Coburg-Saalfeld.

That I shall never under any circumstances, from now onwards, in writing or by word of mouth, mention to Her Highness ... nor to her father, brothers or other relatives, nor to anyone else, anything about the relations and incidents prevailing in the past between His Highness ... and Her Highness his wife, nor about the measures consequently taken by them.

That in future I shall not send, either directly or through other persons, oral or written communications to Her Highness or accept any from her.

That I shall never again have the slightest claim to more money, compensation or to similar presents.

On Luise's own admission, the fabric of the marriage had been weakened during the early days of her second pregnancy in spring 1819. Ernst had become aloof, and never again could Luise refer to him as 'perfection'. It has been asserted, though the evidence is circumstantial, that Ernst was aware that Luise's pregnancy was not due to him – and certainly his treatment of his old friend Alexander zu Solms would support the claim that Ernst suspected him of being the father. Nor was it disputed that there had been indiscretions between the flirtatious Princess and zu Solms.

Ernst had already effectively declared Luise's guilt in the public humiliation of returning her to her family for a while. Now that time had moved on, Albert's questionable paternity could reasonably be disguised. But Ernst literally could not afford to let Luise take the initiative and repudiate *him*, on the basis of not only the Panam memoirs but also his many other infidelities. To get his hands on Luise's considerable Gotha inheritance (for which he had, after all, married her in the first place), he would have to wait until the death of her uncle, the Duke of Gotha-Altenburg, before initiating divorce proceedings If he were to obtain a divorce prematurely, he could then have no claim on this inheritance. But there was no reason not to proceed with a formal separation, and advised by the Iago of the court Maximilian von Szymborski – the chamberlain who, having been appointed as Luise's private secretary by Ernst, was considered by many in the court to be his spy – the Duke now decided to protect his long-term position by doing just that. It would also help reduce the gossip that Panam's memoirs were bound to raise: moreover, Luise's consciousness of her own guilt would outweigh any counter-accusations by her against Ernst. Speaking to Julie von Zerzog shortly before her death, she said: 'I have laid myself bare to you; will you still be able to love me?' Julie comments, 'Only my tears could give an affirmative answer, but I treasured the characteristic openness with which the Duchess understood and confessed the mistakes in her early life.'[7]

But neither Luise nor Ernst seemed to have learnt from the zu Solms scandal. The Landgraf of Hesse-Cassell was due to visit, and when Luise learned that his young sister would accompany him, she wrote anxiously to her friend Augusta: 'She will make a sensation with her beauty. I am frightened for the Duke when he sees her.' Her own admirers at that time ranged from gentleman of the bedchamber Baron Thankmar von Münchhausen, who at twenty-eight was hopelessly in love with her, to the handsome seventeen-year-old Baron Stilfried, who climbed apple trees to look into her windows and, she wrote, 'did a thousand pretty amorous things which amused me'. There was even 'an Austrian *Rittmeister* who lay at my feet, sighed and languished like a turtle dove'. These demonstrations of affection could only have occurred with Luise's encouragement. She had the personality and, of course, the position to encourage these young men and drive them to distraction with desire for her. To Luise, it was just fun, but her play-acting was so effective it led others to believe she was deceitful in character.

In March 1822, Luise was carrying on a flirtation with von Münchhausen. She wrote to Augusta: 'He is full of attention and gallantry. We go for wonderful walks in the woods and fields, quite alone, play, talk and eat together … He is extremely likeable … Julius [von Wangenheim, the *Hofmarschall*] follows my husband like a shadow, so we are both provided for.' It is hard to judge whether this is a comment on Ernst's possible homosexual tendencies, but Luise was known to be sensitive, if not discreet, in her writing.

On 17 May 1822, Luise's father died. Luise, accompanied by her lady in waiting Rosalie Lutzow and chamberlain Colonel von Szymborski, arrived in Gotha too late to see him; Ernst did not get there until five days after the funeral. Her father's death was a very great loss to Luise, who had admired him enormously and had always thought that, while he lived, he had quietly protected her. Julie von Zerzog wrote:

> He [Luise's father] had found the peace which his Luise had to do without for a long time to come … Luise felt in her orphaned soul that she stood alone without a true friend, which she needed so much just then in order to exorcise the spirit of discord penetrating like a creeping poison into the marriage which had begun so happily.[8]

Not long after this, Caroline Bauer was taken to the Rosenau by her cousin Christian Stockmar and presented to Ernst, who had been gored by a stag while out stalking the previous day. She recorded in her diary: 'I saw, in passing, the mother of the young princes – the unhappy Duchess Luise, an elegant, attractive woman with fair locks and blue eyes.'

It was shortly after Ernst's accident that Luise became ill. She wrote to Augusta von Studnitz: 'For two months I have suffered constant pains in my stomach.' Nevertheless, in higher spirits, she added: 'My new *maître de plaisir* is Hans von Thummel,' a relation of Augusta's. But Luise's aura of sadness, recorded by Caroline Bauer, had much to do with her humiliation by Ernst. Madame Alexandre (Pauline Panam) had just published those memoirs, and as Bauer also noted, 'the estrangement between husband and wife grew ever greater'.

Other contemporaries agreed that there was a conspicuous change in both Ernst and Luise's behaviour. Charlotte von Bock asserted that Luise had become vain and uncritical, striving for independence; had fallen under the influence of wicked people; was inclined to secrecy and indulged in romantic ideas; and had gathered around her young courtiers with whom she could enjoy glittering parties. Ernst himself complained to his brother Ferdinand of gossip over the revitalised *Coburgische* court life instigated by Luise, with many balls, fireworks and concerts.

Luise's efforts to break out from the confinement of court life, and her personal loneliness, were not expressed only in the extravagance of glittering balls, but also in more serious enterprises. She had developed social proposals for the relief and economic support of the poor people of Coburg, including a scheme to sponsor apprenticeships for the sons of the poorest citizens with the town's master craftsmen, the costs to be paid out of her private account. This latter proposal was energetically thrown out by Ernst, who as her 'guardian by marriage' administered Luise's fortune under the terms of the marriage agreement of 22 July 1817. After this defeat, Luise then proposed that every poor person in Coburg should be newly clothed, a plan that the authorities thought rash and ill considered: 'These people would have immediately traded the new clothes to the Returnable House.' They tried to keep the public from hearing of Luise's proposals, but Coburg was a small place and the whispers soon started to circulate. It was therefore not surprising that Luise was worshipped by the people of Coburg and surrounding districts: she was on their side against the traditionally authoritarian Duke, who took the view that any radical change would promote unrest. Only later, during her exile in St Wendel, was Luise able to introduce her social reforms, which she underwrote from her own purse – showing that they were not cynical steps taken to curry support or to go against the Duke and his advisers, but arose from a genuine concern for the poorest in society. Not for the first time, we can see similarities between her style and thought and those of Princess Diana some 170 years later – and similar mistakes.

CHAPTER 16

Ernst and Luise: Separation and divorce

The dispute between Luise and Ernst over the management of her private fortune escalated. The Dowager Duchess wrote to her son Leopold:

> The child has impractical ideas ... her plans for the future appear to me to be the greatest danger to her peace and her fortune since she has put together a scheme for independence. These little stupidities have created such fury that von Lindenau buried his head in his hands.

The distressed Baron Bernhard August von Lindenau (1780–1854) was Luise's adviser. Born in Altenburg and a good friend of the Duchess's father, he was a polymath: lawyer, astronomer, politician and art collector.

By now, Luise had come to realise that her marriage had been misguided. The natural companionship that she craved had all but collapsed; she understood that wifely compliance to her husband's demands held no compensation for her. The characteristics of her younger days re-emerged. She needed to be more independent, to pay her own way and to make her own journeys. She wanted to lead a freer life, to be admired and loved and to enjoy her libidinous nature, denied her by her husband, who sought his excitements elsewhere. Luise argued in her usual dangerously controversial way: 'It cannot still be acceptable that a married woman, poor or rich, must always be dependent on her husband's approval.'

She had certainly startled the ducal family, and was placed under close observation by the authorities. The Dowager Duchess commented in her journal: '[I hear] the police may be on her track

because of her political devilry, which could destroy her. God grant
that it is true.'

Matters inevitably deteriorated. From the outset of her son's
marriage to Luise, the Dowager Duchess had set her sights on
the private fortune to which Luise was heiress as the seed corn for
the future financial stability of the House of Coburg. Now she could
see that Luise, who was venerated by the townspeople and farmers,
was not only a very real political danger to her son's authority, but
wanted to squander her fortune on far less deserving causes than her
in-laws! These ongoing disputes only awaited a catalyst that would
lead to a final break – and it came unexpectedly soon.

In the summer of 1824, prompted by Szymborski, Ernst finally
decided to draw the line and have a separation agreement drawn up.
This followed the allegation that Luise was having an affair with a
courtier, Gottfried von Bülow, which became the subject of another
formal enquiry, presided over by Ernst's chancellor, von Opitz. The
Dowager Duchess wrote to her son Ferdinand:

> Ernst wanted me to give you the details of the last 14 days. It has
> been decided that Luise should live in Schloss Eisenberg [the
> home of Luise's stepmother Caroline Amalie] until a verdict is
> reached ... Luise confided to a young maidservant that von
> Bülow had visited her during his 'watch', and could come when
> he wanted. Now more scandalous details emerge daily ...

The Dowager Duchess had certainly already reached her own ver-
dict. When the possibility of a rapprochement between Ernst and
Luise arose in early 1825, Augusta asserted her formidable influence
to prevent this, writing again to Ferdinand: 'Now speak to Ernst,
dear Nantel, and tell him to formally divorce his unfaithful and
badly behaved wife, since the world believes he wants to take her
up again.'

The tally of Luise's alleged affairs grew, with new mention of zu
Solms, plus Freiherr von Stillfried, Gottfried von Bülow and
Maximilian von Hanstein. In 1839 in England, shortly before the
marriage of Victoria and Albert, a 'Tall Story' appeared in a magazine
alleging even further love affairs, including the entire von

Wangenheim family, the *Oberhofmarschall*, Baron Huberman and Baron Münchhausen.

Caroline Amalie, Luise's stepmother, was in despair, not knowing what to believe but not daring to challenge the Duke or his mother. She wrote to Ernst on 6 September 1824, desperately trying to distance herself from the scandal:

> You have heard of the affairs. What is the point, dear Duke, of Luise coming to Eisenberg? It will only create problems. Would it not be better if Luise went to some safe place where she could not add to the scandal and shame? My hand shakes as I write the following words – if she were kept alone, wouldn't that give you time to consider whether an irretrievable breakdown is justified at this stage?

Luise's tragedy was that most of the allegations against her were unproven: the final reason given for the separation – the supposed affair with von Bülow – was subsequently shown to be without substance. Ernst had been passed some affectionate letters from Luise to von Bülow, and merely assumed that there had been an affair. But von Bülow, interrogated by von Opitz, explained that, at a ball at the Rosenau, the Duchess had shown him warmth, expressed affection in words and asked him whether he could love her. He had replied he dared not answer one so highly placed, and the Duchess had then sent him her portrait, with a letter containing expressions of affection.

Von Opitz then examined some of Luise's personal circle: Charlotte (Lotte) Heym, then a lady-in-waiting, on 4 September 1824; the following day, Frau Kahl; and on 6 and 14 September Luise's valet Johann Gottlieb Seelmen. The second examination of Seelman, in the course of the Coburg lower court's investigation into the 'revolt' of 29/30 August 1824 (*see later*), revealed that von Bülow had, in fact, spent two nights with Lotte Heym, the first at Neuhaus and a second in Schwarzberg.

For his misconduct as an officer of the guard having illicit relations with a lady-in-waiting of the ducal household, von Bülow was dismissed from service – a catastrophe for him, rendering him unemployed and with little money. In the summer of 1825 he turned to his father, then chamberlain director in Braunschweig, who made a formal written claim against Luise on his son's behalf, for having implicated him in her affairs. Luise's adviser, von Lindenau, dealt with this. Presumably unconvinced of Luise's innocence of adultery with von Bülow, and well aware that the desperate von Bülows would certainly carry out their threat to make their charges public, to the great detriment of Luise's failing reputation, von Lindenau agreed to 'buy him off' out of the Duchess's private account. The settlement included the payment of von Bülow's debts and a pension for life.

Again, Luise had underestimated the harm that her playful manner could cause. The flirtations that had characterised her young days at Schloss Friedenhof in Gotha had not been cast off with maturity, and the Duke's supporters were keen to recount every one of them to him as conclusive evidence of her adultery. It seemed to Luise's supporters that she had simply embroiled herself in romantic fantasies as an escape from the boredom and loneliness of an unloved wife. But her indiscreet behaviour had cost her almost everything. Nothing could be proven, but to the scandalmongers, and to the many who felt that, given so many allegations, at least some adulterous associations must have taken place, it was a case of 'no smoke without fire'.

The Dowager Duchess, as we have already seen, was anxious to be rid of Luise, whom she now considered a force of harm to the House of Coburg. She knew of Luise's flirtatious behaviour and, rightly or wrongly, believed that she had had a number of liaisons; furthermore, she perceived Luise's attempts to introduce a more liberal and socially responsible regime to Coburg as a political danger. In her view, Luise's political ignorance could bring the whole House of Coburg crashing down: she was a menace who simply had to go. Not to mention the fact that Ernst now had control of the substantial amount of money that his wife had brought on their marriage … Any question about Albert's legitimacy could be dismissed, and Luise silenced for ever, with the promise of benefits to the child she loved so much.

Despite his mother's forcefulness, Ernst still had to be prodded into action; he was not a decisive man, and although he now had little time for Luise, he did not want his judgement in marrying her to be challenged. But his mother's wishes prevailed. With her promptings and those of Szymborski, Ernst finally decided to draw up the separation agreement.

In July 1824, during a period of reconciliation between Luise and Ernst at Franzensbad, Luise wrote to her friend Augusta: 'We lived very comfortably and pleasantly, and I was lauded to the skies, cherished and protected far more than I deserved, and everything I did was good and clever. The Duke went to his mother at Ichterhausen: I will go to Saalfeld.'

But in a longer letter a month later, she describes her last major public function:

> Later we had the opening of the Landtag [Parliament], which began with a festive service and a big court dinner party where I, with tears in my eyes, appeared for the last time before the people in my full regalia as Duchess, covered in silver and jewels. Now comes the worst news, my dear Augusta. You will revile me for my obstinacy, but don't damn me utterly; go on loving me. I have sacrificed everything; don't let me lose your heart's friendship too.
>
> I must begin with my return from Eger. All was pleasant, like the quiet before a storm. Then Szymborski made the bizarre proposal that I should, to some extent, separate from the Duke. I think the plan must originate from the Duke, for I cannot bring myself to believe that a mere functionary would have the effrontery to propose this without his authority. The Duke was friendly to me. We came to an understanding and parted, in tears, for life.

And so it ended without a fight, hardly even a whimper. The penalties for Luise were massive. The greater part of her wealth passed to the House of Coburg; she was exiled for life, and required to leave her children immediately. On 27 August 1824, she wrote, as Ernst required: 'I consent with a heavy heart to a separation, for what mother separates herself without difficulty from her beloved young?

And I loved you dearly. Don't let the children feel deprived of their mother. She loves them twice as much because of it.'[1]

The same day, Luise left the Rosenau for Coburg. On the way, she could not prevent herself from crying, and told the coachman, 'You will never drive me to Coburg again. I must now leave here.'[2]

But then a series of extraordinary uprisings in support of Luise – unparalleled in ducal history – transpired. There are no official contemporary reports of this 'revolt': to avoid further scenes, Ernst, on von Lindenau's advice in a letter from Gotha on 30 August 1824,[3] prohibited any press reports. There are, however, reliable sources that corroborate each other. In her last letter to Augusta von Studnitz from Bad Bruckenau, dated 21 September 1824, Luise related her departure in detail; Julie von Zerzog recorded in her *Denkwürdigkeiten* a similar report from Luise's deathbed confidences. And quite independently, a further source was published in 1862 under the title *Three Days Out of the Patriarchical State* by a Frau Hoffman, who as an eleven-year-old had witnessed the disquiet in Coburg. Her version varies only in minor details from Luise's own account.

According to Hoffman, on the evening of Saturday 28 August, Luise was returning from Schloss Ehrenburg to the Rosenau. From inn to inn, 'where everyone could be found, the news passed like a firefly. Luise was venerated by the people of Coburg, and now they took a stand to protect her.'[4]

Hoffman goes on to recount that there were rumours that a room in the Veste was being prepared for the Duchess, who would be treated in the same way as the unfortunate Anna – the earlier Duchess of Coburg who, after an adulterous affair, had spent most of her life in close captivity there. This aroused high feelings. The night was peaceful, but in the morning of Sunday 29 August, the mood changed. People began to congregate on the streets, and by midday, a large crowd had made their way to the Rosenau – well over an hour from Coburg on foot. Soon, many thousands had gathered in its parklands, and a self-appointed delegation met the Duchess and respectfully asked her to return with them to Schloss Ehrenburg.

Flattered and touched by their loyalty and concern for her, Luise agreed, and when she re-entered the coach, there was a great whoop of rejoicing from the farmers and townspeople, who unhitched the horses and harness from the coach, and pulled it themselves as a mark of their esteem. New teams took over this arduous task at each village, but there was never a shortage of volunteers to bear the honour of escorting Luise to Schloss Ehrenburg. The road to the *Schloss* was thickly lined with people, and the five-mile journey took several hours.

And on her entry into Coburg, Luise was greeted by bunting, banners and all kinds of magnificent decorations. Down through the Holycross, along the Stoneway, via Hospital Street to the Herrengasse, she was met with waves and applause from every window, and lively shouting that seemed to go on for ever. The moment was full of emotion: many women and men wept openly.

Finally, the coach pulled into the forecourt of the *Schloss* and stopped at the main entrance. The Duchess stepped out and entered the building. In a few moments, she stepped alone on to the balcony, and looked down at the crowds, which filled the forecourt as well as the mountain garden behind. She was seen waving a white handkerchief, while weeping in acknowledgement of their welcome.

Then, suddenly, the whole mass of people, as if with one voice, sang the hymn 'Now Thank We All Our God'. 'We want to see you both together!' the crowd shouted. 'Get the Duke! They must be reconciled. We want unity and peace in his house.'

At this, a number of townspeople hurried to nearby Ketschendorf, an hour's ride away, where Ernst was staying with his mother. Confronted with their demand that he return to Schloss Ehrenburg and the Duchess, Ernst must have thought civil war was breaking out: no such populist action had ever before challenged his ducal authority. After a hurried discussion with his mother, he agreed to return to the *Schloss*, so as not to exacerbate the situation. He took with him his two young boys, as both a safeguard for himself and a gesture he knew would help his cause with the crowds, and refused the townspeople's offer to draw his carriage, as they had done for Luise.

It was little after 7pm when Ernst's party reached Coburg. As loudly requested – indeed demanded – by the excited crowds, who had been waiting for some time now, both the Duke and Luise came out on to the balcony. The crowds cheered them and, believing all had been resolved, slowly and peacefully dispersed. However, the next morning, Monday 30 August, the mood changed again. Rumours of skulduggery against their beloved Duchess spread quickly around the town and its environs, and the people had no doubt of the villain of the piece – that foreigner Szymborski, who held the title of personal secretary to the Duchess. Armed with scythes, flails and other agricultural weapons, the farmers joined the townspeople in front of the *Schloss*, and screamed for Szymborski's blood: 'That Pole, that foreigner – whip him, beat him to death, the wrecker of our country, out with him!'

At these first serious signs of personal animosity, Szymborski fled to the residence. A group of Coburgers attacked his home, broke the windows and destroyed his summerhouse and gardens; one of his sons caught out riding was given a beating. The excitement of the crowd in front of the *Schloss* grew more dangerous.

'Out with the foreigner!' they cried. 'Long live the Duchess! Out with the people's curse. Beat this farmers' swindler to death!'

When they began to enter the *Schloss*, the Duke came forward and faced them bravely, dressed in a green coat, long brown gaiters and a white top hat. He stood in front of the torrent of people surging forward, and tried to stop some who attempted to get past him, emphatically ordering them to leave his house. But his voice was drowned out by their frenzy, and he escaped into the *Schloss*, ordering his *Oberhofmarschal*, von Wangenheim, to bring out the militia against the crowds. Von Wangenheim, realising the likely consequences of such an action, wisely refused.

According to Frau Hoffman, the crowd's anger did not abate, and eventually the Citizens' Security battalion appeared to protect the entrances to the *Schloss* – derisively cheered on by the crowd – as the demands for the handing over of Szymborski grew more vehement. At four o'clock in the afternoon, the situation was resolved by deception. A closed chaise and four horses arrived at the door of the *Schloss*, and the crowd surged towards it. A valet cried out that the Dowager Duchess was about to enter it, and they should keep their distance so as not to frighten her – but instead Szymborski jumped in and was driven off as speedily as possible. When news of this eventually reached the crowds, they slowly drifted back to their homes.

Luise's secretary Szymborski had quickly been perceived by the people as a spy who wished to ingratiate himself with the Duke by telling him lies about her. They saw him as a major catalyst in the separation of the Duke and Luise, and once they demonstrated the violence of their hatred for him, he could never return to Coburg.[5] The Dowager Duchess confirmed in a letter to Ferdinand on 6 December 1824 that this was why Ernst had sent him to St Wendel.[6]

Ernst, however, had not only seen his authority as sovereign prince questioned by a popular revolt, but also believed that Luise was the main reason for the unrest – an unforgivable personal humiliation. In a letter to his brother Ferdinand, he defended his stance against the people's uprising as 'a battle to preserve and restore the traditionally established order, [which] can only be good and right from our point of view ... So I will, if necessary, prefer to listen to the oppressor than the oppressed.'[7]

This explains his instigation of a harsh series of arrests, trials and imprisonment of many who had taken part in the 'revolt'. Luise asserted, as always in vain, that she had 'not been the cause of this populist uprising', but only 'a tool of those who desired to pay off grudges against Szymborski, and who had, in fact, made her a prisoner'.[8]

Her stepmother Caroline Amalie, always frightened of any controversy, reproached her in writing: 'You, as First Lady, in denying your husband due deference, have brought yourself into disrepute, and have upset too many people, and made them rebellious.'[9] Luise responded vigorously (but to no avail): 'I have never done anything to undermine the Duke's sovereignty, and am completely innocent of inciting the citizens. I thank God I am incapable of such underhand behaviour, as I hope you will be able to verify.'[10]

After the turmoil, Luise stayed for some days in Schloss Ehrenburg. Von Lindenau arrived on 2 September, on which day she signed the 'deed of separation', now lodged in the Landesarchiv Gotha. It was largely financial: Luise had to renounce all claims to her dowry and other such payments under the marriage contracts of 1817, as well as her guardianship of the children – and the regency that paragraph 15 of the marriage contract had guaranteed her should Ernst die during their children's minority. She also had to cede to Ernst all claims to her Saxe-Gotha-Altenburg inheritance. She was granted an income and use of a residence, which was eventually found for her in distant St Wendel, which Leopold had obtained for the Coburgs with such difficulty after the Napoleonic Wars. But paragraph 10 of the agreement stated starkly: 'Should a divorce come about, no changes in the above stipulations shall take place.'

No causes for the separation were recorded. The preamble only states: 'Circumstances have arisen between HRH Ernst of Coburg-Saalfeld and his wife Luise, born Duchess Saxe-Gotha-Altenburg, which necessitate the separation of these two august persons.' There was no mention in the separation agreement, nor in the subsequent divorce document, of custody of or access to the two young princes.

But the financial provisions of the agreement were particularly convenient to Ernst. Since the marriage contract of 22 July 1817, he had administered Luise's private fortune, and he liberally interpreted the word 'administer' to mean 'use'. For instance, in April 1823, he took a loan from the capital of the trust of 158,000 Rhineland *Gulden* to pay for his purchase of the principalities of Greinburg, Keutzen, Zollhof, Ruttenheim, Prandegg and Aich in upper Austria at 5 per cent interest, or some 7,900 *Gulden* per year. For security, he proposed registering the loan in the Land Registries at Linz and Vienna. But this 'loan', and similar financial transactions, only happened after the death of Luise's father on 17 May 1822, which suggests that she was right to regard her father as her 'quiet protector'. In fact, Ernst neither repaid the capital nor confirmed the contract with the Land Registries. Moreover, only after the divorce did Luise receive the interest as part of her settlement.

Unfortunately, Luise created a further public relations disaster for herself by associating herself very closely, and much too soon after the formal separation from Ernst, with Maximilian von Hanstein. After she left Coburg on 4 September 1824, she stayed at Bruckenau until the middle of November, and Caroline Amalie wrote to her there yet another letter strongly censuring her action: 'For any woman of twenty-four who has fallen so low, to take up with a young man, a lieutenant, a courtier, is very unseemly, and in your case it is terrible.'[11]

Luise (who was actually only twenty-three) justified her decision and, in a spirited written defence, asked her stepmother for understanding:

I am now alone and free. I am still very young and, as you well know, sad. Passion made me rash, or I would have carried out your wishes, but I could not endure loneliness for long. I could have chosen an unknown, and behaved so badly that I would have become hopelessly lost, and humiliated myself before the world. It is better that I choose someone I can trust. It is difficult for a lone woman not to turn to someone; not everyone has your steadfastness ... Please continue to see me as a friend ... This is all that cheers my loneliness and enables me to hold out in St Wendel.[12]

In a final comment on her separation, Luise wrote to Augusta von Studnitz on 21 September 1824:

It was agreed that I should take with me a court household of my own choosing, and go to a *Schloss* belonging to my Uncle Friedrich, Duke of Gotha – I'll give you the details another time. I often went for a walk and was always greeted with cheers ... On 4 September, at the stroke of midnight, I left Coburg accompanied by the Thummels [a court chamberlain and his wife], Thekla, Gran, Brann and Falchen, and took the road to Bruckenau ... Parting from my children was the worst thing of all. They have whooping cough, and they said, 'Mamma is crying because she has to go away while we are ill.'

I remain here until 18 or 20 October, so write to me at Bruckenau – but not for the last time. Write me kind words very soon.

Now farewell, my sweet friend, my dear Augusta. In all circumstances, in every place and climate, for ever your true friend

Luise's continued popularity in Coburg made the Duke hesitate to take divorce proceedings. But her confirmation of her love for von Hanstein, and living with him after her arrival in St Wendel, led Ernst to declare in December 1824 that Luise had been the first to betray their marriage; in his mind, divorce was now necessary and inevitable. Luise's diplomatic and political errors of judgement gave him the opportunity, which he and the Dowager Duchess found irresistible: the House of Coburg's position in this unsavoury affair could be rescued through Luise's natural impulsiveness and carelessness. The Dowager now referred to Luise in her journal as 'she who has become a shameless little sinner and marriage-breaker'. On 11 February 1825, Duke Frederick of Gotha-Altenburg, Luise's uncle, died. Ernst lost no time in declaring that a formal divorce would now follow, on the grounds that 'Luise has openly taken von Hanstein to herself.'

Ernst established a small committee to look into any arrangements that would have to be made for a divorce under the terms of the separation agreement. The committee's presentation, submitted to the Duke on 25 August 1825, began:

This presentation is consequent upon the requirement of Ernst I to look into the matter and work out draft provisions for divorce … Your Excellency has graciously deigned to let us know that His Highness has come to the conviction, for several reasons, that the formality of divorce must not be delayed any further.

It continued to detail quite openly what should happen to Luise's Gotha-Altenburg inheritance should both princes predecease their parents: 'In the unhappy case, which is very improbable, but still possible, and lies in the hands of God, of the early death of the princes … it is desirable that provision be made to secure the Ducal House's enduring possession of the Gotha-Altenburg estate, *which matter becomes the main consideration* [author's italics] …'

The presentation continued with a warning to Ernst:

However, it is known from the negotiations of last year [over the separation agreement] how little von Lindenau was disposed to proceed with such a matter, and it is hardly to be expected that he would receive it more favourably at present … There would be a better expectation of success after His Highness obtains actual possession of the estate, or at least when the Duke of Nassau's guardianship of the princes has become a reality … Until then at least, we believe it could be useful to avoid taking any official step towards a formal divorce.

The committee further warned the Duke: 'And considering the close connection between formal divorce and the interests of the princes, it might not be useful at all to take unilateral steps without the agreement of the Duke of Nassau, the princes' guardian.'

On 31 March 1826, the vice chancellor and members of the Justice Collegiate Board confirmed the divorce document. It cites in its short preamble:

> After His Highness Duke Ernst of Saxe-Coburg-Saalfeld by way of his esteemed letter of the 13 February 1826 deigned to reveal to us how HRH Luise had submitted her wish for a complete dissolution of the marital bond ... and after thorough consideration of the prevailing circumstances and consequent conviction that the present marital bond cannot respond to the natural and legal purposes of a marriage, we have decided to concede to this wish, and grant the dissolution of the ducal marriage.

Ernst had managed to obtain from Luise a written statement that she wanted a divorce – certainly disingenuously, since he knew very well that she did not, as she had written to him on several occasions. However, he conspired and connived, and eventually acquired Luise's consent in a letter of 29 October 1825, in which she wrote: 'You want the divorce, so I will not refuse my agreement.' Thanks to the smoke and mirrors of the Coburg court, this became *her* application for divorce.

On 4 December, she set out her conditions: 'I now receive 13,000 *Gulden*. The house in St Wendel, together with its garden house and garden, to be left to me free of charge and for life.' And finally, 'the right to see my children at least every two years'.

Luise obtained most of her conditions, but her request for access to the children was simply ignored. She was never to see them again.

Paragraph 4 of the divorce document reads: 'His Serene Highness ... will allow Duchess Luise the use of the estate of St Wendel and the garden estates of Niederweiler and Gutersberges.'

In paragraph 10, Luise had to confirm that she 'acted from free will, and has made the above-mentioned decisions unalterably and irrevocably'. The Coburg court officer, Graf von Trenberg-Fischler, wrote to Ernst on 16 December 1825 that, in his opinion, 'People will find the agreement insufficiently generous, and to the disadvantage of the Duchess.' This was ignored by Ernst. Luise nevertheless signed it in St Wendel on 28 February 1826, and Ernst in Coburg on 27 March 1826.

In a revealing letter of 16 October 1824, Luise had written from Bruckenau to Ernst with tacit admissions of serious guilt:

> Herr von Lindenau has given me your message and ... I gratefully acknowledge the <u>leniency</u> [Luise's underlining] and kindness of your conduct, and hope to give you proof of my gratitude by changing to a quiet and peaceful life in St Wendel. I don't want to give you any further cause for dissatisfaction, nor for a formal divorce.
>
> Should divorce in the end become necessary, against my wishes, *yet I would still recognise you as the father of my children, as a sympathetic husband, as my best friend and guardian* [author's italics], since I believe that you will now and always care for my well-being and afford me the protection you promised me earlier in Coburg. Allow me to give you my news from time to time, and let me hope to receive some from you and my beloved children. It would be dreadful not to hear anything from them.
>
> Lindenau has also told me that Szymborski is being transferred to St Wendel. After the past events, his proximity cannot be pleasant to me, but I shall do everything I can to live with him on a friendly footing.
>
> I beg you to remember me to your esteemed mother, and to greet the other relations, and moreover not to forget your Luise.

Poor Luise: she was never to hear from the children, and any letters sent by her to them were intercepted. And given Szymborski's part in her downfall, on the occasion of the Coburgers' demonstrations, it was to say the least insensitive – but in character – for Ernst I to send him to be Luise's neighbour in faraway little St Wendel.

One must ask why Luise showed so little spirit in her own defence. Von Lindenau, a close friend of her late father, a man of distinction and ability, could also surely have done better for his client, unless there was some underlying fault in her case that had to remain secret. Luise had many points in her favour for the negotiations. Her husband had had indiscreet affairs, without consideration for his teenage wife; the Panam scandal in particular could have been resurrected to strengthen her bargaining position. Ernst continually left her alone for long periods in pursuit of his own pleasures, and made it clear by his conduct, as acknowledged by Luise in Julie von Zerzog's *Denkwürdigkeiten*, that he had little interest in her as early as her confinement with Albert. The citizens of the Duchy, with their adoration of her, would have given Luise moral support – just as in modern times, popular support strengthened the resolve and direction of Princess Diana. So why did Luise supinely eschew all her rights, all her bargaining power, and meekly accept the extraordinarily harsh terms of the separation and divorce?

One could argue that, in 1824, it was a man's world, in which it was expected that the woman would always submit to the will of her husband, particularly a reigning Duke. But that argument does not stand up to the total banishment of Luise from her homeland; to her acceptance of becoming a 'non-person' in Coburg and to her family; and, more particularly, to never again having communication with or direct news of her adored children. So why should Luise describe her husband's actions as 'fair' and 'lenient'? The youthful mistakes she made in her marriage, as recorded in the *Denkwürdigkeiten*, would have had to be of a very serious nature – and Luise herself would have to have recognised their magnitude – for her to accept all the blame and endure such cruel punishment.

The biographer D A Ponsonby writes: 'It seems impossible that [Luise] could have allowed herself to be driven from them [the children] except for some very grave reason. Even if she herself were guilty of actual infidelity, she was in a position to defy Ernst and Szymborski too. The whole of Coburg was for her.'[13] So her dismissal on such punitive terms, and their acceptance by von Lindenau, must surely have been based on behaviour acknowledged by all parties as well beyond the bounds.

CHAPTER 17

St Wendel

St Wendel was the chief town of the principality of Lichtenberg, an area of 465 square kilometres with some 20,000 inhabitants, formed of the cantons of St Wendel, Grumbach and Baumholder. In 1815, the Congress of Vienna formally granted this territory to Saxe-Coburg-Saalfeld – and the period between 1816 and 1834 when Ernst I controlled it illustrates more than anything else his administrative and political inadequacies.

On obtaining legal possession on 11 September 1816, Ernst guaranteed his new subjects an impartial administration of justice and undisturbed religious freedom. He subsequently declared: 'It was never my intention to unite the countries of Coburg and Lichtenberg, but rather to give Lichtenberg its own regional constitution.' In the same breath, he went on: 'I always intended to establish a governor there under the personal direction of the family.'

Not surprisingly, this cynical duplicity kindled strong sparks of hostility among the population. Within three years, having realised that the principality was a liability to his exchequer and a constant source of civil problems, Ernst entered into negotiations to sell or exchange it – which naturally angered the Lichtenbergers further. In 1818, he was negotiating with the Prussians in Aachen; in November 1820 with Bavaria; in 1821–22 with Austria. He tried Prussia again the next year, and Bavaria again in 1824, but all to no avail.

In 1821, Ernst integrated the departments of justice and administration into one body, which was not conducive to an independent judiciary, and was disliked by the Lichtenbergers. (By contrast, in 1808 Prussia had separated these departments in their neighbouring territory.) Then, having created the Provincial Council as a democratic plaything, he declined to summon them to meet. Matters came to a head on 14 February 1829, when Ernst appointed Peter Conrad as *Burgermeister*, or mayor, of St Wendel. The townspeople saw this appointment as unconstitutional, and therefore an illegal intrusion on their rights, which they were not prepared to tolerate. The unrest escalated so badly that the next spring Ernst had to send the Coburger *Oberhofmarschal*, Ernst Habermann, to St Wendel to pacify the people.

The local authorities presented Habermann with a list of complaints, and he at least succeeded in calming the situation and prevented an outright revolt against the Coburg government. But on 13 December 1830 Ernst introduced the Lichtenberg and Prussian customs contract, without consulting the Provincial Council, which led to a big increase in smuggling to avoid taxes. Dangerous confrontations between customs officers and smugglers followed, and in May 1832 Ernst had to ask Prussia for troops to quell angry demonstrations. Despite this, a demonstration on 27 May planted a freedom forest, there was a citizens' rally on 1 June, and a further demonstration on 13 June. On 9 July, renewed occupation by Prussian troops presaged the usual repression, committees of enquiry, arrests, interrogations and sentencing. Finally, on 26 June 1833, Ernst contracted to transfer the legal and sovereign rights of Lichtenberg, debt-free, to Prussia, which formally took over on 31 May 1834 in a welter of public parades and acclamations from the townspeople of St Wendel, delighted at their transfer from the authority of the Coburgs they despised.

The Coburg administration of Lichtenberg had been a disaster. While its neighbours, controlled by the Prussians and the Duke of Oldenburg, had benefited from investment by their masters, who also supported their domestic policies by allowing them a great deal of autonomy, Ernst had exploited his territories. He had failed to grant Lichtenberg any true self-rule, nor had he seen any need to consult the local dignitaries, and as a result the Lichtenbergers, quite reasonably, had viewed him as a tyrant. It was all very different from the doctrine of enlightened monarchy pursued so successfully by Leopold, Victoria and Albert, ably supported by Stockmar.

All of which goes some way to explain why it was convenient in

1824 for Ernst to exile Luise to St Wendel, some 300 miles from Coburg. Before her arrival, the ducal governors there received detailed instructions on how they should behave to the Duchess: 'Her Serene Highness ... deserves full respect, [but] will have no influence on government. Any points she may raise will be submitted to the Duke alone.'[1]

Ernst wanted to ensure that Luise withdrew into a quiet life, and would have no official standing. He personally appointed the household that accompanied her to St Wendel, and they were not the same people who had been with her at Bruckenau. Her entourage included lady of the bedchamber Amalie von Uttenhoven (who after the divorce became lady-in-waiting to Luise's friend and Ernst's sister Sophia von Mensdorff-Pouilly); Carl Wilhelm von Spessart, the chamberlain; an assistant chamberlain; a chamber woman; a dresser; a valet; a cook; and a coachman. Von Spessart had been instructed to inform Ernst of 'every incident that touches the Duchess, and everyone who has personal contact with her'.

Luise arrived in St Wendel from Bruckenau in mid-November 1824. Originally it had been planned as a staging post, since the separation agreement proposed that Luise would reside in Gotha-Altenburg. However, as we have seen from her letter to Ernst, her stepmother Caroline Amalie was already reluctant to house her and, after Luise's public association with Maximilian von Hanstein, flatly refused to.[2]

Ernst actually found this refusal quite convenient. As he wrote to his brother Ferdinand on 4 December 1824, and was supported by a letter from their mother the Dowager Duchess two days later: 'Luise's presence in St Wendel, although a burden, is preferable to having her dangerously close to Weimar and Gotha, where so many people intrigue shamefully against me.'[3] He therefore extended Luise's 'asylum' in Lichtenberg – and even von Lindenau agreed that 'it was a suitable place for her to stay, and likelier than any other to reduce the unfortunate princess to political oblivion.'[4]

In December 1824, Luise wrote to her sister-in-law Sophia: 'I live here alone, very quietly; one day seems so much like another that I never know the date.' She complained of the terrible disrepair of the residence (now the town hall), and informed Sophia that

'Maximilian von Hanstein holds office as my Master of Horse, and lives with me in the Residence.'

On 25 February 1825, she wrote to Ernst:

I received your letter of the 13th yesterday, and hasten to reply to it today so that you can see it is not my fault I was silent until now. The death of my uncle [the last Duke of Gotha, on 11 February 1825] saddened me very much. He was a loving relative. I take your assurance that you will manage the practicalities of that for me as a token of your friendship, and have high hopes of your kind inter-cession. Obviously, I welcome the upturn in my financial situation, since to date I have had to cut back even on virtual necessities, but can now look forward to a trouble-free future. I truly appreciate your desire to help me take possession of my estate, and shall never be ungrateful. Never doubt, either, that I want our separation to be amicable, *and hope no circumstances will arise to cause you to demand a divorce* [author's italics]. Naturally, I assure you that it certainly won't be my fault if our friendly rela-tionship is disrupted.

Since I have received hardly any news of my children, I must ask you to let me have more frequent information through Schutz. I am also waiting impatiently for the carriages bearing my possessions …

I have read your decree in answer to the presumptuousness of [*illegible*] in the Frankfurt newspaper, and found it very right and proper. Please kiss the children for me, and convey my respects to your mother and my regards to Princess Caroline.

With best wishes for your well-being

Luise

No reply from Ernst has been found, if one ever existed. On 27 May 1825, Luise wrote again:

I am writing to ask you to transfer to me the lease of the St Wendel Park. You will laugh about this, but I have become a great marks-man and shoot really well. The park borders the gardens of Gudesberg, and would therefore bring me a pleasant distraction from my quiet way of life …

When are our children going to Gotha? Kiss them from me, and please convey my respects to your mother and Aunt Caroline. Hoping to receive a kind word from you soon, I close,
Luise

There is no confirmation that she was ever granted the lease, and the *Denkwürdigkeiten* reports that Luise was desolated by the lack of news of her children. For example, she wrote to Julie on 8 January 1828:

Although I am infinitely happy with my dear Max, I still often have depressing hours. My little Albert had the measles, and no one thought to tell his distant mother – Lindenau mentioned it in passing, having known about it for a fortnight. The lack of consideration for me pained me a great deal. In such moments, the only trust that remains to me is in He who cares for everyone, nor forgets any of His creatures.

As to her request that Ernst remember her – that never stood a chance. She had become a non-person in Coburg, and after the divorce, he ensured that there would be no further direct association between him and Luise, ordering that any necessary communication should be through either Lindenau or the Coburg chancellor von Opitz.[5]

On 18 October 1826, Luise married Maximilian von Hanstein (1804–1884) in the small town hall in St Wendel, close to the basilica church in Fruit Market Square, and from references to Max in her subsequent letters, it was undoubtedly a love match. Ernst gave the necessary dispensation from the delay legally required for a second marriage, and Luise's uncle, the Duke von Hilderburghausen, regularised its social inequality by elevating von Hanstein to the position of Graf von Poelzig and Beiersdorf. But members of the ducal government at St Wendel were forbidden to attend the wedding, the banquet or the subsequent celebration, and the Dowager Duchess commented in her journal: 'Now, finally, the knot that was tied with so much splendour and such glittering expectations has been loosed. Through her own carelessness, she is now divorced permanently from her husband and children, and has prematurely nailed her destiny to a man four years her junior.'[6]

Luise never stopped pining for her children. In a letter from St Wendel on 7 October 1828, having just journeyed through Frankfurt, Würzburg, Bamberg and Lichtenfels, she complained: 'I was only six hours away from my children, yet could not be with them.' And the next month, having met Lindenau in Trier, she wrote rather pathetically to Julie that she 'had the happiness of hearing from a woman friend who had seen the princes in the theatre in Coburg, and to hear something of my children … The elder is supposed to resemble the Duke; the younger, me.'

After her divorce and remarriage, Luise did not live exclusively in St Wendel. Now that she was her own mistress, she did what she had always wanted to do: travel. She and Max undertook many journeys to Paris and Frankfurt, among other cities. She wrote to her friend Elise Kumer that she had been 'four months in Paris, then by the Rhine, later in Baden', and continued: 'If all goes as planned, this autumn [1829] I will travel to the South of France for my health.'[7]

In June 1829, after many ignored requests for portraits of the princes, the Dowager Duchess declared herself willing to fulfil Luise's dearest wish. Luise wrote to 'Malchen' (Amalie von Uttenhoven):

What upset me about the portraits of my children is that Ruprecht [the Coburg court painter] is away. I wanted the portraits done in pastel, one of each child, the same size so that they can hang next to each other, and with the children in their everyday clothes. But I am very pleased that the Dowager Duchess is happy to grant my request, and apparently the court painter Schadt will do the work.[8]

At the end of September 1830, the President of Lichtenberg, Georg Wilhelm Bruckner, brought over the portraits, and Luise wrote to a friend: 'I envy her [the Dowager] the joy of seeing my children. When may I share that happiness? It is too hard to have no hope of this! And cruel of him, who well knows what it means to love one's children. I often make plans to see them, if only from a distance.'[9]

It didn't take Luise long to get involved with the social life of St
Wendel. Despite her assurances to Ernst that she would lead a quiet
life in her backwater, she began to participate in masked balls, the-
atrical performances and other such entertainments. In no time, the
popular Luise, seen in St Wendel as a victim of the hated Coburg
establishment, was wholly accepted. As she had been venerated
among the citizens in Coburg – though vilified by the establishment
– so she was in St Wendel, where indeed the collective memory of
her remains strong today. She wrote to Elise Kumer: 'On my birthday [21 December 1825] there was a very popular masked ball here,
where everyone has been very supportive.' And on her next birthday,
she wrote: 'I received a new proof of the locals' devotion to me, in
that they sang me a serenade, although they had been forbidden to
do so. I am very happy here.'[10]

The basic reason for this veneration was not Luise and
Maximilian's participation in St Wendel's social life, but the
considerable money that Luise spent in supporting the town's poor
generally or individuals and families in dire need. Even though
mortally ill in Paris, on 21 May 1831 she asked her sister-in-law
Christal von Rauchhaupt to give six *Thaler* in her name 'to Sergeant
Schmidt in St Wendel, whose child has been ill', and the next month
ordered Court Master Gran to give money to other poor families
with sick children.[11]

However, a few months earlier, in January 1831, Luise and
Maximilian had lost patience with the St Wendel authorities over the
question of renovations to their residence. They had been complaining about this for years without result, and in November 1830 the
St Wendel Council had written to Maximilian that the town
considered it beyond its responsibility to pay for the necessary
redevelopment of the dilapidated building.[12] Maximilian had
responded furiously that, since the Duchess and he could no longer
accept their living conditions, they 'would leave St Wendel for ever,
although sadly', referring to their 'very happy time' there.

This had galvanised the burghers into an immediate request to
Ernst in Coburg to authorise the works at his expense, pointing out
in the process their own economic arguments: 'We all hope that
the Duchess Luise will continue her present generosity to the poor,

thereby keeping her annuity circulating in St Wendel, which will profit the local tradesmen most of all. She is a patron of the poor, and lately has disbursed more than 2,000 *Gulden* as charitable gifts.' The panicked counsellors feared a future in which 'the almost unbearable burden of the support of the poor would once again fall entirely upon [them]'.[13] They were supported by Ernst Habermann, once again visiting St Wendel, who wrote to Ernst that Luise's putative departure 'meant an annual financial loss of turnover for the town of at least 20,000 *Gulden*'.[14] The burghers further declared, in another note to Ernst, that if he didn't sanction the required renovations, they wanted the Graf von Poelzig and the Duchess to be given a cost-free site for development in order to keep them in St Wendel.

What the burghers of St Wendel didn't know was that Luise had already made plans to leave the town, and had met von Lindenau to discuss this – although the onset of her terminal illness while in Paris in February 1831 forestalled the move.[15]

Luise liked travelling with Max, and decided to visit Paris despite suffering severe abdominal pains shortly before her departure. She ignored her doctor's warnings, and they travelled with Baron Franz Xaver von Zach (1754–1832), whom she had known from childhood as a respected friend of her father. He had been the Colonel Court Master and Astronomer of the Seeberg Observatory at Gotha, and Luise had written to Julie von Zerzog about his relationship with her grandmother, with whom von Zach had travelled through France and Italy until her death in 1827: 'Duchess Charlotte von Gotha was on the left hand [i.e. having an affair] with Herr von Zach.'[16] Von Zach was also ill, with painful kidney stones, which he wanted to have treated in Paris.

On 5 March 1831 Luise suffered a huge haemorrhage at the opera, which resulted in her being taken unconscious from the theatre and confined to bed under close medical attention. Twelve days later, she wrote to Malchen about it:

> I was very ill, as they know in St Wendel. My condition was made worse by the journey, and now in Paris is deteriorating daily. I was, however, able to go out, and allowed myself to be enticed to see

the performance of *Der Gott und die Bajadere* at the Grand Opera House. There I had a violent haemorrhage, a lump the size of an orange. I fainted and was carried home quite unconscious. I am being looked after in bed, and still have some pain.

Max arranged for the doctor to call – the King's favourite doctor, Karl Christian Mark, a German by birth. He shook his head, politely asked my permission to investigate, and sent me a 'Madame Bois' wine. It was found that the cell tissue of every tube had accumulated mucus to such a degree that if I had not come to Paris, I would have been dead in a few months … Doctor Mark prescribes that I do not even sit, but only lie down. He gave me pills to take. I asked him how long the treatment was likely to take. He answered that he could not confirm, since the accumulation had existed for years, but that at best it would be two months, perhaps even a year. I am not allowed to travel, which could be life-threatening. Imagine my situation if there is a war! But still I thank God that I travelled here, or I might have died in misery, since the German doctors weren't aware of my condition!

… I have got really thin. My hips have almost disappeared, and my breasts have dropped more and more. I become even more slender than you, my dear Malchen!

I can't praise the Graf [Max] enough. He has inspired me and looked after me day and night … In the mornings he reads aloud to me, then we chat, and if I begin to be sad he makes jokes and plays tricks until I have to laugh. Zach comes to us for the whole afternoon and evening.

The Graf's love and von Zach's friendship make me happy. Max talks everything away … and does it as though his only happiness is in my company; von Zach walks half an hour each way to reach me, despite the pain it causes him in his 77th year … They are wonderful people.[17]

Maximilian and von Zach consulted more doctors, who agreed that Luise was mortally ill with cancer of the uterus (*Mutterkrebs*). Yet cruelly, within a week of this news, the Coburg court gossip was alleging that she had given private details of her divorce, and the earlier amorous adventures of the Coburgs, to the Duke's *bête noire*

Pauline Alexandre Panam (whose son Duke Ernst had finally knighted as Ritter von Hallenberg in January).[18] But much more seriously, the gossip also asserted that Luise had said that the princes Ernst and Albert 'are not Ernst's real sons'.[19]

Von Zach, disgusted, immediately wrote to Amalie von Uttenhoven: 'The Grafin von Poelzig [Luise] never stooped as low as the dishonourable people now propagating despicable and unwarranted slanders against her. She will soon be in another place, free from their petty intrigues ... Luise is ill beyond recovery. The doctors have all given up on her ... Her illness is natural, but terminal: there is no prospect of remission.'[20]

At the beginning of July 1831, Luise deteriorated further. Christine von Rauchhaupt wrote from St Wendel: 'The coachmen who returned from Paris to St Wendel three weeks ago described the terrible condition of the Duchess, and since then, according to the latest messages, it has deteriorated still further. Why has the good lady to suffer? She doesn't deserve this: she is so good and charitable. Now, apparently, she is so emaciated that she is just skin and bones, a shocking sight, and the constant pain is so bad that one can hear her screams some twelve houses away.'[21]

Luise had still not accepted that her illness was life-threatening. She wrote to her lady-in-waiting Julie von Stuhs on 3 July:

> My illness is a mucus congestion, and constipation of all the tubes' cell tissue. This is not mortal, but it is difficult and will take time to heal. I have pain in the lower abdomen, back and stomach, no sleep, no appetite and no natural functions, all torments which tire me terribly. I eat nothing but a cup of bouillon, a cup of tea and some *compôte*. To drink I have an extract of a herb called 'bittersweet'; for medicine, enemas, baths, injections, the application of ointments with a [*illegible*] touch on the lower abdomen [*illegible*], and an embrocation on the legs which is supposed to dissolve the knots. My mother [stepmother Caroline Amalie] wrote me a warm letter, which I enclose.[22]

But clearly her attitude changed during the month, because on 25 July, Luise dictated her will to her nurse Anna Metz, in the presence of a lawyer and another witness. She named Maximilian as her sole heir, and bequeathed him everything Ernst had withheld from her in her lifetime: the jewellery and furniture; a pension of 3,000 *Thaler* from the family inheritance; saved capital of 25,000 *Thaler*; and 25,000 *Gulden* she had inherited under the codicil of Duke Friedrich IV's will.

On 1 August, she dictated a final codicil to Anna Metz:

> If the Heavens call me from Paris, I want my body to be taken to Germany by my husband, if that is where he settles. Should he choose another place, take me there. I would like to live with him, but if death separates us I want my body at least to remain close to him. I therefore state that I don't want to be buried in the churchyard, but somewhere my husband chooses.

Luise Grafin von Poelzig, born Princess von Sachsen-Gotha-Altenburg, died on 30 August 1831 at four o'clock in the afternoon. Von Zach wrote:

> No one suspected it at just that moment. Anna Metz asked the Duchess, a few minutes before she passed away: 'Tell me, Your Highness: do you still know who I am?' There was a dying smile, a nod, and in a moment she was no more. The noble lady had not struggled with death, had not been aware of passing away: she just came to an end.[23]

Von Zach composed an obituary, from which this is an extract:

> The good Duchess, who never anticipated her death, did not mention her former hardships, either during her illness or in her healthy days. *She avoided, at least so long as I had the honour of knowing her, speaking of the person who had been involved with her* [author's italics] ... I never perceived resentment or bitterness in her. As far as I can judge, I believe her mistakes and so-called crimes did not originate from wickedness, for she was a gentle creature, but from thoughtlessness and impulsiveness.[24]

At the news of Luise's death, Caroline Amalie, despite her former severe criticisms of her stepdaughter, wrote to Ernst: 'My dear Duke, So I must also endure the fact that the child I reared with such love goes before me ... It is a very bitter feeling that the beloved House [of Gotha] is now quite extinct.'

There is a document in Luise's handwriting, sealed on 9 June 1824, in the State Library in Coburg,[25] but although the body of it is clearly in Luise's handwriting, the date and signature raise questions. In it, Luise writes:

> Since my beloved Max von Hanstein promised to follow me anywhere, even if my destiny changes, I vow to him solemnly that I will not part from him in any circumstances until death, which dissolves all ties, calls me away from him. And then my children must strictly obey my instructions to behave as my grandmother did, for which there is documentary evidence.
>
> Should he form another intimate relationship, either marital or unofficial, that is his choice, and I endorse it unconditionally. In that case, my uncle's personal fortune [that of the former Duke of Gotha-Altenburg], which I am free to dispose of however I like, goes to him after my death, and only after *his* death, if no child of ours lives, reverts to the princes [Ernst and Albert]. No one may rescind this except Max von Hanstein, should the relationship become a problem to him – if he commences a new relationship. This is my final decision. God be with him.
>
> Ehrenburg, 9 June 1824, signed Luise Herzogin [Duchess] Saxe-Coburg-Gotha [seal of Herzogin affixed]

Since we know from contemporary evidence that Luise's and Max's mutual affection and loyalty continued to the end, in Luise's case, and far beyond that in Max's, why is there a question about this document's authenticity?

The date 9 June 1824 is the key. In June 1824, Luise was still living with Ernst; her letters to Augusta von Studnitz of that date and later in August 1824 (*see page 141*) don't ring true if the date on this document is correct. Remember, too, that on 27 August Luise wrote to Ernst consenting very reluctantly to the separation he demanded.

In view of these facts, it seems highly unlikely that Luise would have drawn up a formal document committing herself to Max in June: she was clearly unaware of her future until late August. Moreover, on 20 November 1826, she wrote to Julia Stuss that she had been with Max for two years, which would date the start of their association some five months later than the date on the document. That also fits with her stepmother Caroline Amalie's letter of November 1824, citing her relationship with Max as the reason she would not receive her in Gotha, which was why Luise had to move to St Wendel – and, of course, it was only in December 1824 that Ernst decided to proceed with the divorce, on the grounds that, as he then stated: 'Luise has openly taken up with von Hanstein.'

Dr Josef Dreesen of Holstum, Eifel, in Germany, a historian of that period, has told me that Luise's signature on the document is questionable – it is much heavier and more laboured than the writing in the document itself. Also, Luise usually signed herself 'LuisehzS' or 'Luise HzS' – Herzogin zu Sachsen – which is not the case here: the striking squiggled 'S' in the first line by her signature is not repeated in the third line thereunder, while the capital 'E' for Ehrenburg is also untypical. But the shaky signature *is* similar to that in her will, made shortly before her death.

It is generally accepted that the document was written by Luise, apparently when she and Max arrived at St Wendel in November 1824, to assure Max that Luise had complete confidence in him, and would look after his financial security should she predecease him. He would have needed some such guarantee, since otherwise his prospects were grim – he had certainly burnt his boats with the Coburg authorities!

So could the document have been found by Ernst or his agents, and deliberately backdated and signed with a forged signature to blacken Luise's name? That would have offered Ernst many advantages, and was well within his moral compass. With that letter in his hands, Ernst would have had no problem in securing a divorce on the grounds of Luise's infidelity; the Coburgers would have lost their loyalty and love for their beautiful Duchess, and the damaging and embarrassing riots of August 1824 would never have occurred.

But for just those reasons, the answer must be no: had Ernst had the document before September 1824, he would certainly have aired it as publicly as possible, but there is no record that he did. So the likeliest interpretation is that the document *was* written by Luise, in November 1824 at the earliest, and certainly within a few months of that, but not signed. If it was a private document for Max, a statement of intent not a formal deed, there was no need of a signature then.

Yet the signature was in Luise's later laboured handwriting, similar to that on her will written shortly before her death. So perhaps she suspected that Ernst would contest that will (as he did, in his sons' names): Luise was well aware by then of Ernst's chicanery over her personal inheritance and, in 1827, had even considered suing him for his unlawful handling of it.

So it seems reasonable to assume that the mismatch between date and signature has a simpler explanation. Luise would have realised that, if she added her signature to the document and backdated it by a few years, that would make it much more difficult for Ernst to contest her will on the grounds of Max's undue influence over her during her terminal illness. So the document she had written as a letter of intent was backdated to 9 June 1824, and to ensure its authenticity further, the seal of Luise, Duchess of Coburg – which she had not been entitled to use since her divorce in 1826 – was affixed to it. Given her circumstances, it is unlikely that she would have given much thought, if any, to what she might have been doing on 9 June 1824, some seven years earlier. It was left to history to prove the date erroneous. And in this typical Coburg saga, remember that the grounds for separation made no mention of Maximilian von Hanstein, but only of von Bülow's alleged illicit association with Luise.

Luise's death should have put the whole tragic episode to rest, but the problems continued. Her body was embalmed, so that it could be brought back to Germany, but then a strange odyssey began. Ernst, typically, fought against Luise's Will in the names of his sons. The coffin containing Luise's body was taken to Saarbrücken and from there to Ottweiler, where it was placed in a guesthouse. After the required approval from Maximilian, the ducal government and the town council of St Wendel, it was brought to the Gartenhaus at Niederweiler in St Wendel, whose citizens offered to guard the body pending confirmation of the burial arrangements.

The argument between Ernst, in theory on his sons' behalf, and Maximilian was not confined to the financial conditions in the will, but extended to the burial rights. Ernst claimed these for himself, but Maximilian stood his ground in support of Luise's wishes, so the Duke's efforts to have her buried in either Alfassen or Niederhinxweiler, both Catholic parishes near St Wendel, broke down. Finally, fearful of its confiscation by ducal agents, *Notar* Stephen, a local pro-Luise lawyer, 'kidnapped' the coffin on Maximilian's behalf and safeguarded it in his own house.

On 21 August 1832, more than a year after Luise's death, Maximilian at last reached an agreement with the Duke over her estate and prepared to bury his wife in peace. He was granted Luise's jewellery, the furniture and silver in St Wendel, and an annuity for life of 3,000 *Gulden* from her personal inheritance from her uncle, the late Duke of Gotha-Altenburg, backdated to Luise's death. All other claims were settled by a one-off payment of 10,000 *Gulden*. Ernst also had to commit himself to the cost of caring for Luise's servants for life. At last, Maximilian could bury Luise in a 'respectable place' in Lichtenberg. He chose the Protestant church in Pfeffelbach, near St Wendel.[26]

On 19 December 1832, the coffin was brought there by hearse, accompanied by many local dignitaries and twelve pallbearers chosen by the magistrates. The *Burgermeister* of Berschweiler record-ed the events:

Today, about 11 o'clock, the coffin bearing the body of the supreme lady Her Highness the Duchess arrived on a hearse from St Wendel, accompanied by President von Szymborski, Government Adviser Riotte, Government Adjudicator Sebald, Major Plankner, President of the Parliament Cetto, Judge Gobel, Investigating Judge Weisgerber and *Oberburgermeister* Conrad, as well as many other officials, town councillors, and citizens from St Wendel, to the sound of the knells in Pfeffelbach.

The report continues with a detailed description of the crypt, and notes that a suitable memorial speech was given.

But even in Pfeffelbach, Luise was not left in peace: nor did her children observe the wishes she set out in her will. In 1846, after the death of Ernst I and fourteen years after her interment, her son Ernst II had her coffin raised and reburied in the royal crypt in the Moritzkirche in Coburg. Many years later, during the nights of 15 and 16 August 1860, the coffin was disturbed again, and transferred to the newly built mausoleum in the cemetery at Glockenberg in Coburg.[27] There she lies today, beside her first husband, Ernst I von Sachsen-Coburg and Gotha, and his second wife. In autumn 1860, Victoria and Albert visited the mausoleum and laid a wreath on her tomb – the closest Albert had been to his mother since her sad departure just after his fifth birthday.

Maximilian remarried in 1833, to Marie Therese von Carlowitz, with whom he had three children. He died on 18 April 1884, when he was seventy-nine years old. There is no evidence that he knew of – or, if he did know, objected to – either of the relocations of Luise's coffin.

Ernst I also remarried, in the autumn of 1832, six years after his divorce from Luise. The new duchess, Princess Mary of Württemberg, was his niece, the daughter of his sister Princess Antoinette and the Duke of Württemberg, and was one year older than Luise. Caroline Bauer records that, while she was acting in St Petersburg, Mary, who was staying at court, regularly attended her performances at the German Theatre, but: 'She always looked remarkably serious. Never did a smile brighten her sulky face, nor did she ever applaud.' And on 3 April 1835, Ernst's sister Sophia wrote to her brother Ferdinand: 'Ernst neglected his second wife Marie in pursuit of hunting and shooting ... It was always a stupid decision of his to marry again, and to that moody Marie too! Perhaps it was God's punishment for his sinful weakness for sex.'

Nothing had changed, apparently: this marriage, too, lacked romance, and the couple were often apart. But at least this time Ernst's wife, who knew what had happened to Luise, was content to be Herzogin of Coburg in name only.

Following his father's death in 1844, Ernst II followed in his footsteps and, in the 1860s, descended to selling honours as a way of increasing his income. Indeed, a 'cash for honours' black market grew up in Coburg.[28] His memoirs make no comment on his mother's exile from court and her family, nor indeed on her early death. He only states offhandedly:

It is known from the publications of the Queen of England respecting my brother's life how short a time we enjoyed the advantage of growing up under our mother's eyes, and how quickly our family happiness was clouded over after promising to be imperishable ... But I will not repeat these matters here ... After my mother's death, my father took as his second wife the Württemberg princess Marie, his niece, who remained childless.

CHAPTER 18

Albert's paternity

The evidence that Albert was unlikely to have been fathered by Ernst I can be gleaned from many sources. Letters and Julie von Zerzog's faithful *Denkwürdigkeiten* clearly disclose that the real breakdown of the marriage came in 1819, during Luise's pregnancy with Albert. Nothing was the same after his birth. Luise sank into melancholia, and it was not long afterwards that Ernst took the remarkable step of having her sent away for the first time, to her father's *Schloss* in Gotha in 1821. Her subsequent and final exile in 1824 to St Wendel, never again to set foot in Coburg or its surrounds, never to see or hear from her children, was cruel by any standards, but particularly harsh given Ernst's own scandals. His family, in their various letters over many years, referred to his weakness for sex, his pursuit of hunting and shooting, and his neglect of both his wives. Had he thought Luise had just had a serious flirtation and nothing more, it might well have been forgiven and forgotten, for morals were not a high priority in the court of Coburg during his reign. Caroline Bauer wrote in her memoirs: 'In Coburg the very sparrows on the roof twittered stories of the amours of both Duke and Duchess.'

However, while a habit of flirtatious conduct and the occasional discreet liaison might be overlooked, the birth of a son fathered by someone other than the Duke was definitely a step too far. But to dispatch Luise immediately in 1819 would have risked raising public doubts about Albert's paternity. The House of Coburg might not have survived the resulting gossip, and its reputation, as well as that of Albert himself, could have been indelibly besmirched. Ernst was also anxious not to lose the Gotha inheritance, which he could not have claimed had he moved before his wife's uncle in Gotha died, since a divorced Luise would have been no part of Coburg.

Therefore it was only prudent not to part from Luise until the question of the inheritance had been settled through her to the House of Coburg – as the loyal Szymborski, who had great influence over Ernst, no doubt advised him.

Luise's constant references to her 'mistakes' as a newly-wed, and her meek acceptance of the very disadvantageous divorce settlement, give further validity to this argument. And even her highly respected close friend, Baron von Zach, acknowledged in his 'obituary' of her that she had made mistakes.

As for Albert, he immediately became his mother's favourite, which was much commented on and criticised at court; to German minds at the time, the elder son was the *Erb Prinz*, the heir and rightful favourite in the household. But it was Albert who had the personality, the good looks and the intelligence.

His early education and development were arranged first by his grandmother, and subsequently by his uncle Leopold with guidance from Stockmar. It was Leopold who prepared Albert for marriage with the 'Mayflower', his cousin Victoria, the heiress presumptive to the crown of England. More and more, his father Ernst was marginalised in the principal decisions on Albert's upbringing – nor, as the facts demonstrate, did he ever appear to concern himself with such matters.

There is no doubt that Albert was quite unlike any member of his direct family – except, of course, his mother. From his earliest childhood, he wanted to excel and please his teachers, and worked more than conscientiously. His brother Ernst later wrote in his memoirs:

By nature we were neither bodily nor mentally much alike. From the earliest childhood, my brother was the best loved. His physical development did not keep pace with the quick unfolding of his remarkable mental powers ... It was the exercise of his intelligence that, later, so often gave him an advantage over others, and about which the Emperor Napoleon [III] once characteristically said to me: 'His mind is so accurate that one is always afraid of entering into a debate with him; he is always right.'

Leopold, writing to Victoria in 1864, said: 'He was always an intelligent child and held a certain sway over his elder brother, who rather kindly submitted to it.' And Christoph Florschütz, the children's teacher, wrote: 'His studies were a pleasure to him, not a task; his perseverance and application were only equalled by his facility of comprehension.'

Later, well after Luise's expulsion – since he would not have dared to criticise her in such terms in her previous position as the Duke's wife – Florschütz further emphasised the differences between the brothers:

> Difficulties indeed there were, which showed themselves at the very outset ... Amongst these difficulties was the partiality shown in the treatment of the children by their mother. Endowed with brilliant qualities, handsome, clever and witty, possessed of eloquence and of a lively and fervid imagination, Duchess Luise was wanting in the essential qualification of a mother. She made no attempt to conceal that Prince Albert was her favourite child. He was handsome and bore a strong resemblance to herself. He was, in fact, her pride and glory.

In July 1820, Luise wrote in her court French: '*Albert est toujours beau, gaie et bon et a sept dents. Il marche déjà quelquefois tout seul, et dit "papa" et "maman". N'est-ce pas un petit prodige pour dix mois?*' (Albert is always beautiful, happy and good and has seven teeth. He already walks a little on his own, and says 'papa' and 'mama'. Is he not a little prodigy for ten months?)

When Albert was two, she continued her praise: '*Albert adore son oncle Leopold, ne le quitte pas un instant ... Il est charmant de taille, blond et yeux bleus.*' (Albert loves his Uncle Leopold, and never leaves him for a moment. He has a delightful figure, is blond with blue eyes.)

The historian D A Ponsonby has a contrary view, however. In *The Lost Duchess*, she ponders, 'Was it the overweening partiality for Albert that first made tongues whisper that he was not Ernst's child?', but goes on to answer herself: 'No.'

Another sign of his difference was that, unusually for a Coburg, Albert demonstrated from an early age a marked distaste for the opposite sex. 'At the age of five, at a children's dance, he screamed

with disgust and anger when a little girl was led up to him as a partner; and although later on he grew more successful in disguising
such feelings, the feelings remained.'[1] Indeed, Stockmar wrote in his
memoirs: 'He [Albert] will always have more success with men than
with women, in whose company he shows too little enthusiasm, and
is too indifferent and retiring.' This characteristic was also much
remarked upon at the English court when he first came to see
Victoria, as he kept himself aloof from the many young women who
wished to meet the handsome prince.

Victoria told Melbourne prior to the engagement that one thing
that pleased her very much was 'that he never paid any attention to
any other woman'. Melbourne unwisely responded: 'No, that sort of
thing is apt to come later.' Victoria was not amused! But her judgement was correct: it never did come later in Albert's case.

Ernst was distant from his children and largely uninterested in
their development. Once, when asked by a relation if the children
studied diligently and behaved well, Ernst answered dismissively: 'My
children do not misbehave, and they know they must learn something in order to become able men, so I don't trouble myself further
about them.'

Indeed, as Ernst II commented in his memoirs: 'He would never
suffer the least complaint of bodily inconvenience, even of pain ... I
remember we once [winter 1828–29] rode from Coburg to Gotha
and suffered fearfully from the cold.' Anyone who has travelled even
in recent times along the now well-kept roads in the Thuringian hills
will know how long and tiring the journey of more than fifty miles
on horseback and rough tracks must have been: winter in Thuringia
can be bitter. The boys were only twelve and ten at the time, and by
all accounts Albert's physique was not strong: to require young boys
to make such a journey was inconsiderate at best.

Ernst was absent for some time over the next winter too, and
Albert wrote at his grandmother's direction to say 'how sorry we are
at your staying away so long'. In 1831, the year of Luise's death, Ernst
was again away for long periods – in Italy with his current mistress
– during which Albert wrote many letters to his father, but there was
no mention of his mother's death. And in 1839, when Albert had
planned to spend his twentieth birthday at the Rosenau, his father

insisted for reasons of his own that they go to Gotha. Albert's obedience only increased the tension between them.

One of Albert's uncles, Count Mensdorff-Pouilly, said that 'he had a natural talent for imitation and a great sense of the ludicrous' – qualities certainly inherited from Luise, who since childhood had captivated everyone by her liveliness and sense of fun. This characteristic was seen at its best in Albert's university days, where he felt at home and relaxed among the students.

Ernst I, however, was unconcerned with Albert's happiness in England following his marriage, anxious only to exploit every possible advantage from it. He wrote to Albert that his brother Ernst was short of money, and suggested that he ask Victoria to give him an allowance – the conduct not of a sovereign duke, but of a vulgar money-grubber. That, alas, was Ernst I, but it certainly wasn't Albert. In November 1840, just nine months after his wedding, his father's greed goaded him to fury. 'Always money, money, money,' he wrote to his brother. 'I return Papa's letter to you. The principles he reveals in it can really sting one to one's heart ... God help you and your affairs.'

Years later, Albert's eldest daughter Vicki wrote: 'Papa always said that he could not bear to think of his childhood. He had been so unhappy and miserable and had often wished himself out of this world.'

Albert had seen Ernst and Luise quarrelling. There were frequent occasions, mentioned by Florschütz, when he turned suddenly pale, fell asleep at meals, or fainted away without reason – physical signs of strong emotions suppressed. There can be little doubt that Ernst II and Albert's young lives would have been harsh and loveless but for their two grandmothers, Augusta and Caroline, who shielded them from the Duke's bullying. Stockmar realised early on that Albert needed to be taken out of his home environment, and Leopold required no prompting to bring that about.

It is intriguing that no Coburg court gossip about Albert's legitimacy or otherwise was recorded at the time of his birth. Nor is there any evidence that Melbourne questioned his paternity; Victoria's own journals cover her and Albert's courtship fully, and if Stockmar had felt any disquiet, he too would surely have made some reference to it. In his letter to Victoria of 16 October 1839, Melbourne makes it clear that he relies only on 'Her Majesty's happiness', thus appearing to absolve himself from any state or other responsibilities as to the correctness of the marriage.

But there are a number of candidates for Albert's real father, who need to be mentioned if only to be rebutted, clearing the way for more acceptable arguments.

Luise's second husband, Maximilian von Hanstein, one rumoured possibility, is highly unlikely. At the time of Albert's conception in 1818 he was just fifteen, and there is no evidence that Luise had yet met him: he only joined the Coburg battalion in 1822, and their love affair began in late 1824.

Then, in 2003, at a dinner party I attended in New Rochelle, New York, Ann Burger, a fellow guest, introduced herself to me by saying: 'I suppose you know you're sitting next to a relative of your royal family?' She claimed that one of the ancestors of her family – the von Meyers – had been at the Coburg court and had had an affair with Luise, from which liaison Albert was born.

At the time, I had only heard of the von Meyern family. Wondering if the similarity in the names could have created a confusion, I replied carefully that more than one family claimed that honour. Nevertheless, Ann agreed that I could visit her home and inspect family papers, including a copy of her family tree. She also suggested that her elderly cousin Walter Eberstadt, who had written a family history, albeit of a later period, might have more information: his ancestors had lived in Germany's oldest ghetto, in Worms-on-Rhine, in the seventeenth century.

In 1849, Walter Eberstadt's maternal great-great-grandfather Ferdinand von Meyer became mayor of Worms, having been ennobled to a barony by Ernst I in 1844 – 'von Meyer Strasse' exists in Coburg today. He had, however, come from impoverished stock, and couldn't have been a close associate of Luise's in 1818.

Another candidate – the one usually mentioned as the prime suspect – was the similarly named Ferdinand Freiherr von Meyern-Hohenberg. He is first alleged as Albert's father in 1915, in a pamphlet written in Germany by Max W Foss, *England als Erzieher*, which states categorically that von Meyern was then a Jewish chamberlain at the Coburg court and that Albert was half Jewish. 'Prince Albert of Coburg, the Prince Consort,' Foss wrote, 'is without doubt a half

Jew, so since his time, Jewish blood has been circulating in the veins of the English royal family, as well as in those of the Hohenzollerns.'

One has to question Foss's motive for producing such a bold, uncorroborated statement: written in 1915, at an important stage in the Great War, it reeks of political propaganda. It was given a hint of respectability when Lytton Strachey wrote in his 1921 book *Queen Victoria* – but again without corroboration:

> The Ducal Court was not noted for the strictness of its morals; the Duke was a man of gallantry and it was rumoured that the Duchess followed her husband's example. There were scandals; one of the Court Chamberlains, a charming and cultivated man of Jewish extraction, was talked of.

However, the accusation is vague to the point of meaninglessness. In 1791, Ferdinand Freiherr von Meyern-Hohenberg became *Kammerjunker* (gentleman of the chamber) at the court of Coburg; he was promoted to *Reisemarschall* (in charge of all journeying), and in 1815 was appointed *Schlosshauptmann* (captain of the castle); he died in 1841 as *Oberhofmarschall* (high court marshal), the highest position at court. There is no evidence that he was Jewish, and it is hard to believe that, in the narrow world of Schloss Ehrenburg with its notoriously lax morals, his putative fatherhood of Albert could have been kept secret. Luise and Ernst might have kept silent, for the sake of the child's future and the Coburgs' reputation, but it is inconceivable that von Meyern-Hohenberg would have been subsequently promoted so highly.

We can also eliminate as candidate the objects of Luise's flirtations: von Bülow, von Stillfried, von Münchhausen and others whose relationships with the Duchess don't accord with the date in 1818 when Albert was conceived.

Alexander Graf zu Solms, however, is within the timescale. The fact that he and Ernst had been close boyhood friends and remained regular companions did make the rift between them significant and serious: remember that zu Solms accompanied Ernst to Gotha in December 1816, when the latter became engaged to Luise. Ernst later

(1819) complained in a letter to his brother Ferdinand about a liaison between zu Solms and Luise, which sparked off the first quarrel with Ernst she ever admitted to. She wrote to her friend Augusta von Studnitz:

> The good Bock [Charlotte] has been unutterably stupid. You'll laugh when you hear about it, but it made me cry. She accused me of loving Graf Solms, and scolded him for being in love with me – which made him die with laughter, but also feel quite proud that such an honour could be conceived likely. Had [Ernst] been sensible he would have laughed too, but he took it seriously, and was very angry with me. It all ended in tears. Now he watches me, which he never used to, and he misconstrues everything.

Alexander zu Solms had a reputation as a ladykiller, which would have helped anyone who wished to imply intrigues between him and Luise. That he was exiled to St Wendel in 1819, subjected to a court enquiry that took over two years to run its course and had been an intimate boyhood friend of Ernst, who had personally taken action against him and denied him his promised promotions, clearly show that the Duke took Charlotte von Bock's allegations against zu Solms seriously. The timing of his alleged affair with Luise corresponds with the time of Albert's conception. It was reported by Luise herself, and noticed by the court, that Ernst's affection for her waned dramatically during her pregnancy with Albert.

Ernst's boyhood friend never left St Wendel, and today lies in the cemetery there. Although he was slowly promoted to the rank of lieutenant-colonel – a lowly rank for a Graf who was a close friend of the Duke – he was never forgiven for his transgressions. The cumulative evidence against zu Solms makes him one of three serious candidates for Albert's paternity – although against this one must weigh the strenuous denials by both Luise and zu Solms, and the court of enquiry's inability to establish any wrongdoing beyond flirtation, which seems to indicate the foolish side of Luise's nature rather than anything more sinister. And surely, if zu Solms had really fathered her favourite son, Luise's relationship with him would have been to some extent rekindled during their mutual exile to St Wendel? Yet there is no evidence for this.

★ ★ ★

A second and more intriguing candidate is one Friedrich Blum. Since 1819, the story has been passed down through the Blum family – who lived in Tukums in Latvia until they moved to England in the great immigration of the 1890s – that one of the family was responsible for the birth of Luise's second child. Although it sounds far-fetched, their account is at least consistent, and Blum's deathbed testimony is supported by the affidavit of a contemporary family member.

Apparently the young man, who wanted to experience life outside his small town, got an introduction through his father's influential German friends in Latvia to the ducal House of Coburg. Certainly a contemporary handwritten note in papers held at the Staatsarchiv at Coburg lists a Friedrich Blum as a member of the household at Schloss Ehrenburg, and the 1818 and 1819 *Staats Kalender* states that he was a *lacquais* (lackey) – an under-servant, usually either a footman or an under-groom of the chamber – to the Dowager Duchess Augusta. But the name does not appear in later calendars, although those of his colleagues do, suggesting that he was no longer in service at the *Schloss*. But could a lowly lackey have had an affair with Luise?

Nearly a century later, in the late 1890s, Victoria, at her liberal best, recorded a similar case.[2] This time, the princess had been an unmarried virgin, and when her pregnancy became obvious, it was discovered that the father was a footman who, owing to some antiquated rule, had the nightly task of bringing the lamps into the girl's bedroom. The parents, horrified at their daughter's plunge from grace, turned her out, but Queen Victoria was more horrified at their lack of sympathy: 'It is too awful and shameful and almost sinful to send the poor baby away. I hear from a reliable source that the family have forbidden that poor unhappy girl's name ever to be mentioned … I think it is too wicked.'

Victoria might not have been so liberal-minded had she known of a thirty-year-old case that directly affected her own family, and was only finally resolved on 30 September 2004. The petitioner, George Nicholas Donald Locock, had applied for an order to exhume the body of his grandfather Henry Frederick Leicester Locock from St Nicholas's churchyard in Sevenoaks, Kent, to prove via DNA that he had royal ancestors, a belief based on anecdotal evidence: his father had told him that his grandfather, whom the

Lococks had adopted, was the illegitimate son of Princess Louise, a daughter of Victoria and Albert. The court ruled against him on the grounds that the principle of a Christian burial was final, and human remains, once interred, should not be disturbed.[3]

The Blum story is based on anecdotal evidence supported by a statutory declaration. According to an affidavit made by Lawrence Bloom on 14 January 2004, his uncle David Bloom, then close to death, had revealed that his grandfather Sam Bloom, who had been brought up in Tukums, had told him the following story, which he had heard from his own parents: When Sam's ancestor Friedrich Blum had been a working member of the court of Coburg, he had had an affair with the 'Princess' [*sic*]. A baby had been born who had been accepted as a prince of the family and whose name had been Albrecht. 'Such expressions of this matter,' said Lawrence Bloom in the affidavit, 'had been passed down from each generation in hushed whispers as though it had always been an unseemly source of pride to mention it.'

Lawrence goes on:

> The manner and the certain confidentiality in which my uncle gave me this information which was in my understanding at that time as being a testimonial given in the full expectancy of his early death assured me at that time and has ever since that time of the truth and sincerity of his statement.

This affidavit, sworn before a solicitor and accordingly witnessed, is certainly strong, both in the law of evidence in England and in Hebraic religious law. Anecdotal evidence is very important in Hebraic law, since the first stipulation in the Passover service is that 'it is our duty to narrate the departure from Egypt, and all those who relate [it] are to be praised', while a leading text on English law, *Phipson on Evidence*, states: 'In tracing pedigrees, family tradition appears to have been resorted to long before the establishment of the hearsay rule. Indeed, before jury trial itself was developed, such matters were "tried" by witnesses who stated circumstantially the sources of their knowledge, which included family hearsay and reputation.'

The Coburg records note that Blum married the widow Gertraud Lleicht, born Poseker, who brought to the marriage two children,

Margaretha and Anna. From this marriage was born a daughter Erneste Henriete Sophie, who in 1829 was confirmed as Christian. Possibly Friedrich Blum had given up his Judaism in order to assimilate into Coburg life: he would have had a strong motive to do so. In the opinion of the Coburg archivist Dr Nöth, it is unlikely that the lackey Blum was Jewish, since 'a Jewish servant in the lower ranks of the royal household is inconceivable, although as an adviser on a higher plane, it would be very possible.'

In 1897 and 1898, a substantial part of the Blum family left Tukums and arrived in London. This was the time of the great emigration of Jews, mainly from Russia and Poland. These were the people who responded to the deepening virulent anti-Semitism then encouraged and provoked in tsarist Russia. For the most part, parents encouraged their young male offspring to leave notwithstanding the fact that their chances of ever seeing them again were remote. The immediate cause for these departures was to avoid the oppressive compulsory conscription into the Tsar's army. This was not short-term national service but a period of not less than twenty years of bullying and physical violence meted out to young conscripts who were used as military fodder for any and every action.

But in this case, Jacob Blum (b. 1856) came to London with his two elder sons – Nathan (b. 1876) and Sam (b. 1883) – to find work and accommodation. They anglicised their name to Bloom and took up residence at 8 Canon Place, Mile End, Old Town, Stepney. A year later they arranged for Jacob's wife Anna (*née* Freedman) and Nathan's young wife Leah (*née* Tankel), and Jacob's other children – Kay (b. 1879), Chave (b. 1882), Louis (b. 1889), Bessie (b. 1890) and Rebecca (b. 1893) – to join them. The 1902 census declares that Nathan was a bootmaker, and to help with their living costs, they had taken in a lodger, Barnet Levy, who was then twenty-two years old.

It is Nathan Bloom who closely resembles the Prince Consort as seen in a photograph taken when the latter was about forty years old. The family, including Nathan's younger brother Sam and their children and successors, have never wavered in their belief that Friedrich Blum was both their direct antecedent and the father of Albert, the Prince Consort. Today, Nathan's last surviving daughter, Renée (b. 1911), lives quietly in St John's Wood, London.

Unfortunately, no proof has emerged linking the Blum family of

Tukums with Friedrich Blum, the one-time lackey of Coburg, but if this bridge could be completed, the evidence for paternity would be difficult to rebut. There are marked physical similarities between Albert and descendants of the Blum family in their later years, and it is probable, given the well-documented situation between Ernst and Luise in 1818, that in those dark corridors on the first floor of Schloss Ehrenburg, Friedrich Blum could have satisfied a lonely and sensuous Luise. Nor is it beyond belief that Luise could have invited his attentions – some years later she approached von Bülow while he was on guard duty at the Rosenau. Would not a young man – who, if photographs of his descendants are anything to go by, was probably handsome – approached by a princess who well knew the arts of flirtation, have accepted a brief liaison, perhaps almost taking it as a command, or perhaps because he was flattered and excited by the prospect? In the circumstances that then existed at Schloss Ehrenburg, the difference in rank between duchess and lackey would scarcely have mattered. Indeed, Luise might have felt much the safer for it: if Friedrich Blum revealed any hint of the encounter and she denied it, who would have believed a lackey's over the royal word – and indeed, what penalties might he have incurred?

Certainly no one would have guessed at such a liaison: no glances exchanged at court, no 'paddling of palms' in the corridors, or secret trysts that might have been noticed. Would it have been so very different from the much-recited liaison, some 170 years later, between Princess Diana and her police protector?

Moreover, one must remember the prevailing culture at the court of Coburg, noted by so many contemporary witnesses. In 1818, Luise was still just seventeen, and had recently discovered from the courtiers that her husband was a freewheeler in sexual escapades. Would it have been so surprising, in the circumstances, that a young, lively and imaginative woman known for her independent spirit, left alone for long periods by her husband, had exercised her own right to indulge occasionally? The separation and divorce were both instigated by the Duke. In these sordid circumstances, combined with the continuity of the Blum claim, there remains a powerful argument for Friedrich Blum as a candidate for the paternity of Albert.

CHAPTER 19

Return to Leopold

The intriguing question of Albert's paternity cannot be concluded without commenting on one further possibility: Leopold.
This view is gaining momentum in current German history circles,
and were it to be demonstrated as historical fact, the consequences
would be sublime. Here is the handsome Prince Leopold, ambitious
beyond belief and supported in his quests by his mother, the
Dowager Duchess Augusta. He had gained the prize of Europe by
winning the hand of Charlotte, the heiress apparent to the British
crown, much against the will of her father, the Prince Regent (later
George IV), only to lose it tragically almost at once through the
death of both his wife and their stillborn son. To have fathered
Albert, and to have subsequently taken extreme care of his education
and development in order to prime the marriage to Victoria, could
be seen as a dramatic fulfilment of his thwarted dream. Albert would
replace his stillborn child by Charlotte, and his 'own child by Luise'
could be manoeuvred into marrying that of his sister Victoire. At the
same time, he could preserve this most holy of secrets from anyone,
including the records of history. Luise would do nothing to upset
Leopold, and certainly not her beloved child Albert; nor would she
ever acknowledge an illegitimate son by her husband's brother. Once
again, the words of von Zach, in his obituary of Luise, come to mind:
'She avoided moreover, at least so long as I had the honour of knowing her, speaking of the person who had been involved with her.'

There were opportunities and motivation for both Leopold and
Luise in 1818, at the time of Albert's conception. Following
Stockmar's advice, Leopold stayed in England for some months
after Charlotte's death, but he returned to Coburg in the autumn of
1818, free from his long period of mourning and no doubt alert to

opportunities to indulge himself with the ladies of that permissive court. To Luise, in need of comfort and the love that had not been forthcoming from Ernst, Leopold was her charming, handsome, intelligent and single brother-in-law. Although I have been unable to trace the exact reference, a German scholar told me that both he and some of his colleagues recalled an entry in the Dowager Duchess Augusta's journal during January 1819 that read: 'Leopold and Luise are inseparable, and should have no further contact with each other.' About the same time, Caroline Bauer reports Luise as stating: 'I do not know whom I love more, Ernst or Leopold.'

In the close confines of the *Schloss*, Leopold would have had no difficulty in meeting with Luise – nor, given the family's past conduct in such matters, would he have felt any moral scruples about sleeping with his brother's wife. He must have been aware, since the whole court was, of Ernst's lack of affection for Luise, and would certainly also have been aware of her physical need for fulfilment. And the lively, flirtatious Luise was a very attractive young woman. To Leopold, she must have represented temptation without responsibility.

There are both physical and intellectual similarities between Albert and his uncle. Albert was serious-minded, unlike his father and brother – but very like Leopold, the active architect of the rise and rise of the Coburg family. And from the start, Leopold took a distinctly paternal interest in Albert – recall Luise's letter saying how the two-year-old adored his uncle. It was Leopold who ensured, primarily through Stockmar, that Albert served an apprenticeship in governance, Leopold who took the lead in choosing Albert's university and decreed his subsequent grand tour. Moreover, the friendship between Leopold and Luise was lifelong; he kept in touch with her after her exile to St Wendel, and met her on several occasions during her post-1824 travels.

That he had more than a brother-in-law's influence on Luise is borne out by a letter to Leopold from his mother Augusta, dated 13 October 1822, in which she complained of Luise's growing independence, and asked him to remonstrate with her: 'She is in awe of your superiority, and greatly respects you. If you take her to task, she will yield.'[1]

It has also been suggested that, when Luise found she was pregnant with Albert, she guiltily tried to abort the foetus by infusions of chemicals into the uterus which allegedly caused the cancer that killed her in 1831. Certainly, depending on the chemicals used, it is medically possible for a cancer to form and have mortal effect in that timescale. It is a matter of record that, in 1822, some four years after the putative attempted abortion, Luise was complaining of serious pains in her lower abdomen, and she was never able to conceive with Maximilian.

Without DNA testing, the truth may never be known: look at how the question of the identity of 'Anastasia' rolled on for years, subject to much civil litigation, until DNA gave conclusive evidence. And in today's context, it is right to ask if it matters whether or not Albert was legitimate, illegitimate or Jewish.

But in the context of the 1820s, it did matter. If the story, true or not, had come out, the reputation of the House of Coburg might have been ruined, which would have negated any chance of a marriage with Victoria, and the Coburgs would not have been ruling over most of Europe on the eve of the First World War. It is impossible to conjecture how history might have evolved, but it certainly would have been different.

Even today, when monarchy and aristocracy, their influence and authority much diminished since that war, are finding their relevance increasingly questioned, the blood line remains critical. This is what gives a royal family its mystique, and confirms its supremacy over any republican president. What divides a royal from a pop-star, film-star or footballer is the basic respect for the blood line. If that can be proved false, a major prop in the edifice of monarchy is removed. The House of Saxe-Coburg-Gotha may have an irreparable break in their blood line. But if it could be proved that Leopold was Albert's father, it would not have been broken, and the Coburg heredity would remain intact.

Science may yet prove what historic documents can't: whether or not Luise had an affair in 1818, from which illicit liaison Albert was born. But her own deathbed reflections, faithfully recorded by Julie von Zerzog in her *Denkwürdigkeiten*, hint strongly at this. And whatever else may be said about the House of Coburg during the first half of the nineteenth century, there is clear and irrefutable evidence of intrigue and conspiracy on a grand scale. 'Family business' it most certainly was.

Endnotes

CHAPTER 4

1 Grey, *The Early Years of His Royal Highness the Prince Consort*, pp. 375–86.
2 Stockmar, *Memoirs*, vol. 1, p. 12.
3 Knight, *Autobiography of Miss Cornelia Knight*, p. 5.
4 Castlereagh, *Letters*, vol. 4, p. 211.
5 Benson and Esher, *Letters of Queen Victoria*.

CHAPTER 5

1 Strachey, *Queen Victoria*, p. 5.
2 C Stockmar, *Memoirs*, vol. 2,
3 Strachey, *Queen Victoria*, p. 81.
4 E von Stockmar, *Denkwürdigkeiten aus den Papieren des Baron Stockmar*, p. 14.
5 Ibid., p. 4.
6 Ibid., p. 15.
7 C Stockmar, *Memoirs*, vol. 1, p. 72.

CHAPTER 6

1 RAY 69/26.
2 C Stockmar, *Memoirs*, vol. 1, p. 97.
3 British State Papers 1829/1830, p. 455.
4 Wellington Papers, Southampton University Library, WP1.
5 Ibid.
6 Hansard, Parliamentary Debates, 3rd series, vol. 1 (1830), cols 52–3.
7 Greville, *The Greville Memoirs*, vol. 1, p. 351.
8 C Stockmar, *Memoirs*, vol. 1, p. 151.
9 Ibid., p. 162.

CHAPTER 7

1 Palmerston Papers, Southampton University Library, MS62.
2 Neale, *The Life of Field Marshal HRH Edward Duke of Kent*, p. 15.
3 Duff, *Edward of Kent*, p. 76.
4 Anderson, *The Life of Edward, Duke of Kent*, p. 4.
5 Neale, *The Life of Field Marshal HRH Edward Duke of Kent*, p. 7.

6 Anderson, *The Life of Edward, Duke of Kent*, p. 86.
7 Porter, *Overture to Victoria*, p. 108.
8 Anderson, *The Life of Edward, Duke of Kent*, p. 89.
9 Porter, *Overture to Victoria*, p. 109.
10 Anderson, *The Life of Edward, Duke of Kent*, p. 89.
11 C Stockmar, *Memoirs*, vol. 1, p. 77.
12 RA M3/3, 24 May 1819 (cited Woodham-Smith, *Queen Victoria*, p. 30).
13 RA M24/23, 31 May 1819 (cited Woodham-Smith, *Queen Victoria*, p. 30).
14 Martin, *The Life of the Prince Consort*, vol. 5, pp. 1–2.

CHAPTER 8

1 C Stockmar, *Memoirs*, p. 113.
2 Hudson, *A Royal Conflict*, p. 16.
3 RA M3/36, 1 April 1821.
4 Benson and Esher, *Letters of Queen Victoria*, vol. 1, p. 18.
5 Ibid., p. 11.
6 RAY 203/81.
7 Benson and Esher, *The Girlhood of Queen Victoria*, vol. 1, p. 280.
8 Hibbert, *Queen Victoria*, p. 19.
9 RA MP 116/111 232 March 1830.
10 Charlot, *Victoria, the Young Queen*, p. 59.
11 Longford, *Victoria R.I.*, p. 43.
12 RA 115/58, 22 August 1835.
13 Hudson, *A Royal Conflict*, p. 26.
14 RA M5/84, 2 September 1835.
15 Greville, *The Greville Memoirs*, vol. 2, p. 388.
16 Ibid., vol. 3, pp. 374–6.
17 Ibid.
18 RA QV, 9 November 1837.
19 Weintraub, *Albert*, p. 55.
20 Benson and Esher, *Letters of Queen Victoria*, vol. 1, p. 61.
21 Ibid., p. 62.
22 Ibid.
23 Ibid., p. 63.
24 Ibid., p. 91.
25 Ibid., p. 94.
26 Ibid., p. 95.

CHAPTER 9

1 Benson and Esher, *Letters of Queen Victoria*, vol. 1, p. 141.
2 Ibid., p. 148.

3 Ibid., p. 190.
4 Ibid., p. 193.
5 Ibid., p. 199.
6 Jagow, *The Letters of the Prince Consort*, p.13.
7 Benson and Esher, *Letters of Queen Victoria*, vol. 1.
8 Charlot, *Victoria, the Young Queen*, p. 171.
9 Jagow, *Letters of the Prince Consort*, p. 58.
10 Greville, *The Greville Memoirs*, vol. 4, pp. 239–40.
11 RA VJ, 10 February 1840.
12 C Stockmar, *Memoirs*, vol. 2, p. 38.
13 C Stockmar, *Memoirs*, vol. 2, p. 41.
14 RA U2/5, 19 June 1842.
15 Woodham-Smith, *Queen Victoria*, p. 231.
16 C Stockmar, *Memoirs*, vol. 2, pp. 466–7.
17 Greville, *The Greville Memoirs*, pp. 329–30.
18 RA VJ, 26 February 1838.
19 RA A 11/12, 8–13 June 1837.
20 RA VJ, 20 June 1837.
21 RA Z482/12, 17 August 1837.

CHAPTER 10

1 C Stockmar, *Memoirs*, vol. 2, p. 600.
2 Greville, *The Greville Memoirs*, vol. 6, pp. 68–9.
3 Martin, *The Life the Prince Consort*, vol. 1, pp. 247–9.
4 C Stockmar, *Memoirs*, vol. 2, p. 363.
5 Blackburn, *The Peculiarities of German History*, p. 43.
6 Lepsius, *Die Deutschen Parteien vor 1918*, pp. 64–5.
7 Palmerston Papers, Southampton University Library, MS62.
8 Cannadine, 'The Last Hanoverian Sovereign?', p. 129.
9 Ibid., p. 140
10 E von Stockmar, *Denkwürdigkeiten aus den Papieren des Baron Stockmar*, p. 662.
11 Benson and Esher, *Letters of Queen Victoria*, vol. 2, p. 181.
12 Ibid., p. 194.
13 Greville, *The Greville Memoirs*, vol. 6, pp. 63–4.
14 Strachey, *Queen Victoria*, p. 227.
15 Ibid., p. 232.
16 RA A79/58, 8 October 1850.
17 Greville, *The Greville Memoirs*, vol. 6, pp. 315–61.
18 RA VJ, 20 December 1851.
19 Connell, *Regina v Palmerston*, p. 147.
20 David Brown, 'Palmerston and the Press 1846–1855', *History* 86 (2001), 41–6.

21 Connell, *Regina v Palmerston*, p. 167.
22 St A Co LA A 7206.

CHAPTER 11

  1 *The Times*, 22 June 1850
  2 Hansard, vol. 112, p. 905.
  3 RA VJ, 1 May 1851.

CHAPTER 12

  1 Albert, *Collections of the Principal Speeches and Addresses of HRH
    The Prince Consort*, p. 134.
  2 Hibbert, *Queen Victoria*, p. 388.
  3 *The Times* (London), 7 October 2002.

CHAPTER 14

  1 Julie von Zerzog, *Denkwürdigkeiten aus dem Leben der Herzogin
    Luise von Sachsen, Grafin von Polzig, geb. Princessin von Sachsen-
    Gotha-Altenburg* ('Memories from the Life of Duchess Luise of
    Saxe, Countess of Polzig, born Princess of Saxe-Gotha-
    Altenburg'), p. 436. Future references use the abbreviation
    Denkwürdigkeiten.
  2 St A Co (endorsed HF. 1 Bd. 24).
  3 Zerzog, *Denkwürdigkeiten*, p. 438.
  4 Bauer, *Memoirs*, p. 64.
  5 St A Co Koháry A231.

CHAPTER 15

  1 St A Co LA A 6005.
  2 St A Co LA A 6082.
  3 Zerzog, *Denkwürdigkeiten*, p. 440.
  4 Ibid., p. 439.
  5 St A Co LA A 6006.
  6 Ibid.
  7 Zerzog, *Denkwürdigkeiten*, p. 451.
  8 Ibid.

CHAPTER 16

  1 St A Co LA A 6008.
  2 St a Co A 835, fol. 39.
  3 St A Co LA A 6008.
  4 St A Co A Nr 835, p. 39.
  5 St A Co A 835.
  6 St A Koháry A57.

7 St A Koháry A124.
8 St A Co LA.A 6008.
9 St A Co LA A 6009.
10 St A Co. LA A 6009, p. 3.
11 St A Co LA A 6009.
12 St A Co LA A 6009, p. 2.
13 Ponsonby, *The Lost Duchess*.

CHAPTER 17

1 LA SW.382 401.
2 St A Co LA A 6009.
3 St AQ Co Koháry, p. 105.
4 St A Co. Stockmar II A, p. 25.
5 St A Co LA A 6005.
6 St A Co LA A 5572 No 31.
7 St A Co LA A 6150.
8 St A Co LA A6150.
9 Ibid.
10 St A Co LA A 6151.
11 St A Co LA A 6014.
12 St a Wendel C 1/57, FOL. 15–18.
13 St A Co Min. Nr 9, p. 46.
14 St A Co Min. R 830 Report of Ernst Habermann of 25/11/30.
15 Zerzog, *Denkwürdigkeiten*, p. 445.
16 Ibid., p. 447.
17 St A Co LA A6150.
18 St A Co LA A 6509, Sophia to Ferdinand Mainz 31.1.30.
19 Ibid., Maximilian von Poelzig to Herzogin Auguste, Paris, 25.4.31; Bericht des Militz, 29.4.31.
20 Ibid., Franz Xaver von Zach to Amalie von Uttenhoven, Paris 26.4.31.
21 St A Co LA A 6015.
22 St A Co LA A 6152.
23 St A Co LA A 6015.
24 Ibid., fol. 9.
25 Coburgische Landesbibliothek MS460 (appendix).
26 St A Co LA A 6017.
27 St A Co LA A 6019.
28 Ritter, *Deutsche Sozialgeschichte, Dokumente und Skizzen*, vol. 11, p. 80.

CHAPTER 18

1 Grey, *The Early Years of His Royal Highness the Prince Consort*, chaps 1–6.
2 Buckle, *The Letters of Queen Victoria*, p. 858, paras 35–6.
3 *Times* [London] *Law Report*, 29 October 2004.

CHAPTER 19

1 St A Co Stockmar II A Nr. p. 251 ff.

Bibliography

Albert, Prince Consort, *Collections of the Principal Speeches and Addresses of HRH The Prince Consort* (London: John Murray, 1862).

Anderson, William, *The Life of Edward, Duke of Kent* (Ottawa: Hunter Rose, 1870).

Aronson, Theo, *Grandmama of Europe: The crowned descendants of Queen Victoria* (London: Macmillan, 1974).

Aronson, Theo, *Heart of a Queen: Queen Victoria's romantic attachments* (London: John Murray, 1991).

Ball, T F, *Queen Victoria: Scenes and incidents of her life and reign* (Toronto: Willard, 1888).

Bauer, K, *Memoirs* (London: Remington, 1885).

Bennett, Daphne, *King without a Crown: Albert, Prince Consort of England, 1819–1861* (London: Heinemann, 1977).

Benson, A C and Esher, Viscount, *Letters of Queen Victoria: A selection from Her Majesty's correspondence between the years 1837 and 1861*, 3 vols (London: John Murray, 1907).

Benson, E F, *Queen Victoria* (London: Longmans Green, 1935).

Blackburn, D and Eley, G, *The Peculiarities of German History: Bourgeois society and politics in nineteenth-century Germany* (Oxford: Oxford University Press, 1984).

Bolitho, Hector, *Albert the Good and the Victorian Reign* (London: John Murray, 1954).

Bolitho, Hector (ed.), *Further Letters of Queen Victoria* (London: John Murray, 1938).

Bolitho, Hector, *Victoria and Albert* (London: John Murray, 1938).

British and Foreign State Papers, 1829/30.

Brown, David, *Palmerston and the Politics of Foreign Policy 1846–1855* (Manchester: Manchester University Press, 2003).

Buckle, G E, *The Letters of Queen Victoria* (London: John Murray, 1926).

Cannadine, D, 'The Last Hanoverian Sovereign? The Victorian monarchy in historical perspective', in A L Beier, D Cannadine and J M Rosenheim (eds), *The First Modern Society: Essays in English history in honour of Lawrence Stone* (Cambridge: Cambridge University Press, 1989).

Castlereagh, Viscount, *Letters*, St John's College Cambridge.

Charlot, M, *Victoria, the Young Queen* (London: Blackwell, 1991).

Connell, B (ed.), *Regina v Palmerston: The correspondence between Queen Victoria and her foreign and prime minister, 1837–1865* (New York: Doubleday, 1961).

Corti, E C (trans. J McCabe), *Leopold I of Belgium* (Unwin: London, 1923).

Creevy, T (ed. Sir H Maxwell), *The Creevey Papers, 1793–1838*, (London, 1904).

Dahrendorf, R, *Society and Democracy in Germany* (London: Weidenfeld & Nicolson, 1968).

Dreesen, J, *Ein Porträt* (St Wendel Museum, 1999).

Duff, D, *Edward of Kent: The life story of Victoria's father* (London: S Paul, 1938).

Eberstadt, W, *Whence We Came, Where We Went: From the Rhine to the Main to the Elbe, from the Thames to the Hudson* (New York: WAE Books, 2002).

Ernst II, Duke of Coburg, *Memoirs*, 4 vols (Coburg: Coburgische Landesbibliothek, MS460, 1888).

Esher, Viscount, *The Girlhood of Queen Victoria*, 2 vols (London: John Murray, 1912).

Eyck, F, *The Prince Consort: A political biography* (Bath: Chivers, 1959).

Fisher, H A L, *A History of Europe* (London: Edward Arnold, 1936).

Foss, Max W, *England als Erzieher* (pamphlet, 1915).

Fulford, Roger, *The Prince Consort* (London: Macmillan, 1949).

Greville, G C F, *The Greville Memoirs: A journal of the reign of Queen Victoria*, 8 vols (London: Longmans Green, 1896–99).

Grey, C (under direction of Queen Victoria), *The Early Years of His Royal Highness the Prince Consort* (New York: Harper, 1867).

Hansard Parliamentary Papers, vol. 112.

Hibbert, C, *Queen Victoria: A personal history* (London: HarperCollins, 2000).

Hobhouse, H, *Prince Albert: His life and work* (London: Hamish Hamilton, 1983).

Howard M N (ed.), *Phipson on Evidence* (London: Sweet & Maxwell, 13th ed., 1982).

Hudson, K, *A Royal Conflict* (London: Hodder & Stoughton, 1994).

Illustrated London News, 6 July 1850.

Jagow, Kurt, *Königen Viktorias Madchenjahre* (Berlin: Kiepenheuer, 1938).

Jagow, Kurt (ed.), *The Letters of the Prince Consort, 1831–61* (London: John Murray, 1938).

Knight, Cornelia, *Autobiography of Miss Cornelia Knight*, 2 vols (London: W H Allen, 1861).

Lepsius, M R, *Die Deutschen Parteien vor 1918* (Cologne: Ritter, 1973).

Longford, Elizabeth, *Victoria R.I.* (London: Weidenfeld & Nicolson, 1964).

Marshall, T H, 'Citizenship and Social Class', in *Citizenship and Social Class and Other Essays* (Cambridge: Cambridge University Press, 1950).

Martin, Sir Theodore (under direction of Queen Victoria), *The Life of the Prince Consort*, 5 vols (1875–80).

Neale, Erskine, *The Life of Field Marshal HRH Edward Duke of Kent* (London: Richard Bentley, 1850).

Netzer, Hans-Joachim, *Albert von Sachsen-Coburg-Gotha: Ein deutscher Prinz in England* (Munich: C H Beck, 1938).

Palmerston Papers, Southampton University.

Pemberton, W B, *Lord Palmerston* (London: Batchworth, 1954).

Ponsonby, D A, *The Lost Duchess: Louise of Saxe-Gotha* (London: Chapman & Hall, 1958).

Porter, McKenzie, *Overture to Victoria* (Toronto: Longman & Green, 1961).

Rhodes, J R, *Albert, Prince Consort: A biography* (London: Hamish Hamilton, 1983).

Ridley, Jasper, *Lord Palmerston* (London: Constable, 1970).

Rimmer, A, *The Early Homes of Prince Albert* (London: Blackwood, 1883).

Ritter, G A, *Deutsche Sozialgeschichte Dokumente und Skizzen, Band 1, 1815–1870* (von W Poels).

Stockmar, Baron Christian, *Memoirs ('Biographie Skizze')*, 2 vols (Muller, 1921).

Stockmar, E von (ed. M Muller), *Denkwürdigkeiten aus den Papieren des Baron Stockmar* (Braunschweig, 1872).

Strachey, Lytton, *Queen Victoria* (New York: Harcourt Brace, 1921).

Sykes, C, 'Colonel Sibthorpe', in *History Today*, 1951.

The Times, 22 June 1850.

Tooley, S, *The Personal Life of Queen Victoria* (London: Hodder & Stoughton, 1901).

Turner, M, *Osborne House* (London 1989).

Weintraub, S, *Albert: Uncrowned king* (London: John Murray, 1997).

Wilson, A N, *The Victorians* (London: Arrow, 2003).

Wilson, R, *The Life and Times of Queen Victoria*, 2 vols (London: Cassell, 1887).

Woodham-Smith, C, *Queen Victoria: Her life and times* (London: Hamish Hamilton, 1972).

Young, G M, *Early Victorian England* (Oxford: Oxford University Press, 1934).

Zerzog, Julie von, *Denkwürdigkeiten aus dem Leben der Herzogin Luise von Sachsen, Grafin von Polzig, geb. Princessin von Sachsen-Gotha-Altenburg* (O Fischer-Saalfeld, Staatasachiv Coburg HF1 Bd. 24).

Ziegler, Philip, *King William IV* (London: Collins, 1971).

Zwi, R, *Last Walk in Naryshkin Park* (Melbourne: Spinifex, 1997).

Archive reference abbreviations

St A: *Staatsarchiv*/state archive

St a = *Stadtarchiv*/town archive

Co: Coburg

LA A Nr: document number

fol., 281–3: page number

St a St Wendel LA A Nr 500: town archive of St Wendel, document no. 500

St A Co Koháry, 105 = Koháry family archive, folio 105

RA VJ: Royal Archives, Victoria Journal

Index